INNOVATIONS

an English course by Hugh Dellar and Darryl Hocking
for students at upper intermediate level

LTP

Language Teaching Publications

114a Church Rd, Hove, BN3 2EB, England

Tel: 00 44 (1) 273 736344
Fax: 00 44 (1) 273 775361
E-mail: ltp@ltpwebsite.com

ISBN 1 899396 16 0

Reprinted 2001

Note

T5 refers to Extract 5 on the tape.
G17 refers to Point 17 of the Grammar Commentary.

The Authors

Hugh Dellar has taught EFL, ESP and EAP in Indonesia and Britain, where he is now a teacher and teacher-trainer at the University of Westminster. He trains both native-speaker and non-native-speaker teachers. He is grateful to Lisa for her understanding and patience, his colleagues both past and present for their support and for listening, and finally to Dennis Bergkamp, Ralph Ellison, Syd Barrett, Roky Erikson and Tony Adams for inspiration and for getting him through!

Darryl Hocking, originally from New Zealand, graduated from the University of Auckland in Fine Arts, before moving to the UK. He has worked both as an EFL teacher and director of studies. Currently a lecturer in EAP and in-sessional co-ordinator at Goldsmiths College, University of London, Darryl is also a performer and composer with the group Drone Ensemble, who have performed worldwide and released a number of recordings. He would like to thank Rose, Lucia and Isaac for their endurance.

Both authors would like to thank Jimmie Hill and Michael Lewis of LTP for their guidance, advice and encouragement in the development of this course.

Editor: Jimmie Hill
Cover and overall design: Anna Macleod
Printed in England by Commercial Colour Press, London E7 0EW

To the student

How do you learn a language? There is no easy answer to this question. We learn language in lots of different ways. As children we learned our native language by hearing it from everyone we came into contact with. You learn English by coming into contact with it as much as possible and as often as possible. You will meet it in class. You will hear it on TV and in films. You will read it at airports. You will see it on signs in every city in the world. The more you notice the language around you, the more your English will improve.

4a

4b

5a

5b

Grammar Index

Unit 1a : Talking about people

hat's she like? Yes, but what's she really like? A bit on the thin side. No, I wouldn't go so far as to say that! Well, he does take after his father. He's very laid-ba
You've never seen anything like it. She wouldn't say boo to a goose. She's an absolute hoot. I think it's out of a bottle. I know it's not very PC to say so, but do y
he's a really lovely person. Do you fancy him? You'd never think it. His voice is so sexy. I've always thought of myself as a very creative person. It's his aftersha
ally turns me on. No, I don't go for redheads. She can be really bitchy, you know. He's fifty if he's a day. Oh, I just heard it on the grapevine. I'm a friend of a frie

1 Describing people

Think of three people you know – friends or family. Write their initials beside three of the expressions below. Then tell a partner about your choices.

Tick the six adjectives or expressions which best describe you. Then describe yourself to your partner.

Hair
fair
dark
completely white
going grey
losing his hair
almost bald

Age
young
in his/her twenties
elderly
younger than (s)he looks
older than (s)he looks

Height
quite tall
rather short

Looks
good-looking
not very good-looking

Weight
thin
overweight
on the plump side

Personality
amusing
a bit dull
conservative
warm
narrow-minded
independent
fun

Temperament
lazy
hard-working
bad-tempered
easy-going
friendly
moody
energetic
a good sense of humour

Other
religious
musical
sporty
creative
very political
very fit

Look at the pictures on page 8. Use the expressions above to describe one of the people to a partner. Your partner must try to guess who the person is.

2 Who's who?

T1 **Listen to the descriptions of Jenny, Nick, Matt, and Kirsty. Decide who's who. Then work in pairs, trying to remember as much as you can from their descriptions on the tape.**

1. ....

2. ....

3. ....

4. ....

3 While you listen

T2 Simon and Melanie work in the same office. Simon's popped in to Melanie's house after work for a cup of tea. As you listen to their conversation, try to answer the following questions:

1. Do Melanie and Simon have any brothers and sisters?
2. Do Melanie and Simon get on well with the other members of their families?

Listen again and try to fill in the gaps in the conversation.

4 Talking point

Melanie thinks her mum is *a bit too nice*. Is it possible to be too nice? Do you know anyone like that?

Melanie is *an only child*. Do you know any only children? Which would you prefer: to be an only child or be one of 10 or 11?

Do you know anyone who comes from a really big family? How many brothers and sisters did your parents have? What about their parents?

Real English: the brother from hell

This means that he is not a very pleasant person. In fact, he is rather unpleasant. The kind of neighbours who play loud music in the middle of the night are *the neighbours from hell!* Other people's children can be *the children from hell!*

The Brother from Hell!

Melanie: I can't remember. Do you take milk?

Simon: Please, but no sugar. Thanks. It's weird, you know, but I've been to your house . . . . , and I still haven't met your parents.

Melanie: Yes, they're out a lot. My dad works for the BBC and my mum's a, she does sort of . . . . work for a company. You know, like an advertising agency. They're both really busy.

Simon: Oh, they sound really interesting.

Melanie: Do you think so? I find my dad . . . . dull, to be honest. He works late every day, even works some weekends, doesn't read, doesn't go out. I mean, don't . . . . , he's . . . . nice, but I don't know, I just don't have anything to say to him. I think . . . . , we just don't spend enough time together.

Simon: How old is he then?

Melanie: About 55, I think. I can never really remember.

Simon: Oh yeah.

Melanie: But my mum's lovely. She's . . . . , a bit too nice though, sometimes, always trying to look after me. She worries about me leaving home. She's . . . . over-protective, if you know what I mean. I'm an . . . . , so ...

Simon: Oh, I didn't know that.

Melanie: What? You mean you can't tell!

Simon: I don't know. I've never thought about it, I suppose.

Melanie: So, what about you? Have you got any brothers or sisters yourself?

Simon: Yes, I've got one of each, ...

Melanie: Oh right. Older or younger?

Simon: My sister's two or three years younger than me, but my brother's . . . . older. He's about 40 now.

Melanie: Do you get on with them all right? You haven't really talked about them very much.

Simon: Well, my brother, not . . . . well, actually. He's different from me, ... old-fashioned, ... traditional. Well, actually, he's a bit, how can I . . . . , right-wing. You know – things aren't what they used to be, more police, death penalty – that kind of thing. He's . . . . fool, actually.

Melanie: Oh, well, it takes all sorts, I suppose.

Simon: But my sister, she's great. We . . . . We've got the same kind of . . . .

Melanie: Just a pity about the brother from hell, eh?

Simon: Yes. Oh, but he's not that bad. We get on all right, as long as you steer . . . . of certain topics. Anyway, you were telling me about your parents.

Melanie: Oh, there's not much to tell, actually.

5 Modifiers

G1 The words used before adjectives or nouns to make a comment stronger, weaker, or more acceptable are called 'modifiers'. Add adjectives in the spaces to talk about people you know:

1. Very / really + adjective
She's very nice. He's really bossy.
I've got a friend who can be very . . . . at times, but usually she's really . . . .

2. Quite + adjective
He's quite creative – he paints and draws.
My father's quite . . . .
My teacher can be quite . . . .

3. A bit + negative adjective
He's a bit boring. She's a bit immature.
Most of the time I'm calm and friendly, but if I have too much to do I can get a bit . . . .

4. A bit of a + negative noun
She's a bit of a moaner. He's a bit of a workaholic.
I know someone who looks down on everyone else. He's a bit of a . . . .

5. A bit too + positive adjective
She's a bit too nice, if you know what I mean.
I've got a friend who's always giving me things. He's very . . . . In fact, I think he's a bit too . . . .

T3 Listen to and practise saying these examples.

Go back and find examples of modifiers in the conversation between Simon and Melanie. Describe a member of your class to a partner, using as many of these modifiers as you can. See if your partner can guess who you're talking about. For example:

I think A is a bit . . . . .
B is really . . . . .
C is a bit of a . . . . .
D can be a bit too . . . . .
E is quite . . . . .

6 Pronunciation

T4 Listen to the stress and intonation of these examples on tape:

It's QUITE expensive. *(This means it's expensive, but not too expensive.)*

It's quite EXPENSIVE. *(This means you think it really IS expensive.)*

Listen to the following examples on the tape. Each is said in two different ways. Then try saying them yourself, so that the difference is clear.

1. I live quite near the office.
2. She's quite nice.
3. He's quite a good cook.
4. We're quite happy with the colour.
5. He's quite friendly.
6. I think they're quite conservative.
7. The weather was quite good.
8. It's quite interesting.

7 Talking points

Do you agree with these statements?

1. Jeans are a bit old-fashioned nowadays.
2. Tattoos are really cool.
3. Body-piercing is a bit too risky for me!
4. Surfing the net can be a bit of a bore.
5. Long hair is very attractive.
6. Vegetarians can be a bit of a pain in the neck.
7. Alcohol is very dangerous.
8. Parents can be a bit too protective.

Go back and underline all the modifiers. Then make your own statements about four of the above things. Share your ideas with a partner.

Real English: a pain in the neck
If someone is *a pain in the neck*, they are very annoying. You can also use it about a situation. For example: *Parking's become absolutely impossible in the town centre. It's a real pain in the neck.*

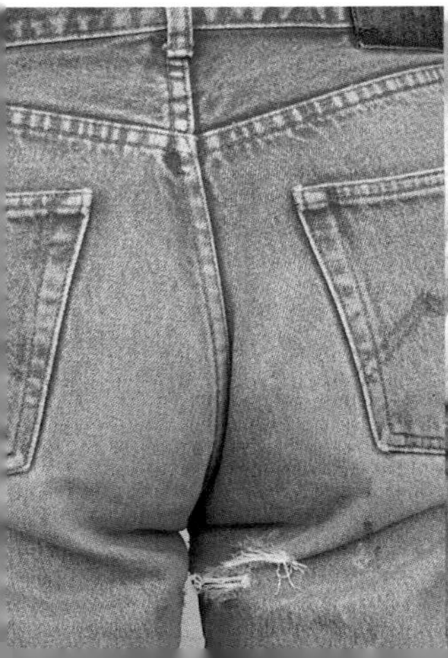

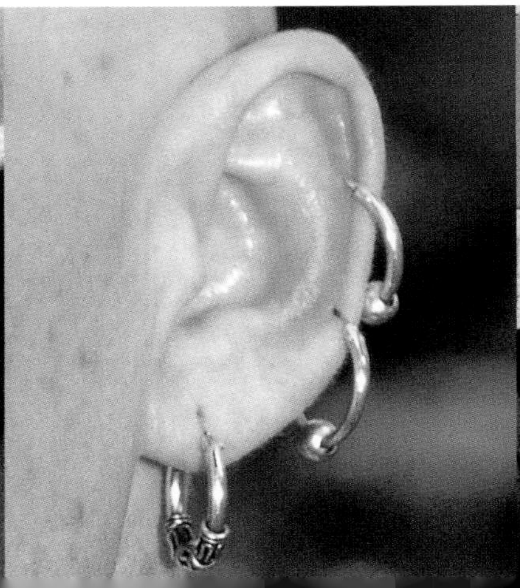
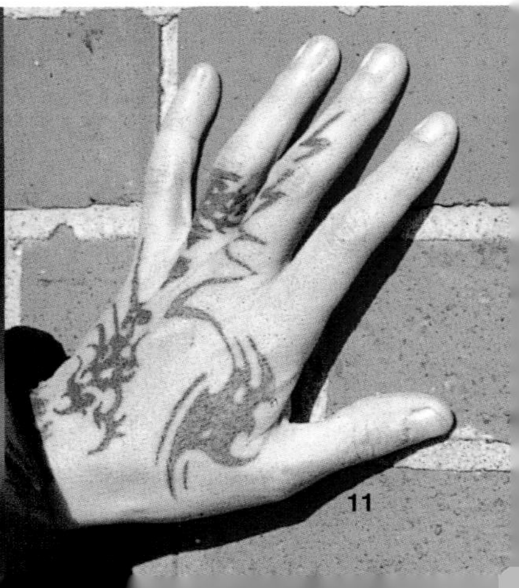

8 Present tenses

I'm Audrey. I'm a journalist. I used to live and work in the centre of London. I got tired of city life, so I decided to move down to the coast.

I love living by the sea. I love the fresh air.

I now work from home. I do a lot of work for one of the big London newspapers.

I'm Andy. I'm a taxi-driver, but in my spare time I do a bit of office-cleaning. At weekends I do a bit of painting and decorating. I'm not a real decorator, but I'm pretty good.

Here are four ways of talking about what you do for a living:

I'm	a journalist / a civil servant / out of work.
I work	in a factory / in IT / as a DJ.
I run	a guest house / a restaurant.
I do	cleaning jobs / a lot of work for the BBC.

Add the verbs to the following. The first two are done for you.

1. I *'m* self-employed.
2. He *works* in advertising.
3. She . . . . . . an architect.
4. You . . . . . . for the government, don't you?
5. He . . . . . . as a waiter at weekends.
6. I . . . . . . in a bank.
7. She . . . . . . a businesswoman.
8. My dad . . . . . . unemployed at the moment.
9. My brother . . . . . . in the army.
10. I sometimes . . . . . . bar work.
11. He . . . . . . the occasional design job.
12. My mother . . . . . . a retired teacher.
13. I . . . . . . on a boat.
14. She . . . . . . her own business.

Talking point

Explain what different members of your family do. Use a dictionary to help you if necessary.

Some people are embarrassed to tell people what they do for a living. For example, your uncle Bill may not want people to know he is a policeman. Your aunt may want to keep quiet about the fact that she is a traffic warden. You might be a tax inspector yourself!

If you did any of these jobs, would you be happy to tell people? Ask the other people in your class what their parents do or did for a living. Here are the most common questions:

What does he do?
What does she do for a living?
What's his job?

With a partner, make a note of the jobs of four parents. For example, Maria's father works in the computer industry.

1. . . . .
2. . . . .
3. . . . .
4. . . . .

Real English: I'm pretty good.

The adjective *pretty* means *beautiful* or *attractive*. As an adverb it means *fairly*. For example: *I'm pretty good at badminton.*

Grammar discussion

G2 **With a partner, discuss the difference in meaning between the verb forms in these sentences. Then look at the Grammar Introduction on page 176.**

1a. My dad works for the BBC as a cameraman.
1b. My dad's working in Manchester this month.
2a. I find my dad a bit dull. He's only interested in making money.
2b. I'm finding my job a bit boring at the moment.
3a. He even works some weekends.
3b. He's working this weekend. He's finishing off a special report.
4a. My mum is a really nice person.
4b. She's being really nice at the moment. I wonder why!
5a. Do you get on with them all right?
5b. Are you getting on with them OK again?

In the examples above, underline the time expressions used with the present continuous.

Grammar in context

Complete the following sentences by choosing the present simple or present continuous.

1. He usually . . . . *(work)* in the centre of town, but this week he . . . . *(work)* from home, because he . . . . *(try)* out a new computer link-up for the company. It could be the thing of the future.
2. Don't you think John . . . . *(act)* strangely at the moment? I mean, he . . . . *(not be)* normally that quiet. Do you think he's OK?
3. My dad . . . . *(run)* his own business, but he's sick at the moment, so my older brother . . . . *(look after)* it for a while. I think they want him to take it over eventually.
4. You . . . . *(not talk)* about your parents a lot. . . . . *(not get on)* with them very well?
5. He . . . . *(be)* very left-wing. I think he . . . . *(still wait)* for the great socialist revolution!
6. We . . . . *(not talk)* to each other just now, actually. He . . . . *(be still)* annoyed with me for forgetting his birthday last year.

Now complete these pairs of sentences with information which is true:

7. My . . . . works . . . .
   My . . . . is working . . . . at the moment.
8. I get on very well with . . . .
   I'm not getting on very well with . . . . at the moment.
9. My . . . . lives in . . . .
   My . . . . is living in . . . . at the moment.

Famous present tenses

These two famous quotations use the present simple. Which is your favourite?

1. Freedom is the right to tell people what they do not want to hear.
2. Foreigners have sex lives; the English have hot water bottles.

Here are some famous sayings. When would you say them?

3. What goes up must come down.
4. An elephant never forgets.
5. It never rains, but it pours.
6. You're making a mountain out of a molehill.

9 Adjectives

Mark each of the following adjectives P or N, depending on whether you think they are Positive or Negative. Use your dictionary if necessary. Then discuss your answers with your partner.

1. religious
2. traditional
3. quiet
4. talkative
5. tidy
6. laid-back
7. conservative
8. ambitious
9. strict
10. business-minded
11. nice
12. individual
13. messy
14. liberal
15. hard-working
16. sensible

Underline the main stressed syllable in each adjective.

Look back at the adjectives used to describe people on page 9. Which is the most positive for you? Which is the most negative?

Make a list below of the four most positive adjectives and the four most negative adjectives you can use about someone:

Positive	Negative
1.	1. . . . .
2.	2. . . . .
3.	3. . . . .
4.	4. . . . .

Compare your lists with a partner.

Judging by appearances

Work with a partner. Decide what you think these people are like. Use more than one adjective for each person. Begin *He/she looks …*

FULL-TIME JOB!

Every English-speaking child knows the nursery rhyme about the old woman with lots of children:

There was an old woman who lived in a shoe.
She had so many children she didn't know what to do.

Nicola Pridham must understand the old woman's problem very well. She is expecting her 20th child and she's only 40! She and her husband Kevin already have 12 sons and 7 daughters.

Kevin Pridham is a self-employed builder, but what he earns is not enough to feed and clothe their large family. Every week their grocery bill comes to £400. They go through 35 loaves of bread and 25 boxes of breakfast cereal per week.

If you have a child in Britain today, researchers have shown that it will cost you almost £100 per week when you take into consideration food, clothes, pocket money and all the other expenses involved in bringing up children.

Before they are 18 you will have spent almost £100,000 per child. This means that Nicola and Kevin will have to find two million pounds! You can be fairly sure that the Pridham children will be handing clothes down to each other and getting little jobs to provide themselves with pocket money.

10 Talking point

What do you think of the Pridhams' decision to have so many children? Would you like to be one of the oldest, youngest, or middle children in a family of that size?

Do you think there should be a limit on the number of children people can have?

Work in pairs and prepare a shopping list for one week's food for a family of 20 in your country! Then work out the cost.

11 How much / many?

Answer these questions on your own, then work in pairs and ask each other:

1. How much is your grocery bill per week?
2. How much bread do you buy per week?
3. How much breakfast cereal do you go through?
4. How much pocket money did you get as a child?
5. How much pocket money is normal for a ten-year-old child in your country today? What about a 16-year-old?
6. How much do you spend on newspapers per week? Magazines per month?

12 Emphasising

T5 We often use more than one adjective to describe things or people. These adjectives are often emphasised by using the same adverb before each adjective:

It was really cold and really windy.
She's very nice, very interesting.
It was extremely long and extremely boring.

We use two *different* adjectives with a similar meaning:

He's a bit strange, a bit weird.
He's a bit old-fashioned, a bit traditional.
It was really scary, really frightening.

Listen to those six sentences on the tape, and practise saying them.

Now talk about the pictures opposite using two adjectives and the same adverb. For example:

What a bike! It's really big and really fast.

Really nice, really warm

Underline the adjectives and adverbs which make this sound interesting:

Didn't you go to Turkey last summer?
> No, we went to Thailand. It was really nice, really interesting.
Whereabouts did you go?
> Well, first we went to Bangkok, which was a bit too crowded, a bit too mad for me, so we went off to the islands instead, which were really beautiful, really relaxing.

Now describe the following to your partner in a similar way:

1. your last holiday
2. the best place you've ever been
3. food from your country
4. your best friend
5. your home town

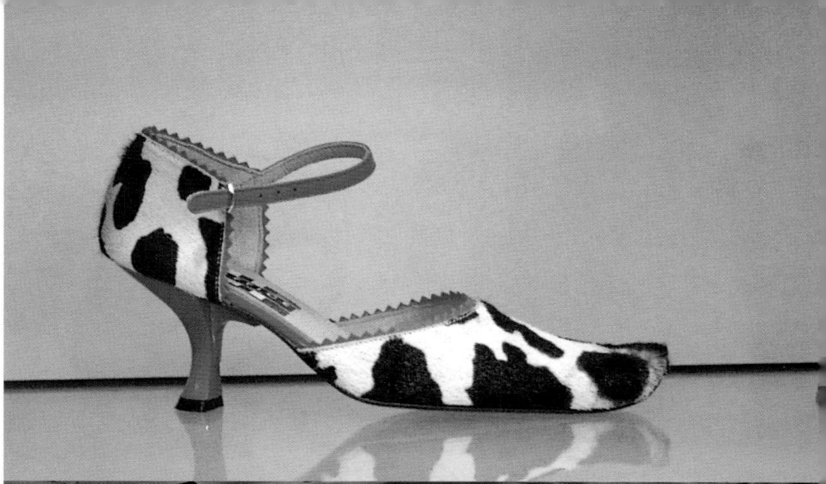

13 Softening

We use the expressions in colour to soften what we are going to say. We do this when we disagree or have something negative or unusual to say.

1. So how do you get on with your brother?
   > Well, actually, not really all that well. I find him a bit too laid-back for me.
2. So what does your dad do for a living?
   > Well, to be honest, I'm not really sure. I think he's some kind of businessman or something.
3. I find Nigel really dull, don't you?
   > Well, to tell you the truth, I don't agree. I think he's really lovely. Maybe I just know him better than you do.

Here are 6 responses, each using one of the above softening expressions. Work in pairs and try to work out what the first person said:

1. Well, actually, no, he doesn't. He hates it.
2. Well, to be honest, I thought it was awful!
3. Well, to tell you the truth, I don't want to either!
4. Well, to be honest, I'd rather spend the evening doing my homework.
5. Well, to tell you the truth, I can't think of anything more boring.
6. Well, actually, I'm already going with someone.

The new girlfriend

Do you like the photograph of your brother's girlfriend? She's the one in the picture!

She's got a shaved head, a tattoo on her right arm, and wears a ring through her nose. She watches videos a lot. She's got a degree in philosophy. She's a brilliant singer.

Work in pairs and have conversations using these ideas and the highlighted expressions above.

1. So what do you think of his girlfriend?
2. She's got lovely blonde hair, hasn't she?
3. Do you find her good-looking?
4. Why don't you ask her to come round?
5. Is she interesting to talk to?
6. Isn't she interested in anything?
7. Does she like you?
8. Do you think they'll get married?

Unit 1b : Friends and relatives

s a bit strange. A bit of an odd-ball. What a nose! I think she had it done in America. He's brighter than you think. She's not really my sort. Do you think he woul
. I wouldn't like to meet her on a dark night. We get on like a house on fire. I keep meaning to write. Men with beards usually have weak chins. Too spotty for r
old head on young shoulders, as they say. There's no insanity in my family. She's really easy to talk to. Didn't you hear he's passed away? She's one in a milli
got his head screwed on. I wish she'd pull her socks up. No, I'm not with anyone at the moment. I think they've split up, gone their separate ways. I'd never ha

1 Collocations

Before you read the text, try to fill in the missing words from these collocations. Check your answers after you have read the text.

1. When a married couple split . . . . . . , it means that they stop living together.
2. If you are convicted – found guilty – of a crime, you are usually given a prison . . . .
3. If you contact someone, you get in . . . . with them.

2 While reading

In the conversation on page 10, Melanie said that she didn't really have anything to say to her dad, because she didn't spend much time with him. Read this article about a son who, after 25 years, only recently found out who his dad was, and has since been making up for lost time. When you have read it, answer these questions:

1. Why has Bronson spent so long in prison?
2. How often have father and son met in the past 25 years?
3. What does Charles Bronson plan to do?

SURPRISE FOR JAILBIRD DAD

There are many happy stories about children being reunited with the famous parents they did not know they had, but perhaps one of the most unusual is that of a 25-year-old chef from Liverpool, who was recently told that the father he had never known was in fact Britain's most dangerous man.

Originally jailed for robbery and burglary, Charles Bronson has spent 22 of the last 26 years in prison. Much of this is because he has repeatedly taken hostages in jail and attacked fellow prisoners. He is a man of incredible physical strength and has a terrible temper.

Twenty-five years ago, he became a father, when his son, Michael, was born. However, he split up with the boy's mother when he began his first prison sentence three years later. Last year, though, an old friend found Bronson's son in Liverpool. The news that his father was the infamous 'most dangerous man in Britain' came as a total shock to the son, who decided to get in touch with his father. When Bronson first heard from his son, he said, "I was on a mission of madness but now I'm on a mission of peace. All I want to do now is get home and have a pint with my son."

When the two finally met in prison, Michael said that he got on with his father immediately. "I gave him a great big hug. It was very nice to meet him." He also said that they looked very similar, except for his father's large, bushy beard. Bronson himself said, "I'm delighted to be back in touch with my son. It's taken twenty-two years to get him back in my life."

When Charles Bronson is eventually released, father and son want to open up a restaurant. Mike plans to be the chef – while Bronson intends to be the security on the door!

Real English: have a pint
This means *go to a pub and have a pint of beer.* One pint is 568ml.

3 Comprehension check

Are the following statements about the text true (T) or false (F)?

1. A 25-year-old chef is Britain's most dangerous man.
2. Charles Bronson is a very weak man.
3. Bronson's son was aware of his father's past.
4. Charles Bronson was pleased to meet his son.
5. Michael has a large beard.
6. Father and son have plans to go into business together.

4 Vocabulary check

Find words from the text to complete the following sentences:

1. If you haven't met someone for 50 years, it can be a very emotional occasion when you are . . . .
2. If you are found guilty of breaking into someone's home and stealing from them, you are guilty of . . . .
3. Sometimes one country tries to put pressure on another country by taking some of its citizens . . . . Sometimes these . . . . are killed; sometimes money has to be paid for their release.
4. If you are famous for something bad or evil, you are . . . .
5. If you put your arms round someone, you are giving them a . . . .
6. If a beard is . . . . , it means that it is large and very thick – like a bush!

5 Talking point

If you were Charles Bronson's son, would you have visited your father? What do you think Michael said to his wife when he went home after meeting his father?

Do you think locking people up for a long time is a good idea? What effect does prison have on people? What about their families?

Can you think of alternatives to prison?

Real English: have it put down

In answer d. in exercise 6, if an animal is seriously ill or badly injured, you take it to the vet and he *puts it down*. Another way of saying this is he *puts it to sleep*.

6 Giving bad news

Notice how the highlighted expressions warn the other person that bad news is coming:

I haven't seen Mary for ages. How is she?
> Oh, haven't you heard? She was made redundant last month.
Oh, that's awful. She must've been really upset.

How's your mother?
> Well, actually, she passed away last month.
Oh, I AM sorry to hear that. Is your father all right?
> Oh yes, he seems to be coping very well.

Can John make it to the party?
> I'm afraid not. We're no longer together.
Oh, I'm sorry about that. Is everything OK?

Match up the following two-line conversations.

1. Can you give me a lift home?
2. Do you think I could get that camera back off you sometime soon?
3. Have you heard from Jan recently?
4. Is your grandfather any better?
5. So, has Peter had his results yet?
6. Are you feeling all right, Steve?
7. Hello, how are you?
8. I thought you had a dog.

a. I'm afraid not. We're very worried about him. But then, he IS 90.
b. Oh, fine thanks. Well, actually, I think I'm getting the flu, so I'd stay away if I were you.
c. I don't know how to put this, but I think I lost it last night while I was out. I'm really sorry, but I've searched everywhere and I can't find it. I'll get you another one. I'm extremely sorry.
d. We did. But unfortunately it ran out into the street and was run over. I'm afraid we had to have it put down.
e. I'm sorry, I'm afraid I can't. I lost my licence last week – had a bit too much to drink and got stopped by the police!
f. Well, actually, I haven't – not for about six months – we had a bit of an argument last year.
g. Well, actually, no. I've just had some very bad news.
h. Well, yes, I'm afraid he has. He didn't pass – so he's got to re-sit part of his exams in July.

T6 Go back and underline the expressions used to introduce the bad news. Then work in pairs reading the two-line dialogues.

7 Role play

What do you think has happened in the situations in the pictures opposite?

Imagine you are in one of these situations. A friend has just rung you, not knowing what has just happened. For example:

Hello, is that you, Jack? This is Ron in Sydney.
> Hi, Ron, how are things down under?
Well, actually, it's like an inferno. Everything's on fire. The bush . . . trees . . . houses . . .
> And are you all right?
For the time being, I think we are.

Work in pairs and continue the conversation.

8 Talking point

Read this extra information about Charles Bronson. Check in your dictionary and underline any expressions which are new to you.

Update on Bronson

Since his son's visit to him in prison, Charles Bronson has continued to be a problem for the prison authorities and his release from jail now seems increasingly unlikely.

Bronson has now taken other prisoners hostage ten times. Along with two murderers, he will be kept prisoner in a special unit, costing £60,000 per prisoner per year. Bronson has already caused over half a million pounds' worth of damage to prison buildings. Not only is he the most dangerous prisoner in the land, he is now also the most expensive.

However, although Bronson has a reputation for violence, he has won prizes in prison for his poetry and drawing. A biography of Bronson is being published, but he will not be allowed to make any money from it. Instead, all the profits will go to children's charities.

When you first read about Charles Bronson on page 17, were you sympathetic to him? How do you react to him now with this extra information? What would happen to Bronson in your country?

Would you be interested in reading his biography? Why / why not?

9 Friends and relatives

Do you say the following in your language?

A friend of a friend is a friend.
A friend of an enemy is an enemy.
An enemy of a friend is an enemy.
An enemy of an enemy is a friend.

Check you understand the following useful expressions for talking about your friends and relatives:

1. I don't really know John Baker. I only know him by sight.
2. Mary's an old girlfriend of mine.
3. We're old schoolfriends.
4. He's her ex.
5. This is my partner, Jean.
6. Bill's just an acquaintance. I don't really know him that well.
7. She's my sister-in-law.
8. I don't know them, but I know of them.
9. I'm his godson.
10. My sister and I are really close.

Are there people in your life who fit the above descriptions? Tell a partner about them.

10 Comparatives

G3 **It is very common to add an adverb or adverb phrase before a comparison:**

much a lot very much	warmer stronger weaker

For example:

I get on	a bit quite a lot a lot much very much	better with my mum *(than I do with my dad).*

Use the following comparative adjectives to complete these examples:

wiser	younger	better
stronger	older	cheaper

1. Could I have some hot water, please? This coffee is a lot . . . . than I expected.
2. We're really pleased. Harry did a lot . . . . in his exams than we thought he would.
3. We had a great time in America. Everything seemed very much . . . . than in the UK.
4. A year spent travelling makes you a little bit . . . . and a lot . . . . !
5. I'm 36 and you say Pete's 40! I thought he was a bit . . . . than me – not older!

Talk about yourself

Using the adverbs above, complete the sentences below in ways that are true for you. You will need to add the names of people in your family.

1. I actually get on . . . . better with my . . . . than I do with my . . . .
2. To be honest, I'm . . . . closer to my . . . . than I am to my . . . .
3. I like my grandparents on my . . . . side . . . . . more than the ones on my . . . . side.
4. I see . . . . more of . . . . than I do of most of my relatives.
5. Personally, I find . . . . easier to talk to than anyone else in my family.
6. . . . . is . . . . more fun than almost everyone else in my family.

Tell a partner about what you have written, and why.

11 An interesting friend

Try to use some of the words and expressions you have learned in this unit to talk about your most interesting friend or relative. For example:

My uncle John is very business-minded. He runs his own company. He's single, very well-off, and much younger than he looks.

or

My grandmother was blind. She lived on her own. She was very independent. She listened to the radio all day and always knew more about what was going on in the world than anyone else.

Do you or your partner have any relatives who sound similar?
Now tell your partner what the rest of your family are like.

12 A family joke

T7 **Here is a joke which you can practise telling each other in pairs. With a partner, decide what the last line is.**

I used to take my girlfriends home to meet my parents, but I couldn't understand why my mum didn't like any of them. If she was fair-haired, my mum said you can't marry a blonde – she'll soon leave you. If she was a redhead, my mum said she would have a bad temper. It was impossible to please her. One night I met a girl who was the spitting image of my mother. She was the same height. Her hair was the same. She even had a similar voice. The only trouble was when I took her home, ... ! *(Answer on page 192)*

Vocabulary

Running and doing

Earlier in the unit, we talked about *running a hotel* and *doing some work*. Fill in run **or** do **in the following:**

1. I . . . . freelance work in my spare time.
2. I . . . . a burger chain.
3. I . . . . my own company from home.
4. I . . . . a lot of work outside office hours.
5. I . . . . an agency for computer programmers.
6. What do you . . . . for a living?
7. Who . . . . the business when you're away?
8. I . . . . a bit of temping when I have the time.
9. I . . . . the marketing operation in Europe.
10. This business doesn't . . . . itself, you know!

Types of people

Earlier in this unit we met the expressions:

She's a bit of a moaner.
He's a bit of a workaholic.

Use the following words to complete the sentences:

bore	loner	snobs
show-off	laugh	weirdo

1. It'll be great to see Tim again. He's a real . . . . .
2. Do we really have to visit your sister-in-law? She's such a . . . . . She just never stops talking!
3. The Blairs won't speak to you if you're from the wrong part of town. They're such . . . . .
4. My nephew is having a few problems at school. He doesn't seem to have any friends. He's a real . . . . .
5. My ex always had to be the centre of attention. He was such a . . . . .
6. That new guy's a bit of a . . . . . I mean, did he tell you he keeps snakes in his bedroom and feeds them on dead mice!

Idioms

The note on page 11 explained *a pain in the neck*. Complete these idioms with the correct word:

1. My car's **on its last** feet/legs. I've already started looking for a new one.
2. Have you seen Paula's new laptop? I bet it **cost her an arm and a** leg/hand.
3. I'm under a lot of pressure at work. My boss is **breathing down my** back/neck all the time.
4. I'm afraid **I've just put my** foot/mouth **in it**. I've just said something to Kate without realising she and Pete have split up.
5. When Frank slipped on that banana skin, **I nearly laughed my** legs/head **off**.
6. Yes, it was funny, wasn't it? I tried to **keep a straight** mouth/face but it was impossible.
7. If you're worried about something, tell me – it's far better to **get it off your** chest/back.
8. I can't even have a morning off. **I'm up to my** eyes/nose **in work**.

Melanie and Simon talked about how they 'got on' with their families. If you get on very well with someone you can say:

We get on like a house on fire.

Complete the idioms in these expressions using moment, eye, wavelength **and** close:

1. We argue about everything. We simply don't see eye to . . . . on anything.
2. There's never a dull . . . . in our house. There's always something going on!
3. I get on really well with my mum. We're really . . . .
4. It's incredible. Although my gran is in her seventies, we really are on the same . . . .

Phrasal verbs with *up*

Michael's parents *split up*. There are lots of common phrasal verbs with *up*. Fill in the correct form of the verb in the following:

fill cheer mix get look pick

1. If the tickets go on sale at 9, we'd better . . . . up early and be there by 8.
2. I'll . . . . you up in the car around 7 and we can go into town and have a bite to eat.
3. You look really sad! . . . . . up! It's not the end of the world!
4. I'll just go to their website and . . . . up the times of their flights to Zurich.
5. We can . . . . up with petrol before we leave.
6. I always . . . . up Pete with his brother Ed. They look so similar.

learning advice

Grammar is part of a language. It helps us to speak and write correctly. But there is much more to a language than its grammar.

English has thousands of words – vocabulary, collocations, idioms, and expressions. We express what we mean mostly by our choice of vocabulary.

If you spend most of your time studying grammar, your English will not improve very much. You will see most improvement if you learn more words and expressions.

You can say very little with grammar, but you can say almost anything with words!

Unit 2a : Your interests

that interest you. It's a hobby. What turns you on? The sort of things you get a kick out of. What things do you do in your spare time? The games you p
s you read. What kind of programmes do you usually watch? What films do you go to? The places you like to visit. The magazines you buy. The evening clas
rument do you wish you could play? What sort of music do you listen to? I only go to classical concerts. I love modern paintings. I've never been to an art gall
rdening. I'm a shopaholic. What do you put on your wall? What languages do you speak? What clubs do you go to? What do you do when you're free? Fashi

1 Free time

Which of the following do you like doing in your free time?
Mark each one in this way:

O if you do it often
S if you do it sometimes
N if you never do it

listening to classical music
going to see bands
going clubbing
playing an instrument
reading
working out at a gym
watching videos
going to art exhibitions
going to an evening class
playing a sport
cooking
going round junk shops
playing computer games
t'ai chi or something like that

Real English: junk
Junk is stuff of little value which you consider useless. For example: old furniture, books, CDs, or other things you have no use for.

Use your dictionary to translate any vocabulary you are unsure of. Find out what you have in common with your partner.

2 Before you listen

T8 **Dan and Helena have only just started going out together. They are not finding it easy to decide what to do with their evening. As you listen, try and decide which statement is most accurate:**

1. They have nothing in common.
2. They have lots in common.
3. They have less in common than they think!

Listen again and fill in the gaps in the conversation.

3 Talking point

Do you and your friends ever have problems trying to decide what to do in the evenings? At what age are you too old to go clubbing? 25? 30? 40? Never?

So what shall we do tonight?

Dan: So what do you feel like doing tonight? Any ideas?
Helena: Well, I'd quite like to see a film, or, I don't know, see if there's any good bands around, if you're into bands.
Dan: Yes, that's an idea. . . . . music do you like, then?
Helena: Oh, all sorts, really, you know, a lot of pop and I quite like blues and jazz and . . . .
Dan: Oh, really? I'm more into dance music myself, so maybe ...
Helena: Well, ..., we could always go and see a film. I like really scary things.
Dan: What? You mean like *Halloween?*
Helena: Yes, that kind of thing, and I also . . . . action movies, you know, car chases, guns, bombs, anything that's fast and exciting.
Dan: Oh, right. To be honest with you, I'm not really . . . . violent films.
Helena: You're kidding! And I thought this was going to be the perfect relationship!
Dan: . . . .! But it doesn't sound like we've got all that much in common, really, does it?
Helena: Oh come on, there must be something we can do!
Dan: Let me think. Well, I suppose we . . . . go clubbing.
Helena: What? Somewhere like Paradox?
Dan: Is that the new place that's just opened?
Helena: Yes, just last week. Right, so . . . . going clubbing, then?
Dan: OK. Why not? Do you go much yourself?
Helena: No, ..., actually. A couple of times a year, I guess.
Dan: Oh, me too now, but I . . . . a lot more when I was younger – almost every weekend. The thing was, though, it just got to me after a while, staying out dancing all night and then having to go to work . . . . in the morning. I'm getting a bit too old for it now.
Helena: Oh, well, that's that off the menu then! So, what shall we do then?
Dan: I don't know. . . . . get a video, and a curry, and have a nice quiet evening in in front of the telly?
Helena: Oh, you've got to be joking! We're not in our graves yet. I mean, that's the kind of thing my parents are probably doing . . . .! Look, it's not what I'd normally do on a Monday night, but let's give clubbing a go! It might be a laugh.

Real English: The thing was . . .

This is a natural way to add extra details or an explanation. *The thing is* . . . introduces a problem, an excuse, or a difficulty of some kind.

4 Pronunciation

T9 Listen to these two conversations and notice the pronunciation of kind of in the second example:

a. I've just bought a new car.
> Really? What kind? [kaind]
b. What kind of car have you got? [kənəv]
> Oh, a Volvo.

Practise the following sentences with the tape:

1. What kind of car is that?
2. What kind of tea do you like?
3. What kind of person is she?
4. What kind of books do you read?
5. What kind of things do you watch?
6. What kind of things do you listen to?

5 Three uses of *thing*

T10 The word thing is one of the most common words in spoken English. Listen, then practise saying these three common structures with thing.

1. *What kind of things* do you like?

What kind of things do you like shopping for?
What kind of things do you like reading?

2. Jazz and blues *and things like that.*

Clothes and shoes and things like that.
I like jogging and running and things like that.

3. I love making *Italian things.*

I love making Italian things, you know, like pasta.
I love old things, like old radios and 78 records.

Using the structures from 2 and 3 above, write your own answers to the following questions:

1. What kind of food do you like?

 . . . .

2. So what kind of things do you usually do at weekends?

 . . . .

3. What kind of music do you listen to?

 . . . .

4. What kind of things do you like watching on TV?

 . . . .

5. What kind of films are you into?

 . . . .

Compare your answers with some other people in the class. Who do you have most in common with?

6 Agreeing

G4 If we share someone's interests we can say:

I really love classical music.
Really? What's your favourite piece?
or So do I. Who's your favourite composer?
or Me too! Especially Mozart.

When we agree with a negative idea, we say:

I don't really like classical music.
Neither do I. or Me neither.

Grammar in context

For each of the following statements only two responses are correct. Cross out the incorrect one in each group.

1. I really love Mexican food.
 > So do I/Me too /So have I. It's great, isn't it?
2. I don't really like much modern fashion.
 > Neither do I/Me neither/Me too. It's dreadful.
3. I'm not really keen on big Hollywood movies.
 > Neither do I/Neither am I/Me neither. They're so predictable.
4. I've seen all the Bond films.
 > So have I/Neither have I/Me too. Some are better than others.
5. I'd love to go to Africa sometime.
 > So do I/So would I/Me too. It sounds amazing.
6. I hate most classical music.
 > Me too/Me neither/So do I. It doesn't do anything for me, I'm afraid.

Auxiliary verb practice

Use So + auxiliary + I **or** Neither + auxiliary + I **to agree with the following:**

1. I prefer coffee without milk.
2. I don't like things that are too sweet.
3. I'm going to stay in tonight and do nothing.
4. I've just booked my summer holiday.
5. I never go abroad.
6. I'd love to meet someone really famous.
7. I was born in Australia.
8. I can't stand sea water.

Real English: What kind of films are you into?

If you are *into* something, you are very interested in it. For example:
She's really into health food.
He's into alternative medicine.

7 Not really keen

If we do not share someone's interests, we often soften the way we express this. Notice how really is used in the following:

I really love classical music and opera.
> Oh, do you? I'm not really very keen on it myself.
or > It's not really my kind of thing, I'm afraid.
or > I don't really like things like that.

Without *really*, these statements would sound quite strong and even rude. Match the following two-line conversations. Then practise in pairs.

1. I love nearly all winter sports.
2. Going out with a crowd of friends and having fun, that's what I really like doing.
3. I'm really interested in politics.
4. I'm really into older music, you know, before 1967.
5. My favourite kind of things are comics and cartoons.
6. I'm really into roller-blading. It's a bit like roller-skating.

a. Oh, it's not really my kind of thing, I'm afraid. I don't really understand what makes all the parties different. They all seem the same to me!
b. Really? I'm not really very keen on them, myself. I once broke my leg skiing and it put me off – for life!
c. Are you? It's not really my kind of thing. I'm always worried I might get hurt.
d. I don't really like things like that myself. I don't see the point of them. I prefer a good novel – the longer the better!
e. Are you? I'm not really that keen on anything before 1980.
f. Do you? It's not really my kind of thing, I'm afraid. I prefer to go out with just one or maybe two people. I hate crowds.

T11 Notice how all the responses give extra information. Go back and underline all uses of really in this exercise.

All the language in this course is carefully chosen to help you to learn useful natural English. Although this activity is teaching the use of *really*, did you notice the following collocations in the examples?

1. winter	5. get . . . . . .
2. have	6. classical . . . . . .
3. interested . . . . . . politics	7. I don't see the . . . . . of it.
4. It's not my . . . . . . of thing.	8. It . . . . . . me off . . . . . . life.

Real English: not that keen

Not that keen is very similar in meaning to *not very keen*. Both are perfectly correct spoken English. For example:

I wasn't that happy about it. *It's not that late.*
He's not that well-off. *It's not that good an idea.*

Listen for this use of *that* when you hear natural English.

8 I really love it

1. With a partner, make sure you can name all the activities in the pictures.

2. Tell your partner whether you like doing these things or not and why. Use expressions from exercises 6 and 7.

Think of *your* three main interests. Find the person or people in your class who you have the most in common with.

9 The -ing form

The -ing form as a verb

G5 **Underline the *-ing* forms in these sentences used to talk about your interests:**

1. I go horse-riding every weekend.
2. I spend all my free time learning English.

Do the following time expressions fit best into pattern 1 or 2? Why?

whenever I can	all my life
most of my evenings	half my life
all my Saturday mornings	quite often
as often as I can	on Tuesdays

Tell a partner which of these things you enjoy doing:

planning your summer holidays
playing the piano/violin/guitar
helping homeless people
raising money for sick animals
collecting things (eg stamps, phonecards etc)
going folk dancing
going to the theatre
studying a foreign language
going camping or youth hostelling
going abroad
surfing the net
gardening or visiting gardens
mountaineering or hill-walking
reading
painting or drawing
singing or acting

Use these ideas to complete these sentences:

1. No wonder John's eyes are so sore. He spends his whole life . . . .
2. This French friend of mine's just got back from New York where he spent most of the winter . . . . at a school in Brooklyn.
3. Kevin feels very strongly about animal rights. He spends a lot of time . . . .
4. Pedro wants to be the next Pavarotti. He spends all his free time . . . .
5. His mother really loves her plants and flowers. She spends all her time . . . .
6. I've spent ages . . . . , and I'm finally off in three days. Two weeks in the sun!
7. Bill has just splashed out £100 on these new boots. You know he goes . . . . nearly every weekend, don't you?
8. Marie works with poor people in the inner city. She spends every Saturday night . . . . at a hostel in the city centre.

Now complete the following about your interests:

I . . . . whenever I can.
I go . . . . quite a lot in the summer.
I spend most Sundays . . . .

Tell a partner what you have written.

The -ing form as a noun

We can use the *-ing* form to talk about an activity which is the subject of a sentence:

Mountaineering can be pretty dangerous.

Use your own ideas and the ideas in the list to complete the following in pairs. For example, the answer to no. 1 might be *Ballroom dancing*. What do you think?

1. . . . . is all right for old people, but not for people in their twenties.
2. I know . . . . can be very dangerous, but there's no need to ban it, just because some people get killed every winter.
3. . . . . around the Greek islands in the summer is great fun.
4. . . . . is all right if you've got the time and the money.
5. . . . . is more useful than learning Chinese – unless, of course, you happen to be Chinese!
6. . . . . is a very worthwhile thing to do.
7. . . . . is something I've always wanted to do, but I've just never had the time.
8. . . . . is all right for women, but not for men.

Now compare your ideas with the others.

Real English: alright *or* all right

In British English some people write *alright* as one word. Others write it as two. Writing it as one word tends to be more informal. In this course it is always written as two words.

Are you a bag person?

Come on, admit it! You can't resist classy carrier bags. You have some cheap and nasty bags from the local supermarket which you put your rubbish in. But somewhere at home you've got a collection of bags that you wouldn't part with for the world. An Armani bag? A Gucci one? Or maybe it's that one from the Duty-Free Shop at Kuala Lumpur Airport? They prove that you're the sort of person you'd like to be.

Recently, a London Gallery held an exhibition to celebrate the carrier bag. They asked 30 top artists and designers to design a carrier bag for 30 shops which took part in the exhibition. The show was a tremendous success because it seems we are all secret carrier bag collectors. Some people go into expensive designer shops and buy the cheapest thing – just to get one of their bags. Others don't even bother buying anything. They just ask straight out for a free bag for their collection. It seems that it's not the bag we want. It's what it represents. That's why we throw away our boring Tesco and Marks and Spencers bags, but make sure our Harrods or Louis Vuitton ones remain in perfect condition.

10 Talking point

Which is your most treasured carrier bag? Where did it come from?

What makes a classy carrier bag?

Do you collect anything else which might seem strange to other people?

11 Time expressions

Below is a list of useful time expressions which tell people how often you do things. For example:

How often do you go skiing then?
> A couple of times a year, I suppose.

If we are unsure or do not know exactly, we say I suppose.

With a partner, number these expressions from 1-10 according to frequency (1 is most frequent).

every month or so	hardly ever
almost every weekend	every day
two or three times a week	every other day
a couple of times a year	every fortnight
once or twice a month	never

1. ....
2. ....
3. ....
4. ....
5. ....
6. ....
7. ....
8. ....
9. ....
10. ....

Go back and find examples of some of those expressions in the conversation.

12 How often do you ...?

Ask your partner:

How often do you . . . ?

1. have your hair cut
2. get up early on Saturdays
3. see your parents /grandparents
4. cook in the evenings
5. work in the evenings
6. see your best friend
7. go clubbing
8. read in English
9. watch films in English
10. buy presents for friends
11. go away for the weekend
12. go to the cinema

Now work with a different partner asking the same questions. Try to use some of the expressions you have learned in this unit so far.

13 Not as often as I used to

T12 **Listen to June, a bus driver, answering some of the questions you have just answered. As you're listening, complete the time expressions below that she uses.**

1. Not all that . . . .
2. All the . . . .
3. Not as . . . . as I'd like to
4. About . . . . fortnight
5. . . . . I can
6. A . . . . of times a year
7. Hardly . . . .
8. Not as often as I . . . . to

14 Talking point

Do you have much in common with the rest of your family? What interests do you share?

Do you think men and women tend to be interested in different kinds of things?

Is it best to marry someone who:

shares all your interests?
shares none of your interests?
shares a few of your interests but has some of their own?

Is there something you would really like to be able to do, but have not yet had the opportunity to do?

Unit 2b : Unusual interests

t what you'd expect. It's not the sort of thing your parents would approve of. A bit off the wall. Something different. Not just what everyone else does. Somethir
mething really individual. But isn't it dangerous? Won't you get hurt? Hunting makes me sick. Do you get a kick out of it? Not everybody's cup of tea. Not really
u wouldn't catch me up in one of these things. Not in a month of Sundays. But people get killed doing that! I wouldn't be seen dead doing that kind
body makes you do these things. Doesn't it cost a fortune? It should be banned. But you're putting other people's lives at risk as well as your own. Wrest

1 An unusual interest

In the conversation on page 24 Helena and Dan discussed things like music, films and clubbing.

However, some people have more unusual interests, such as boxing.

Do you know anyone who has an unusual hobby or interest?

Read this article about Jane Couch, the famous female boxer. What arguments does it give against women boxing?

2 Help with words

To help you understand the text better, here is some help with a few words:

A licence gives you permission to do something.

If something is a spectacle, it is strange or interesting to watch.

If you counter an argument, you give the opposite view.

If you are unstable, you are not mentally fit.

If you commit suicide, you kill yourself.

WOMAN BOXER

The unofficial world women's lightweight boxing champion, Jane Couch, is today waiting to hear whether the British Boxing Board of Control (BBBC) will allow her to continue her career. The BBBC is deciding whether women boxers will be allowed to box officially or whether they will have to remain in the shadowy world of unofficial boxing.

Miss Couch could expect to earn around £100,000 a year if she is given a licence. However, there has been much opposition to the spectacle of women in the boxing ring. There was laughter at the BBBC inquiry this week when it was suggested that women should not be licensed to box because they were biologically and emotionally unstable.

To counter these arguments, Miss Couch's lawyer, Dinah Rose, said sarcastically, "We are all taking a hell of a risk allowing women to pilot aeroplanes, aren't we? Perhaps all women airline pilots should be tested to see if they suffer from emotional instability."

"I would certainly want research on that, if I were responsible for them," replied Adrian Blackson, the BBBC's chief medical officer. "And perhaps we should also say that only men are stable enough to look after children," Miss Rose asked, to which Mr. Blackson could only respond by saying, "That's an interesting question."

Miss Rose went on to suggest that it was men who were more likely to be unstable, to commit violent crimes or commit suicide. Mr. Blackson told the inquiry that until further research had been done, the BBBC should not allow Miss Couch to box.

3 Comprehension check

Are the following statements true (T) or false (F)?

1. The BBBC stands for 'British Broadcasting Corporation'.
2. Women's boxing hasn't been officially recognised yet.
3. Jane Couch earns about £100,000 a year.
4. Dinah Rose thinks women airline pilots should be tested for emotional instability.
5. Men are more likely to commit violent crimes than women.

Real English: if I were responsible ...

If I was responsible / If I were responsible – Both are correct English.

4 Vocabulary check

Complete the following with words from the text:

1. A sports person who wins a very important competition is the . . . .
2. The place where boxing matches take place is called a boxing . . . .
3. If you say something which is the opposite of what you believe, because you want to mock or insult someone, you say it . . . .
4. If you study something in detail to gain new knowledge about it, you do . . . . on it.

Complete the following sentences using words from the text:

5. You can expect to . . . . £30,000 a year.
6. There's a lot of . . . . to the new road.
7. I think we're . . . . a big risk if we don't go to the doctor immediately.
8. If you commit a violent . . . . , you should go to prison for a long time.

5 Violent or dangerous?

Make sure you understand the following.
Are they violent, dangerous, or both?

boxing	bungee jumping	climbing
snowboarding	water skiing	skiing
wrestling	horse racing	canyoning
canoeing	kickboxing	football
sky-diving	hang-gliding	scuba-diving

Should women be allowed to do sports like boxing, which have traditionally been associated with men? Why / why not?

Why do you think so many people like sports like boxing or bullfighting?

Have you got any dangerous interests?

6 How-questions

***How*-questions are useful for asking for more information:**

How much did it cost?
How long did it take you?
How difficult was it?

Make *how*-questions by adding an adverb, an adjective, or a quantity word like much, to the following:

1. How . . . . did it take you to learn to play the guitar as well as that?
   > About 10 years. I started when I was really young, though.
2. How . . . . is your work from your home?
   > About an hour's drive, I think.
3. How . . . . did you move here?
   > Oh, ages ago. In fact, I've forgotten how long!
4. How . . . . does dinner usually cost you?
   > It varies, but I suppose about £8 or £9.
5. So how . . . . have you been learning English?
   > Ever since I can remember. I started when I was really really young.
6. How . . . . can you speak Chinese?
   > I guess I'm OK, but I could be better.
7. How . . . . is it to learn Chinese?
   > Some people say it's the most difficult language to learn as a foreigner.
8. How . . . . do you go away then?
   > Every couple of months, I suppose, providing I've got the money.
9. How . . . . people do you need in a team?
   > Usually it's 11, but you can also play with 5.
10. How . . . . are you about your exams?
    > Very! But I'm trying not to think about them too much!

Now write questions you would like to ask a partner. Then work in pairs to find the answers.

How much . . . . ?
How often . . . . ?
How long ago . . . . ?
How far away . . . . ?
How difficult . . . . ?
How easy . . . . ?
How many . . . . ?

Grammar check

G6 Look at this simple grammar rule:

Many is used with plural nouns:
How *many people* do you work with?
There are too *many cars* on the road these days.
Much is used with nouns which are uncountable:
There isn't *much time.*
I don't have very *much money* on me.

Add much or many in these sentences:

1. How . . . . . . hours did you say you worked?
2. How . . . . . . time have we got?
3. I don't actually know how . . . . . . children they've got.
4. There aren't . . . . . . students in this town.
5. I don't know how . . . . . . money to take.
6. When we were first married, we didn't have . . . . . . furniture – just a table and two chairs.

Here are some common expressions containing much. Match them to the responses below:

7. Have you seen much of John recently?
8. What's wrong? You're not saying very much.
9. I don't think much of his new girlfriend.
10. There's not much I can do, is there?

a. No, I'm not feeling very well.
b. No, there's not much anyone can do.
c. Yes, as a matter of fact, I bumped into him yesterday morning in Woolworth's.
d. Don't you? I think she's great fun.

Real English: Do you go clubbing much?
Much is also used to ask how often someone does something. Look at these examples:
Do you go away much? Do you see your parents much? Do you see much of Mary these days?

Interviewing Jane Couch

Write six questions you'd like to ask Jane Couch, the female boxer.

1. . . . . ?
2. . . . . ?
3. . . . . ?
4. . . . . ?
5 . . . . ?
6. . . . . ?

In pairs, take turns pretending to be Jane Couch and use your six questions to interview each other. You will need to use your imagination.

Scottish Kickboxers

Two Scottish women, Kate Kearney and Teresa Dewan, are two of Britain's top kickboxers. During the day Kate works in a shop selling hats to wealthy Glaswegian ladies, while Teresa works in credit control for a car hire company. Kate is currently Scotland's female champion kickboxer.

In a sport normally dominated by men, the two women are proud to be the only two Scots in the British team.

Some critics of the sport believe that women should be barred from taking part. Kate and Teresa couldn't disagree more. In fact, they enjoy fighting against men. The women usually win. Teresa said, "We give them a good fight and beat them. They usually go off in a huff – you should see their faces. A man never likes to be beaten by a woman."

Both women think there is nothing better after a hard day's work than to get into the ring and have a good fight. Apart from their jobs all they have got time for is training. Kate said, "I love fighting and I am confident we will be world champions."

Real English: in a huff

If you are *in a huff with* someone, you are upset because of something they have said or done.

7 Talking point

Can you think of other sports where women can beat men? Golf? Tennis? Football?
Do you think this will be the same 50 years from now?
Do you think your national football team will ever include a woman?

8 Interests

G7 In English, the word *hobbies* suggests things like stamp collecting or making model aeroplanes, and is often associated with being pre-teenage. Most adults don't have hobbies; they are *interested in things* or they *do things*. However, people do sometimes talk about the hobbies they used to have when they were younger. For example:

I used to collect cans when I was younger, like Coke cans. I lived near the sea and I'd find them on the beach. I grew out of it after a while and I can't remember what happened to all the cans.

I used to have a train set when I was younger, but I just lost interest in it once I got into music.

Think of two hobbies you used to have when you were younger. Tell your partner as much as you can about them. Try to use the following:

1. I used to collect . . . . when I was younger. I kept them in a . . . . I grew out of it when I was . . . . . years old.
2. I used to play . . . . when I was younger.

9 Would and 'd

G8 Here are some expressions using would, wouldn't or the contracted form 'd. Complete the two-line dialogues below using them:

a. I would if I could, but I can't, I'm afraid. I've got to leave early today.
b. Well, I'd quite like to go somewhere exotic.
c. If you'd rather, we could always stay in instead. I don't mind either way.
d. I wouldn't if I were you! It's really hot!
e. That'd be great, if you could.

1. I'm not really very keen on going out tonight.
. . . .
2. If you want a ticket, I'll get you one.
. . . .
3. Could you possibly give me a lift home?
. . . .
4. I've no idea where to go on holiday.
. . . .
5. I think I'll have the Madras curry.
. . . .

Grammar in context

Now complete the sentences below by adding one of these expressions:

that'd be great	If you'd rather
I'd quite like to	I would if I could

1. So what do you feel like doing tonight?
> . . . . go out for a meal, if that's all right with you.
2. Do you want a lift?
> Oh, thanks. . . . . I'm in a real hurry to get home.
3. Look, it's not that I don't want to see you. . . . . , but I just can't. I'm out of the country all that week.
4. . . . . go to the party on your own, that's fine by me.
5. Well, if you could persuade Jim to come to the lecture this evening then . . . . , but don't worry if you can't.
6. I'm really sorry you can't come with us tonight.
> Well, you know, ... , but I've really got to finish this work.
7. I'm really very tired. . . . . go to bed, if that's all right.
8. . . . . come a different weekend, that's fine. It's all the same to me.

Here are three common expressions with 'd and wouldn't:

You'd never catch me in a boxing ring!
I wouldn't be seen dead wearing leather trousers!
I wouldn't go parachuting even if you paid me!

Use them to say something amusing about yourself.

Real English: Do you want a lift?

You ask this question when you offer to take someone in your car. Look at these examples:

Could you give me a lift to the station?
You couldn't give me a lift, could you?
I'll give you a lift if you want.

This is different from the expression *thumb a lift* which means that you are hitch-hiking.

10 Reaching decisions

With a partner, try to agree what to do in each of the following situations. Use the highlighted expressions with *would* in exercise 9.

1. An important guest is visiting your home town. You have been asked to take them out and show them the best it has to offer. What would you suggest to them?

2. You and a friend have just won £1,000 in a lottery. How would you most like to celebrate?

3. You and some friends are totally broke, but want to have a nice day out tomorrow. You have absolutely no money to spend. Where would you go?

Once you have reached your decisions, join up with another pair and reach a group decision.

11 Checking you understand

Good listeners check they understand what is being said to them. This encourages the speaker to give more information. You might have to interrupt to do this. Look at the following very useful 'checking' technique.

I love music.
> What? Do you mean just listening to it or actually playing an instrument?
Both, really. I play the drums in a band at weekends and I've got piles of CDs at home.

Practise these conversations with a partner. Use the ideas in italics with the pattern above.

1. I'm really interested in boxing.
watch it / box yourself
> . . . . ?
No way! You'd never catch me in the ring! No, I just love watching it.
2. I really love American football.
watch / play
>. . . . . ?
Oh, I'm in a team. We play every Sunday.
3. I really love Chinese food.
go to Chinese restaurants / make it yourself
>. . . . . ?
No, I make it myself – all the time. You must come round sometime.
4. I'm really into art.
go to galleries / paint yourself
> . . . . ?
No, I wish I could paint. I just like going round galleries.
5. I'm very interested in culture.
youth culture / Beethoven and things like that
> . . . . ?
Well, all sorts. Fashion, music, dance, clothes, anything, really.

With your partner, make your own dialogues:

1. I really love music.
2. I'm really into food.
3. I'm very keen on sport.

12 Boxing joke

T13 **Practise telling the following joke in pairs. Think about which words to stress and where to pause. Who tells the joke better, you or your partner?**

When I was a kid, we couldn't afford a TV, so one day, my dad drilled a hole through the wall, which meant we could look into the house next door. After that, we used to watch the boxing and the wrestling every night . . . until we finally realised that the neighbours didn't have a TV either.

Vocabulary

Idioms

Use these words to complete the idioms:

accounting own street taste cup

1. I must admit, I don't really like this kind of music. It's not really my . . . . of tea.
2. If you're into action movies, you really should go and see *Explosive Device*. It should be right up your . . . .
3. You like Disney movies! I can't believe it! Oh well, each to their . . . .
4. My favourite kind of food is cheese – blue cheese. I know it's an acquired . . . .
5. You're into techno music? Well, there's no . . . . for taste, I suppose.

Match the idioms to the meanings below:

a. I don't really like that kind of thing.
b. I'm sure you'd like it.
c. It's something you learn to like gradually.
d. Different people like different things. (2 idioms)

Expressions with *thing*

Use the following common expressions in the situations below:

It's just not the done thing.
It's just one of those things.
for one thing
the thing is
one thing after another
don't know the first thing about

1. I've had such a dreadful day. It's just been . . . . since I got up.
2. I don't know why you're asking me. I . . . . cars. Ask Mark.
3. I'm sorry to hear you've lost your job.
   > Yes, well, ... , I guess. We could all see it coming.
4. Whatever you do when you're in Indonesia, don't use your left hand to offer or take things. . . . .
5. I'd love to come with you, but, ... , I've already agreed to go out with Samantha.
6. So why don't you like him, then?
   > Well, ... , you can't trust anything he says, and for another, he's a bit of a show-off.

Time expressions

Use these words to complete the time expressions below:

small dawn morning
last start night

1. I'm not at my best first thing in the . . . .
2. We'd better have an early night. We've got a really early . . . . . . in the morning.
3. I woke up in the middle of the . . . . . . and just couldn't get back to sleep.
4. The party went on till well after midnight. We didn't get home till the . . . . . . hours.
5. . . . . . . thing at night, before I go to bed, I switch off everything electrical and pull out all the plugs. It's a habit I can't get out of!
6. I was up at the crack of . . . . . . this morning.

Now underline the time expressions above.

All right

Match up these short conversations. Each one contains a different use of all right.

1. Are you feeling all right now?
2. I'm really nervous about making the speech.
3. Is everything all right, sir?
4. Is your coffee all right?
5. Shall we take the car?
6. Just listen to that wind. I hate flying in weather like this!
7. Is it all right if I borrow your video for the weekend?

a. Well, actually, it's a bit cold.
b. Yes, thanks. The room's perfect.
c. Yes, thanks. I'm much better.
d. Yes, all right. It'll be quicker than the train.
e. Yes, sure – so long as you're careful with it.
f. Don't worry, it'll be all right on the night.
g. Now, calm down. Everything's going to be all right.

Review : Units 1 and 2

1 Tenses

Choose the correct form:

1. I'm looking/I look for a new job at the moment.
2. My dad likes/is liking playing golf a lot.
3. I do/'m doing odd jobs now and again.
4. She's running/runs her own business from home and always has.
5. I work/'m working this weekend, I'm afraid.
6. How often are you having/do you have your hair cut?

2 Multiple choice

Choose the correct alternative:

1. He's (a) a bit of a show-off.
   (b) a bit too show-off.
2. He's (a) quite fun to be with.
   (b) a bit of fun to be with.
3. (a) To learn English is not easy.
   (b) Learning English is not easy.
4. I don't really like this kind of food much.
   (a) > Me neither.
   (b) > Me too.
5. I don't really like places with lots of people.
   (a) > So do I.
   (b) > Neither do I.
6. I like jazz and blues and
   (a) those sort of things.
   (b) that sort of thing.
7. Pete spends a lot of time out in the country
   (a) hill-walking.
   (b) to hill-walk.
8. I spend (a) as often as I can studying.
   (b) most of my evenings studying.
9. How (a) many (b) much people are coming tonight?
10. (a) I had gone
    (b) I used to go
    swimming in the lake a lot when I was younger.

3 Expressions

The following expressions all occurred in units 1 and 2. Use them in the sentences below:

I'm afraid I can't	haven't you heard
not really keen	one of those things
to tell you the truth	I would if I could

1. You must be really looking forward to seeing your parents again.
   > Well, ... , I'm not actually.
2. Where's Jim? Hasn't he turned up yet?
   > Oh . . . . ? He's been taken ill and rushed to hospital.
3. Look, it's not that I don't want to see you. I mean, ... but I just can't get away from work until after 7.
4. Could you look after my kids on Friday for a few hours?
   > No, sorry, ... I'm already doing something else.
5. I'm sorry I broke your vase.
   > Don't worry about it. It's just . . . .
6. So what do you think? Do you like my new tie?
   > No, I can't say I do really. I'm . . . . on that colour.

4 Conversation

Put the jumbled conversation below into the correct order. The first line is correct.

a. So do you feel like doing anything tonight?
b. Oh really. I didn't know you had a brother. How old is he?
c. Well, actually, I'm already going to see a film with my brother.
d. You mean action movies and that kind of thing.
e. Yeah, that kind of thing. So what were you thinking of doing tonight, anyway?
f. And do you get on with him all right?
g. Yeah, he's great. We get on really well. He's into the same kind of films as me.
h. About 32 or 33, I think. I can never really remember. He's a good bit older than me.

1 a	2	3	4	5	6	7	8

5 Collocations

Match the verbs on the left with the best collocations on the right:

1. do	a. . . . . . . for myself
2. run	b. . . . . . . the net
3. go	c. . . . . . . self-employed
4. surf	d. . . . . . . for the weekend
5. work	e. . . . . . . a lot of work
6. go away	f. . . . . . . well with my family
7. get on	g. . . . . . . clubbing
8. be	h. . . . . . . my own business

6 Adjectives

Match the adjective on the left with its opposite on the right:

1. liberal	a. dark
2. rude	b. interesting
3. talkative	c. normal
4. lazy	d. poor
5. weird	e. conservative
6. dull	f. friendly
7. tidy	g. hard-working
8. well-off	h. quiet
9. fair *(hair)*	i. messy

7 Real English

Match 1-8 with the follow-up comments in a-h:

1. What's all that noise?
2. I think boxing is all right for men but not for women.
3. So, do you see her much?
4. So, how long have you been collecting phonecards, then?
5. Can you get there by seven?
6. What's your little brother like then? Is he OK?
7. How do you get on with your in-laws?
8. He's great, isn't he, that new teacher?

a. That's a pretty conservative view, isn't it?
b. Do you think so? I'm not that keen on him myself.
c. It's the neighbour from hell again.
d. No, not really. Not since she's moved away.
e. Pretty well, I suppose, all things considered.
f. No, not really. The thing is, I'm supposed to be meeting Jim at 6.30.
g. I suppose I've always been into it, really.
h. You're joking, aren't you? He's a total pain in the neck!

8 Vocabulary quiz

Answer the following 20 questions with a partner. Then compare your answers with another pair. Who got most answers right?

1. If you have a car, do you need a driving licence or a driving permission?
2. If you want to do well in your career, are you ambitious or greedy?
3. Do vegetarians drink milk and eat cheese?
4. If you hardly ever do something, does it mean that you do it very often or very rarely?
5. Where does a retired teacher teach?
6. If you are messy, are you tidy or untidy?
7. If someone kills themself, do they commit suicide or suffer from suicide?
8. If you are keen on another person, do you want to start a relationship with them or not?
9. If someone with red-hair is called a red-head, what is someone with blonde hair called?
10. Where are you likely to be if you are having a pint?
11. If you were a laid-back sort of person how often would you be in a huff with someone – often or hardly ever?
12. Is a biography a book someone writes about their own or another person's life?
13. Do criminals make crimes or commit them?
14. If you get up first thing in the morning do you get up very early or before the rest of your family?
15. A friend of yours is described as narrow-minded. Does it mean they are open to new ideas or are their ideas fixed in a negative way?
16. If you have no brothers or sisters, are you a single child or an only child?
17. If bad neighbours can be described as neighbours from hell, do we describe good neighbours as neighbours from heaven?
18. Do you make a sport or play a sport?
19. Does a boxing match take place in a ring or a square?
20. How well do you know an acquaintance?

Unit 3a : Big decisions

e. I've decided it's time to leave home. I can't make up my mind. Good for you! I'm sure it's the right decision. I don't want to get stuck in a dead-end job. It's
l. You don't get a second bite at the cherry. It's a once-in-a-lifetime opportunity. I've got something important to tell you. I don't know if you want to hear this,
ouldn't mind becoming a doctor. It was the biggest decision of my life. You'll meet lots of interesting people and see lots of interesting places. I'd never do that e
me. It just feels the right thing to do. How come you're marrying her and not me? What on earth made you do that? I've finally decided to stop smoking. It's a

1 Tough decisions

What is the most important decision you have ever made in your life?
Did it turn out well or badly?

On your own, put the following decisions in order from the most difficult to make (1) to the easiest to make (8).

deciding to change your job	__
deciding to get married	__
deciding to start a family	__
deciding to work abroad	__
deciding to stop smoking	__
deciding to get divorced	__
deciding to move house	__
deciding on a name for your child	__

Compare your answers with a partner. Can you think of any other tough decisions not listed above?

2 Who did what?

T14 **Now listen to these three people talking about their experiences of the above. Listen carefully and write down their decision.**

3 What a nightmare!

Check you understand the expressions below. Use a dictionary to help you translate any vocabulary you're unsure of.

I felt really pleased with myself.
It was total chaos.
It was a real weight off my shoulders.
I couldn't stand it any more.
What a nightmare!
After that, it was plain sailing.

Listen to the three people again and tick the expressions when you hear them.

Use the expressions to talk about experiences you have had.

1. ....   2. ....   3. ....

4 While you listen

T15 Phil and Jason are both in the same evening class and are chatting during the coffee break. Listen to them talking about some big decisions.

As you listen, try and answer the following questions:

1. What big decisions has Jason made?
2. Why?

Listen again and try to fill in the gaps in the conversation.

5 Talking point

Crawley is a nice quiet town in the country about half an hour by train from London. It's near Gatwick Airport, so there are a lot of jobs. It's got good schools and few social problems. Where would you rather live – London or Crawley?

Would you like to move to another town – or even another country – or are you happy where you are?

Forty a day!

Phil: Just time for a quick smoke. Oh sorry, do you want one?

Jason: No, thanks. I gave up years ago.

Phil: . . . . ! I've given up even trying to give up!

Jason: Yeah, it's a nightmare, isn't it?

Phil: . . . . ! I don't know how you managed it.

Jason: Well, it's funny, but it was my job that did it. I mean, ... , and you know it's destroying your lungs, don't you, and I knew I wouldn't be able to become a fireman if I didn't give up.

Phil: So what's becoming a fireman got to do with it? Is it the fire risk or something?

Jason: No, it's just that . . . . pass a physical to get in, and I wouldn't be able to do that if I was smoking 40 a day.

Phil: 40 a day! Just as well you gave up! So . . . . you decided to become a fireman anyway?

Jason: Mm, I'd have to think about that. I suppose it all goes back to when I got out of college. I wanted to do something exciting and different, you know, and a friend of my dad's was in the local fire brigade.

Phil: Oh, right. So, ... , ... ?

Jason: Yes, he helped me get the job. I mean, I knew I didn't want to . . . . sitting in an office pushing bits of paper round a desk or stuck in front of a computer screen!

Phil: Yeah, I know exactly what you mean. I'm half-blind already! So . . . . move to London, then? Was it for work or because of a relationship or what?

Jason: Well, it was mainly work, but also because I was just . . . . where I was living at the time.

Phil: It was down in Crawley, wasn't it? It's pretty quiet down there, isn't it?

Jason: Quiet? Yeah, it's dead. There's absolutely nothing to do there.

Phil: . . . . ?

Jason: What? Becoming a fireman?

Phil: No, no, moving to London, I mean.

Jason: Oh yeah, ... I love it. I don't think I could live anywhere else now.

Phil: No, it's the same for me. It gets you after a while, doesn't it? It's like a drug.

Real English: Good for you!

This is a common way of congratulating someone. For example:

I've just passed my driving test.
> Good for you!

6 Pronunciation

T16 The following sentences using question tags are taken from the dialogue. Listen to them on tape, then practise saying them:

1. It's a nightmare, isn't it?
2. You know it's destroying your lungs, don't you?
3. It gets you after a while, doesn't it?
4. It was down in Crawley, wasn't it?
5. It's pretty quiet down there, isn't it?
6. So, he helped you, did he?

Do you use tags when you speak English? Say the examples again without the tags. What difference does it make? Translate the examples into your own language. What is different about number 6?

7 Question tags

G9 Here are four reasons why question tags are important for you:

1. They are very common and natural.
2. They help you to keep a conversation going.
3. You will sound friendly if you use them.
4. If you use them, you don't need to ask so many direct questions (which can sound aggressive).

Grammar check

Add the correct question tag to these statements:

1. This weather's dreadful, ... ?
2. It's not as bad as last week, ... ?
3. We've been here before, ... ?
4. He used to live in Barcelona, ... ?
5. That cost a lot, ... ?
6. He didn't get the job after all, ... ?
7. It doesn't really matter, ... ?
8. They got married in a hurry, ... ?

These common tags all follow the same rule:

positive sentence = ... tag
. . . . sentence = ... tag

Positive-positive tags

G10 Another kind of tag uses a positive tag after a positive sentence. For example:

So he helped you, did he?

These often express surprise and start with *So* to show that we have just realised something. Look at this example:

I used to spend hours walking in the hills.
> So you actually grew up in the north of Scotland, did you? I didn't realise.

Add the correct tag in these situations:

1. I grew up in Switzerland actually.
   > So, you grew up in Switzerland, ... ? That explains why you're such a good skier!
2. My first wife came from Germany.
   > So, you've been married before, ... ? I didn't know that.
3. Look, we've got to be at the station by 7.
   > So, we're getting the early train now, ... ? You've changed your mind again!
4. And we'll be in Calcutta for a week.
   > So, you're going to Calcutta, ... ? My brother's been there. Watch what you eat. He was ill for a month afterwards.

8 Talking about jobs

Which 9 jobs can you see in the pictures opposite?

surgeon	mechanic	builder
chemist	social worker	soldier
bouncer	policewoman	pilot
fireman	postman	model

Now complete the following sentences in ways that are true for you by adding the relevant jobs to each:

I wouldn't mind being a . . . . .
I'd quite like to be a . . . . .
I could never be a . . . . .

Compare your answers with your partner and explain your choices. The vocabulary below might help you explain why a job does or doesn't really appeal to you.

On the positive side:

I imagine it'd be really rewarding.
I think it'd be a really creative job.
I imagine it'd give you a lot of freedom.
I'm sure the money would be good.
It wouldn't be all that demanding.
You'd meet a lot of people.

On the down side:

You'd have to work really long hours.
I imagine it'd be really stressful.
I think it'd get really boring after a while.
It'd be dangerous.
It'd be dirty.
I've got a feeling it'd drive me mad.
The money wouldn't be very good.
You'd end up doing the same thing every day.

GREAT BRITAIN

SMOKING
POLICE
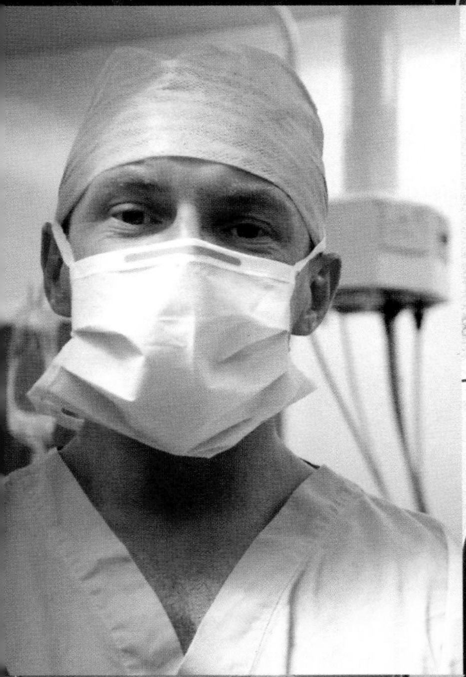

EVENT
SECURITY

9 How come?

How come is an alternative way of saying why. Look at these examples:

Why did you decide to move to London?
How come you decided to move to London?

Why did you decide to do that then?
How come you decided to do that then?

Why are you leaving early?
How come you're leaving early?

Practise saying the above expressions.

Re-write the following sentences so that they start with why:

1. How come you paid so much for your car?
 . . . .
2. How come you got here so early?
 . . . .
3. How come you refused the invitation?
 . . . .
4. How come you didn't accept the job in LA?
 . . . .
5. How come you're so interested in Tibet?
 . . . .
6. How come there's no beer left in the fridge?
 . . . .

Now put how come or why into the gaps below:

7. So . . . . you're studying English?
8. So . . . . did you choose this school?
9. So . . . . did you decide to do that then?
10. So . . . . you chose to study that?
11. So . . . . do you want to go to Iceland?
12. So . . . . you decided to move there then?

Ask your partner two interesting questions starting with How come.

10 Explaining your decisions

Here are six expressions for explaining why you made certain decisions. Put the words in the correct order.

a. got with we just each other bored
 . . . .
b. always I've been in it interested
 . . . .
c. always to wanted I'd
 . . . .
d. just with up I fed it got
 . . . .
e. just I felt it like
 . . . .
f. him of friend recommended mine A
 . . . .

Now put them into the correct situation below:

1. Why did you decide to write a book?
 >. . . . .
 ever since I was at school.
2. So how come you went to Dr Martin?
 >. . . . .
 and I'm glad I did. He's wonderful.
3. So why did you decide to stop dancing lessons?
 >. . . . .
 I mean, it was fun to begin with, but it started eating up all my free time.
4. So what on earth made you decide to dye your hair grey?
 >. . . . .
 I thought it might make me look more mature.
5. So what made you study Greek philosophy?
 >. . . . .
 believe it or not!
6. So why did you and Jane split up?
 >. . . . .
 It's sad, I know, but that's life, I suppose.

Tell a partner about:

1. something you did because you had always wanted to do it.
2. something that someone recommended you do.
3. something you got fed up doing.
4. something you've always been interested in.
5. something silly you just felt like doing.

Real English: What on earth ...?

When we are surprised or shocked, we often use *on earth* in questions. For example:
What on earth made you do that? Who on earth told you that? How on earth did you manage to do that?

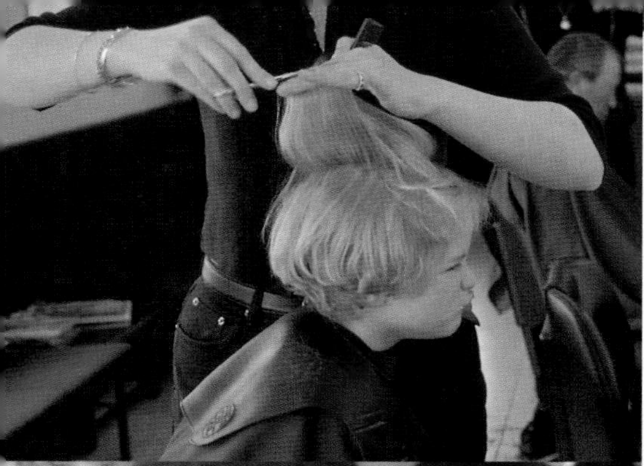

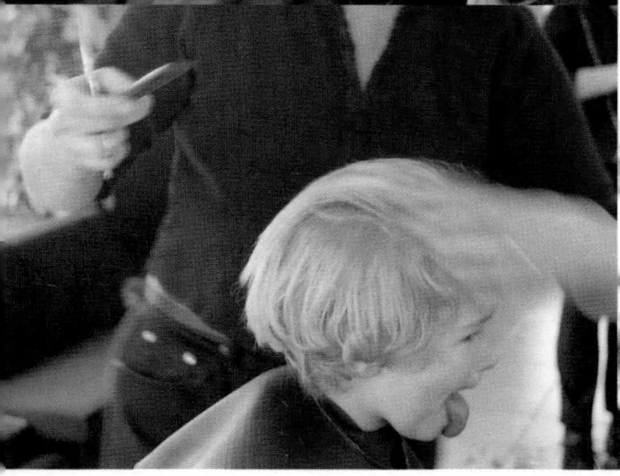

11 While reading

Yael Gregory is from New Zealand, but now lives in Brighton on the south coast of England and works as a hairdresser. While you read, decide if these statements are true (T) or false (F):

1. Her parents sent her to live in England.
2. Yael is married.
3. Yael planned to become a hairdresser.

12 Talking point

1. **Would you leave your family to go and live and work on the other side of the world?**
2. **Yael left school and got a job. Is this better than going to college or university?**
3. **How long do you need to know someone before deciding to get married?**

Q: Why did you decide to leave New Zealand?

YG: Well, my mother's English, so it wasn't such a big decision. When I was about six, we came over to visit my grandmother, so England wasn't such a strange place to me. When I left school, I felt it was a good time to get away and have a change. You see, I'm a Sagittarian! My parents didn't try to stop me coming. My brother had gone to work in Japan. I also had a schoolfriend who was living in England at the time, and of course, I could come over here and stay with my grandmother.

Q: What's the biggest decision you've ever had to make?

YG: I think it must be deciding to get married. It's both a personal and a legal decision. I'd known my boyfriend for 12 years before we decided to get married. When we first met, I thought he was a fun sort of person to be with and when you're only 20 you don't think about getting married and buying a house or having kids, but now that I'm 30, things like that are more important. I mean, I'd never have a kid without getting married.

Q: How come you became a hairdresser?

YG: Well, I had always cut my mum's hair, and she had always cut mine, and my dad's, and my brother's. When I came over here, I didn't really plan it. One day I answered an advert in the local paper for a job which offered training. The money was terrible to start with, but I worked hard. I love people. I find them really interesting. And I'm good at talking! When I first started work as a hairdresser, I got a job in Haywards Heath – about 20 miles from Brighton. If I made a mess of people's hair, I didn't want to meet them in the supermarket!
Eventually, I think I want to go and study. My father thinks I should go to university and get what he calls 'a real job', but at the moment I really enjoy doing what I'm doing. I like the people I work with and I love living here. What more could I ask for?

13 Jokes!

T17 Complete these 'How come?' jokes below by adding the correct response.

a. I wanted to be near my mum!
b. Because I left the plane tickets on it!
c. They didn't look!
d. I want to be ready in case there's an accident!

1. How come you drive with your brakes on?
   > . . . .
2. How come you were born in New Zealand?
   > . . . .
3. I wish I'd brought the piano with me.
   > How come?
   . . . .
4. When I was a kid, I ran away from home. It took them six months to find me.
   > Six months! How come it took them so long?
   . . . .

14 Gerund and infinitive

Verb check

G11 Look at these two patterns:

I've just finished reading it. Verb + gerund
We decided to leave early. Verb + infinitive

Some verbs can take either pattern, but the meanings may be different:

I clearly remember posting your letter.
I must remember to post your letter.

Mark the following:

G: if they only take the gerund
I: if they only take the infinitive
G/I: if they can take either

1. try *to do/doing*	9. enjoy *to do/doing*
2. ask him *to do/doing*	10. avoid *to do/doing*
3. promise *to do/doing*	11. begin *to do/doing*
4. suggest *to do/doing*	12. prefer *to do/doing*
5. forget *to do/doing*	13. carry on *to do/doing*
6. expect *to do/doing*	14. manage *to do/doing*
7. love *to do/doing*	15. start *to do/doing*
8. remember *to do/doing*	16. plan *to do/doing*

Now cross out the impossible verb forms.

Grammar check

Verbs often work together in specific patterns. Underline the correct form in these examples and cross out the wrong one. For example:

I'm tired of working/~~to work.~~

1. Why did you decide *to learn/learning* English?
2. Well, because I wanted *going/to go* to America.
3. Well, because I was interested *in travelling/ to travel*.
4. Well, because I was fed up *with working/ to work* in the evenings.
5. Well, I was really bored *with doing/to do* the same thing every day at work.
6. Because I was trying *getting/to get* into university and I needed it for my exams.
7. Because I was hoping *to go/going* to Australia for six months.

Grammar in context

Now, with a partner, think of 2 possible answers for each of the following questions, using the words given. Begin your answer with Well, because . . . .

1. So why did you leave your job?
   I wanted . . . .
   I was fed up . . . .
2. So how come you decided to move to Milan?
   I was bored . . . .
   I was interested in . . . .
3. So why did you break up with your fiancé(e)?
   I wanted . . . .
   I didn't want . . . .
4. So how come you decided to become a dancer?
   I was interested in . . . .
   I hoped . . . .

In the conversation on page 41, can you remember why Jason decided:

1. to give up smoking?
2. to become a fireman?
3. to move to London?

Which gerund describes the watersports below?

15 Summarising

One way in which we keep conversations going is by checking that we understand what the other person means. We do this by 'summarising' what we think their main point is.

Back in 1989, I moved to New York.
> New York? Why?
Well, I just couldn't find any work over here.
> Right, so you went to look for a job, then?
(go/look for/job)
Yes, exactly.

Write 'summary' questions in each of the gaps below. Use the words in brackets as a guide.

1. There were only two other people there and I was much better qualified than either of them.
   > So . . . . , then?
   (think/got/job)
   Yes, definitely. Well, I hope so, anyway.
2. So why did you take up the guitar?
   > Well, I wanted to play with some friends.
   So . . . . , then?
   (want/play in a band)
   > No, not really, we just play for fun.
3. So why did you decide to take up golf?
   > Well, everyone else in the office played.
   Right, so . . . . ?
   (think/help/career)
   > Yes, and it has! I'm now MD.
4. How did your exam go?
   > It was pretty tough, actually. I found it really hard.
   What? So . . . . , then?
   (think/failed)
   > Well, let's just wait and see.
5. I feel terrible.
   > Well, I did tell you not to mix your drinks.
   I think I'm going to go back to bed.
   > So . . . . , then?
   (not/go into work)
   No, could you give the office a ring and say I've got flu?

Talking point

In the last example someone gives the excuse of having flu when they really have a hangover. Have you ever given an excuse which was not true?
Do you ever feel bad about not telling the truth, even if it saves somebody else's feelings?

16 Playing for time

T18 **We often need to pause when we are asked difficult questions, to give us time to think. We do this by using 'delayers'. Listen to the tape and practise saying these 'delayers'.**

So, how come you decided to start karate?

Why did I start karate?
That's a good question.
That's a difficult question.
Well, I'd have to think about that.
I'm not really sure.
Um, I don't really know.
Why? I haven't really thought about that.

With a partner, take turns asking the questions below. Before answering, use delayers to give you thinking time.

1. How come you decided to wear those clothes this morning?
2. Why did your parents call you *(your name)?*
3. What made you decide to sit next to me today?
4. Why do you think everyone ends up learning English and not French, German or Spanish?
5. What makes English so hard to learn?

17 Role play

Pick someone in the class to pretend to be a famous person. For a couple of minutes, the rest of the class should prepare to ask them difficult questions about their life and experiences. The famous person should answer the questions, remembering to use 'delayers' if they need time to think before they answer.

18 Saying you don't know

Sometimes we're asked questions which we really don't know the answer to. Look at the highlighted examples in the following:

Have you got any idea where Karen is?
> No, sorry, I haven't got a clue.
Oh well, thanks anyway.

Do you know where Bristol is?
> I'm the wrong person to ask, I'm afraid. I'm hopeless at geography.

Do you know where I put that book I was reading?
> I've got no idea, sorry.
I'm sure I left it around here somewhere.

Match up the following conversations. Then underline the expressions which mean *I don't know*.

1. You don't know anything about this party tomorrow night, do you?
2. You don't know how this program works, do you?
3. You know that guy I met last month in London? Can you remember where he was from?
4. Do you know Dennis's surname?
5. Have you got any idea where Rose is?
6. Excuse me, do you know where I could get something to eat around here?
7. So, have you got any idea why you were made redundant?
8. Do you know where my mobile is? I've no idea where I've left it.

a. No sorry, I'm afraid I don't. You could try asking Rob. He's our computer expert.
b. I'm afraid not, but if you find out about it, let me know.
c. Don't ask me. I haven't seen her all day.
d. How should I know? You had it last. You must've just left it somewhere.
e. No, I haven't got a clue. They just said it was because there was no work.
f. No, how am I supposed to know things like that? I never even met him, did I?
g. Sorry, I can't help you, I'm afraid. I don't live around here.
h. I've got no idea, but I'm sure I'd recognise it if I heard it.

T19 **Listen and check your answers. Practise the conversations in pairs, adding a final response:**

You don't know anything about the party, do you?
> I don't, but if you find out about it, let me know.
Yes, all right, then. I'll call you if I hear anything.

In pairs, try to answer these questions. If you don't know an answer, use the expressions above.

1. Which four countries speak French?
2. What is 100 kilometres in miles?
3. What is the population of China?
4. Name 5 of the republics which used to be part of the old Soviet Union?
5. What is a male duck called? And a female dog? And a baby goat? And a female pig?
6. Where do you think this monastery is?

19 Talking point

Do you worry when you make mistakes in your English? Do you want your teacher to correct you? Some people want to be corrected. Some people think that correction stops them speaking fluently. Decide in your class whether it would be better if your teacher corrected EVERY mistake made in the next two lessons or corrected NO mistakes!

Unit 3b : Flying

aid of flying. I've got no head for heights. This is a no-smoking airline. Smoking is permitted only in the areas designated. I'd never fly them! Can I see your b
s to kiss an ashtray? It's a free country. Passive smoking. I don't have the will power to give up. Smoking isn't allowed until you are inside the terminal buildi
re likely to get killed crossing the road. Mind your own business. I get really nervous just before take-off. It's the safest form of travel. I always fly economy cla
ed like this and unfastened like this. This is a security announcement. Toilets engaged. Would the last remaining passenger on flight BA 2963 to Tangier, pleas

1 Your captain speaking

With a partner, discuss whether you think the following statements about air travel are true or false. Why?

1. Only you or members of your family may pack your luggage.
2. No aerosols are allowed in any luggage.
3. Only two items of hand luggage may be carried on board.
4. No cigarettes or alcohol are allowed on board.
5. The use of mobile phones is strictly prohibited.
6. No toy weapons are allowed on board.

Can you think of other rules about the following things which apply when flying?

1. smoking during take-off and landing
2. using a CD player
3. wearing high-heeled shoes in an emergency
4. where to put your hand luggage
5. using the toilet
6. seats in the upright position
7. wearing seat belts during the flight
8. special seat belts for babies

2 Vocabulary

You're going to read an article that features air travel, the law and smoking. Check you understand the words below, using a dictionary to help you if necessary. Then place them into the correct categories.

air travel: ....

the law: ....

smoking: ....

handcuffed	nervous	cabin crew
touched down	fined	on board
light up	arrested	puff
prosecuted	refuelling	

With a partner, discuss what you think the article is going to be about.

3 While reading

Read this article about a woman whose craving for a smoke landed her in big trouble – at 30,000 feet! When you've read it, answer these questions:

1. Why did Joan Norrish light up on the plane?
2. When was she arrested?
3. What happened to her after that?

THE COST OF A CIGARETTE

A businesswoman's desperate need for a cigarette on an 8-hour flight from America resulted in her being arrested and handcuffed, after she was found lighting up in the toilet of a Boeing 747, not once but twice.

Joan Norrish, aged 33, yesterday became the first person to be prosecuted under new laws for smoking on board a plane, when she was fined £440 at Uxbridge magistrates' court. Ms Norrish, from Radwinter, Essex, said, "I'm such a nervous passenger, and I couldn't have handled the flight without a cigarette. If they'd told me I couldn't smoke before they let me on the plane, I wouldn't have taken the flight."

Ms Norrish first attracted the attention of the in-flight staff when she had her first puff in the toilet after the plane touched down for refuelling at New York's JFK airport. One and a half hours later, she went into the lavatory again, causing passengers to complain to the cabin crew. However, they could find no sign of cigarettes in the toilet, and were concerned that Ms Norrish may have hidden the cigarettes, thus adding to their fears for the safety of the plane.

Relations between Ms Norrish and the crew soon got worse, as Ms Norrish turned violent when the plane landed at Heathrow, where the police were alerted. She was subsequently arrested and handcuffed.

Outside the court, Ms Norrish commented on her fine, "It was quite high, much higher than I was expecting. It all seems like an awful lot of fuss over just a couple of cigarettes."

4 Word check

Find words from the text to complete the following sentences:

1. I quit after two years working there, I just couldn't have . . . . . . the pressure any longer.
2. I've looked everywhere for her. She's just totally vanished. There's no . . . . . . of her anywhere.
3. Since the war ended a few years ago, ... between our two countries have improved.
4. Has the postman been yet? I'm . . . . . . some important mail today.
5. I was going to complain, but I didn't want to make a . . . . I hate it when I feel that everyone's looking at me.

5 Comprehension check

Answer these questions based on the text.

1. Why did Joan Norrish smoke on the plane?
2. Would she have travelled with a non-smoking airline?
3. Was Joan Norrish violent during the flight?
4. After she was fined, was Joan Norrish sorry for what she had done? How do you know?

6 Collocations

Complete these collocations from the text:

1. She did it not once but . . . .
2. She wouldn't have . . . . the flight if she'd known.
3. She . . . . the attention of the crew.
4. The plane . . . . down to refuel.
5. She . . . . violent.

Now use the same words in the following different contexts:

6. We were all . . . . by her generosity.
7. Goodness, it's . . . . cold all of a sudden.
8. At the weekend this café . . . . a lot of bikers.
9. Have you . . . . your pill yet?
10. *You only live* . . . . was one of the best of the Bond films.

Real English: Ms Norrish

This means we do not know if a woman is Mrs or Miss. It is pronounced */Məz/*. It is best to check with someone to see which title they prefer.

7 Talking point

Do you like flying? Why/why not?
What do you do and what do you think about during take-off and landing?
Would you have reported Ms Norrish to the cabin crew? Why/why not?
Do you think the fine she got was a bit excessive or do you think she got what she deserved?
Have you ever tried to stop someone smoking on a train or on a bus? What happened?
Do you think people should be allowed to smoke in public places?

8 Flying vocabulary

Match the two halves of these collocations which are common when you are flying:

1. your boarding	a. entertainment
2. the drinks	b. flight
3. an 8-hour	c. locker
4. the overhead	d. crew
5. your oxygen	e. stopover
6. the in-flight	f. trolley
7. the smoking	g. card
8. the emergency	h. section
9. the cabin	i. exits
10. an unscheduled	j. mask

Have you ever had to use your oxygen mask? Can you remember things falling out of the overhead locker? When was the last time you went on a really long flight? What is the longest flight you have ever been on?

9 Giving explanations

Grammar in context

G12 When we explain why we did something, we often talk about what had been happening (the past perfect continuous) before we did what we did. Look at these examples:

So why did you decide to move out of your old flat?
> It was mainly because I hadn't been getting on with my flat-mates for ages, so I just decided I needed a place of my own.

So how come you started smoking?
> Well, all my friends had been smoking for ages and they'd been trying to get me to start, so eventually I just gave in.

Complete the following, using the same verb structure in colour above and the verbs given.

1. So why did you decide to go to India then?
> Well, I . . . . a lot about it since Sally told me about her trip, so I just took a month off work and went on my own. *(read)*
2. So what made you decide to stop eating meat?
> Well, I . . . . about it for a while. A few of my friends were vegetarians and they . . . . to convince me for ages, so I just decided to give it a go. *(think, try)*
3. So how come you finally bought a computer?
> It was really because for years I . . . . all my writing on this ancient type-writer, so I decided to splash out. *(do)*
4. So how come you two split up, if you don't mind me asking?
> Well, basically, we . . . . constantly for months, and, to be honest, we weren't really enjoying each other's company. *(argue)*
5. I hear you've moved into a flat, Jim?
> Yes, I . . . . in the university hostel since I left home. I thought it was time to get a place of my own. *(live)*
6. So, you and Karen aren't moving back to Sweden after all?
> No, we . . . . second thoughts for a while, so we decided to stay here in Cardiff at least for the time being. *(have)*

Go back and underline the time expressions. Then read the conversations with a partner.

Grammar pairwork

Ask each other the following questions. Use your imagination and the past perfect continuous when you answer.

a. So how come you decided to get engaged?
b. So what made you decide to buy your own flat?
c. So why did you finally decide to get a job?
d. So why did you decide to get rid of your cats?
e. So how come you gave up salsa dancing then?
f. So why on earth did you get rid of your TV?

Tell your partner about a big decision you've made, and then explain the background to that decision, using:

I'd been ...ing.
I hadn't been ...ing.

Real English: Basically, ...

This is a common way to introduce an explanation:

So why do you need to learn English, then?
> Well, *basically,* my boss told me I had to.

How come you sold your car?
> Well, *basically,* I just couldn't afford to keep it running.

What other reasons can you give for selling an old car like this one?

10 Adjectives

Strong comparatives

Below are expressions which show that the end result of something was different from our expectations:

How was the play?
> It was really enjoyable – much better than I thought it would be.

What did you think of the mountains?
> They were quite high – much higher than I'd expected.

Using these two examples think of answers to the following questions. Here are some words to help you:

fine	much hotter
great	much nicer
went well	much better
interesting	much easier
nice	
sweltering	

1. How was your exam?
2. What was the weather in Tunisia like? Is it hot at this time of year?
3. So, you've moved into your new house. How did it go?
4. How did you feel about your presentation the other day? Were you happy with it?
5. What did you think of the restaurant? Was it nice?
6. So how was the exhibition? As good as all the advertising said it would be?

Now ask your partner questions about some things you know they have done or seen recently. They should answer as above. Continue the conversations for as long as possible.

Strong adjectives

Remember the way Jason responded in the conversation on page 41:

Phil: It was down in Crawley, wasn't it? It's pretty quiet down there, isn't it?
Jason: Quiet? Yes, it's dead. There's absolutely nothing to do there.

Phil: It must be pretty scary fighting fires in skyscrapers.
Jason: Scary? It's terrifying. I'm glad it hardly ever happens.

Jason repeated Phil's adjective as a question, then added another stronger adjective. Respond to the following situations in a similar way with these strong adjectives:

tiny	terrifying	freezing	dead
boiling	enormous	shocked	gorgeous

1. It must've been really hot in Greece.
   > . . . .
2. Oh, you're from Sao Paulo originally, are you? It's a pretty big city, right?
   > . . . .
3. How's your flat? It must be a bit cold with all this snow we're having.
   > . . . .
4. It's pretty quiet down in Devon, isn't it?
   > . . . .
5. You must've been pretty surprised when you read the report in the papers.
   > . . . .
6. It's a bit small in here, isn't it?
   > . . . .
7. So is he good-looking, then, your new boyfriend?
   > . . . .
8. It must've been a bit scary, going so high up like that.
   > . . . .

T20 **It is important that you can keep conversations going. Here are the next lines from the above conversations. First match them up, then listen before reading the conversations in pairs:**

a. There's no way you'll catch me doing that again!
b. That's why I've decided to have central heating put in.
c. That's why I moved to a small town out in the country.
d. You can hardly swing a cat in here!
e. That's why we made sure the hotel had air-conditioning.
f. That's why I decided to move to the city!
g. You'll die when you see him!
h. That's why I contacted my solicitor straightaway.

11 Second conditionals

G13 **The first conditional uses the present tense:**

If I come with you, I'll miss my son's party.

The second conditional uses the simple past.

If I came with you, I'd miss my son's party.

Complete the paragraph below using these verbs in the simple past. Two are negative:

earn have meet be want exist

Some people spend half their life wishing their lives were better – it really annoys me. "If I . . . . . . a bit more more money – if I . . . . . a better job – if I . . . . . . the right man or woman for me." It drives me mad. There is no perfect job or perfect partner! And people say things like "If I . . . . so busy, I'd do this or that", but that's just an excuse. If they really . . . . . . to do it, I'm sure they could find the time. If the word IF . . . . , the world would be a much happier place.

Make second conditional sentences using the words in brackets. For example:

(you/look better/if/wear/suit)
You'd look better if you wore a suit.

1. I'm sure . . . .
   (Rachel/understand/if/you explain it/her)
2. It's a shame. . . . .
   (if/we have more time/look round/museums)
3. The fact is, ...
   (I/buy one/if/weren't/so expensive)
4. I often think that . . . .
   (if/didn't have any children/I/travel round the world)
5. I often think that . . . .
   (life/be easier/if/everybody just/tell/the truth)

Likely or unlikely

Choose the most sensible verb form – past for an unlikely situation:

If I won a lot of money ...

and present for a likely or more likely situation:

If I pass my exam ...

1. If I meet/met the Prime Minister, ...
2. If everybody thinks/thought like me, ...
3. If I live/lived to be 70, ...
4. If I live/lived to be 120, ...

Now finish the sentences with your own ideas or choose from a-d below.

a. I'd probably have great-great-grandchildren.
b. I don't know what I'd say to him.
c. The world would be a better place!
d. I'll be quite happy.

12 Flying joke

T21 **Try to guess the ending of this joke. Then tell it to each other in pairs and decide who tells it better. These people then tell it to the class who vote on who tells it best.**

Alfred had never flown before and was extremely nervous. He was flying across the Atlantic to visit his sister, who had emigrated to Canada. When he got on the plane he found he was sitting in a window seat. After a few minutes the person next to him arrived – an enormously fat American. Not long after the plane took off, the American fell asleep and began to snore loudly. It was obvious to Alfred there was no way he could get out, even to get to the toilet, without waking the man up.

After the in-flight meal had been served, the plane entered an area of severe turbulence. The American continued to snore. Alfred, however, started to feel sick. He was desperate to get to the toilet. Finally, he was sick – all over the man's trousers. The American didn't wake up, but he just continued to snore. Alfred didn't know what to do.

As the plane touched down, the American finally woke up and saw his trousers. Alfred turned to him and said, ". . . . .?"

(Answer on page 192)

What is your worst flying story?

Vocabulary

Decisions, decisions

Complete the sentences below by adding the correct words from this list:

wise	immediate	wrong
joint	unpopular	right

1. We definitely made the . . . . decision coming by train. It's so much easier than driving.
2. Look, we've got three days to make up our minds about it. It's not as if we need to make an . . . . decision or anything, is it?
3. I've decided to stay and finish my course. It would be mad to leave it now.
   > I think that's a . . . . decision.
4. Oh no, look at the traffic. We made the . . . . decision coming this way.
5. The government's decision to raise income tax to 35% has been very . . . .
6. Some of our friends think it was my idea to give up our jobs and move to the country, but it wasn't. We'd both talked about it for years. It really was a . . . . decision.

Smoking

Complete the collocations below by adding the missing words:

a. a heavy/a chain/an occasional . . . . . .
b. smoke a, light a, put out a . . . . . .
c. king-size, low-tar, mild, menthol, strong . . . . . .
d. . . . . lighter, packet, ends, advertising
e. give up, start, stop, be anti- . . . . . .

Now choose words from above to complete the sentences below:

1. I used to be a really . . . . smoker, you know, 50 a day, but now I'm just an . . . . smoker.
2. I've been trying to . . . . smoking for years now. I wish I'd never . . . . in the first place!
3. Where can I . . . . this cigarette? Is there an ashtray or something around?
4. I saw this old homeless guy in the streets yesterday picking up all the old cigarette . . . . .
5. Cigarette . . . . is banned on television in some countries.
6. The link between . . . . and lung cancer has now been proved.

Watch, see, look

On a long flight, do you watch the in-flight movies? Fill in watch, see, **or** look **in the following sentences. You may need to change the verb form.**

1. Could you have a look on the TV page to . . . . what's on after the news?
2. Can you . . . . anything wrong, doctor?
   > No, your throat . . . . fine.
3. I think I'll . . . . the match on TV tonight.
4. The amount of food at the wedding was incredible. I've never . . . . anything like it!
5. I want you to . . . . him closely. I think he's up to something.
6. Here, ... out of the window. Have you ever seen a car like that before!
7. Can you . . . . my bag while I go to the loo, please?
8. When the sky is this clear, you can . . . . for miles from up here. It's fantastic!
9. Have you . . . . that new film yet? It's great.
10. I've . . . . everywhere for my wallet. I can't . . . . it anywhere.

Idioms

Use the following words to complete the highlighted idiomatic expressions in the situations:

sailing	cake
stone	nothing
done	depth

1. It must've been really hard learning Spanish.
   > No, not really, I already speak Italian, so it was a piece of . . . . . . !
2. Did Lee give you your money back?
   > Eventually, yes, but it was like getting blood out of a . . . . He's so mean!
3. Did you go and give blood in the end?
   > Yes, and I'm glad I did. There was . . . . . . to it! I didn't feel a thing.
4. So how come you decided to quit the class?
   > Oh, everyone else was so much better than me. I felt totally out of my . . . . . . !
5. Did it take you long to get used to living in Greece?
   > Well, the first six months were quite hard, but after that it was all plain . . . .
6. Why not try and get a work permit and stay?
   > That's easier said than . . . . It's fine if you've an EC passport, but I'm Chilean.

learning advice

There are hundreds of thousands of words in English. Nobody knows them all!

Most native speakers know only a small fraction of the total, but they can always say what they want to say. There are three main reasons why they can do this.

Firstly, they know how to combine words in collocations: *make a mistake, get lost.*

Secondly, they know lots of fixed expressions: *by the way, on behalf of, in the middle of.*

Thirdly, they know lots of idiomatic language: *let your hair down, the tip of the iceberg.*

Words almost never occur alone. You will learn best if you learn words in collocations, phrases and expressions.

The Expression Organiser on page 187 helps you to record and translate important expressions.

Unit 4a : Your weekend

really hectic weekend coming up. I think I'll just laze about. Don't you just live for the weekend? Doing anything interesting this weekend? We're popping over
he weekend. Can I crash out on your floor tonight? I always go to the car boot sale. I just love Sunday morning breakfasts. Have a good weekend. Don't ask
there again. I'm going on a picnic in the country with some friends. I usually spend the morning doing the week's washing. I've got to clean the flat. I love ju
just wander around the shops. We're having some people round. It's not my idea of an exciting weekend. What are you up to? Cleaning the car and doing

1 A typical weekend

Here is a list of things people do at weekends. Tick the ones you do. Think of some others.

do the weekly shopping
have a lie-in
buy some new clothes
tidy up your house / flat / room
wander around town
go out with friends for a meal
go to church
stay in and relax
do some studying
get your hair cut
go out for a walk
go to the cinema, the theatre, a concert
clean the car
go swimming
visit your parents / grandparents
play football / play tennis

Compare your answers with a partner.

Real English: What are you up to this weekend?
This is a common way of asking what your plans are. For example: *What are you up to tonight? What are you up to on Saturday?*

2 Planning expressions

T22 Listen to Gavin talking about his plans for the weekend. Tick these expressions as you hear them:

1. I guess I'll probably . . .
2. I imagine I'll . . .
3. I wouldn't mind . . . if I get time.
4. If I get the chance, I'll . . .
5. I hope to . . .
6. Unfortunately, I've got to . . .
7. I'm going to try to . . .
8. I'm planning to . . .

Now use these expressions to tell a partner about your plans for the weekend. Use the ideas in the pictures if you want.

3 Before you listen

T23 **It's Friday evening. Ken and Steve have both just finished work for the day, and are about to go home. Listen to them talking about their plans for the weekend.**

As you listen, try to answer the following question:

What are Ken and Steve doing this weekend?

Listen again and fill in the gaps in the conversation.

Real English: Tell me about it!

You say this to people when they tell you something negative and you want to sympathise because you have had a similar experience. For example:

I've had so many bills to pay this week. I can't believe how much it costs to have my own flat!
> *Tell me about it!*

Are there any more expressions in the conversation which you have not met before or find surprising?

4 Talking point

Who do you think is going to have a better weekend – Steve or Ken?

Do you ever get ***that Friday afternoon feeling*** **or** ***that Monday morning feeling?***

Have you ever been to a party on a boat? What was it like?

How often do you go out for dinner with your parents? What kind of places do you go to?

Are you usually too tired on a Friday to want to go out in the evening?

Thank goodness it's Friday!

Steve: Thank goodness it's Friday! This week's been dragging on forever.

Ken: Tell me about it! So what are you up to this weekend?

Steve: Oh, nothing special, really. This evening, I'm . . . . for dinner with my parents.

Ken: Oh, that should be nice.

Steve: Yes, we're going to this little French place near where I live. The food's great there, and then tomorrow I've got to get up really early – at least for me! – and do some cooking, because I've . . . . some people . . . . in the afternoon. And I'll have to give the place a really good clean as well. And, I'm not sure, but I think . . . . be going out after that – to see a film or something. We haven't really planned anything. What about yourself?

Ken: Well, tonight I'm . . . . going out with some people from my old job, but I don't really feel like it any more. I'm feeling really tired.

Steve: So you're just going to . . . . , then?

Ken: Yes, because tomorrow night I've got a big night. I'm going to my friends Pete and Rachel's party. It's on a boat.

Steve: Oh, that sounds great. ?

Ken: Down by the river. You know, in the docks.

Steve: Oh yes, I know where you mean. I went to a party there myself . . . .

Ken: Right. Is it OK down there?

Steve: Yes, it's great, but it's . . . . big. There's not that much room on the boat.

Ken: Mm, sounds cosy!

Steve: Oh, yes, you can get really close to people! Lots of sweaty bodies!

Ken: I don't think it's . . . . that sort of party!

Steve: Well, you never know. If you're lucky it might become one! – No, I'm only joking, it's actually a great place for a party.

Ken: Good. I'm really . . . . to it. But then on Sunday, unfortunately, I've got to do some things for work.

Steve: No rest for the wicked! Well, listen, I . . . . . give you a ring on Sunday, then, just to hear all about your quiet night out down on the river!

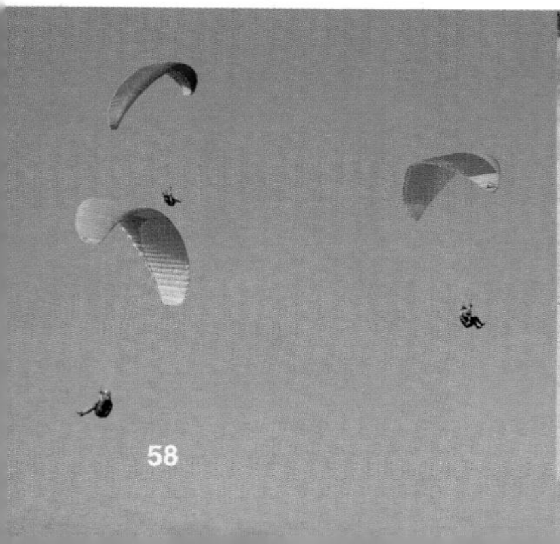

5 Vocabulary check

What is the difference between these words?

a meeting   an appointment   a date

Which do you have with the following people?

1. your doctor
2. your son's teacher to talk about his work
3. your colleagues to discuss working conditions
4. a really attractive person you met at a party
5. your dentist

Form complete sentences with the following:

1. I've got an appointment . . . .
2. I've got a blind date with . . . .
3. I've got a meeting with. . . . .
4. I'm meeting up with . . . .

a. my boss at four, which should last until 6 or so.
b. some friends of mine later for a drink.
c. at the dentist's at 5. I'm dreading it.
d. this friend of a friend.

Now do the same with the following:

5. I'm going to go and visit . . . .
6. I'm going round to . . . .
7. I've got a date with. . . . .
8. I'm meeting . . . .

e. a friend's tonight.
f. some friends later on this evening.
g. a friend of mine in hospital this afternoon.
h. this gorgeous guy/girl I met yesterday.

Real English: a friend's

This is how to talk about a friend's house or flat. For example: We're meeting at *Steve's* before going round to *Stewart and Jane's*.

6 Talking point

What is the difference between a date and a blind date? Have you ever been on a blind date? How often do you have a dentist's appointment?

Do you ever have to go to meetings? Who with? Do you remember your last date, meeting, or appointment? What about your first date?

7 Collocations with *go*

Below are six sentences with go for talking about your plans for the weekend. Delete the wrong collocation in each group.

1. I'm going on a date/a day-trip to Cambridge/shopping tonight/a guided walk.
2. I'm going out to see a film/my friend's up in Yorkshire/a bar tonight/see a musical.
3. I'm going out for shopping/a walk/the day on Saturday/a drink with some friends.
4. I'm going away to the mountains/Brighton this weekend/France for three days/the pub.
5. I'm going out to get something to eat/some things for the house/some shopping/driving.
6. I'm going fishing with my dad/shopping/some shopping/clubbing tonight.

Compare your answers with a partner, then make six statements about what you plan to do next weekend, using the vocabulary above.

Answer the following:

Do you like going to bars?
How often do you go away for the weekend?
When was the last time you went away somewhere?
Have you ever been fishing? What did you catch?
What was the last day-trip you went on?

8 Pronunciation

T24 In the conversation Steve said, I'll have to give the place a really good clean. **Practise saying the following common sentences with** 'll:

1. Right, I'll see you later.
2. It'll be all right on the night.
3. She'll be with us in five minutes or so.
4. What'll you say to your boss?
5. How'll we recognise each other?
6. You'll regret it.
7. I'll see what I can do.
8. There'll be a lot of people you know there.
9. So where'll we meet, then?
10. I'm sure we'll meet again.

9 The future

Four different future forms

G14 Here are 4 common ways to talk about the future:

1. 'll

1. That's the phone. I'll get it.
2. Wait for me. I'll only be a minute.
3. I think I'll have the chicken.

2. going to

1. Look at those black clouds. It's going to rain.
2. We're going to catch the early train.
3. We're going to go to New Zealand this winter.

3. the present continuous

1. We're meeting in town tomorrow.
2. I'm leaving at the end of the month.
3. I'm going out to the cinema tonight.

4. the present simple

1. We leave for Calcutta tomorrow morning.
2. The last bus leaves at 11.15.
3. India play Australia in the final next month.

Discuss with a partner which of the following best describes each group of sentences:

a. We use this form because there is some kind of evidence *now* for the future event. This might be a decision, a plan, or something you can see.

b. We use this form for things which are as certain as a timetable.

c. We use this form for things we've already arranged.

d. We use this form to give a reaction, an opinion or a decision at the moment of speaking.

Grammar discussion

Discuss the questions after these examples:

1. I'm going to tidy up the house tomorrow morning. (When did you decide?)
2. We land at 8 in the morning US time. (How do you know?)
3. I'll call in on the way home from work. (When did you decide?)
4. We're having my grandparents for Christmas dinner. (Is this a plan?)

You will learn best from good, natural examples.

Grammar check

Use the correct form of these verbs to complete the following:

get in   do (2)   go   give   sneeze

1. What're you up to this afternoon? Any plans?
   > I think I . . . . some gardening if it's nice.
2. According to the timetable, the earliest bus . . . . at 7.
3. Did you manage to post that letter?
   > Oh, I'm sorry. I completely forgot. I . . . . it on my way home tonight. I promise!
4. Sorry I can't make it to class tonight. I . . . . out to dinner with some friends.
5. As soon as I pass my driving test, my father . . . . me his old car.
6. Pass me the paper hankies. Uh, uh, uh, I . . . . .

Grammar in context

Complete these sentences with an ending from the list below:

1. I'm just going to have a quiet night in tonight . . . .
2. I've got to work really late tonight . . . .
3. I'm so pleased that my exams are over . . . .
4. My mother's arriving tomorrow . . . .

a. so I'm planning on having a lie-in tomorrow.
b. so I've got to get up really early and meet her.
c. and watch a bit of TV.
d. that I'm going to go out and celebrate tonight.

Now do the same with the following:

5. I've been going out such a lot lately . . . .
6. I'm just going to take it easy tonight . . . .
7. I've got a big night on Friday . . . .
8. I'm just going to stay in tonight because . . . .

e. because my brother's wedding's on Saturday.
f. I've got some things to do around the house.
g. because I was out until 3 last night at a party.
h. that I'm just going to stay in tonight for a change.

SURFING THE NET!

Tim Porter and Chris Gauge, two British sky-divers, look as if they are on top of the world! They went up in a hot-air balloon, jumped from 6,000 feet, then sent an e-mail from the laptop which was fixed to Chris's board. Their e-mail was received by 300 people. After their well-publicised stunt they said they had done it to show people that you can be in touch with friends wherever you are. Sky-diving may not be your way of spending a quiet Sunday afternoon, but an increasing number of people are giving it a try.

The question everyone asks

What if your parachute fails to open? The answer is that parachutes today are far safer and more efficient than 20 years ago. The materials are stronger, lighter and last far longer. Every parachutist or sky-diver must carry a reserve parachute.

How fast do you fall?

If you jump from a plane, you are moving horizontally at the same speed as the aircraft – usually about 100 mph. During the first 10 seconds you fall at about 130 mph. Some sky-divers can reach speeds of over 200 mph on their way down, but they must slow down to about 110 mph before they can open their parachute safely.

Why do people do it?

The simple answer is that some people can't live without taking risks. Some people get a kick out of chasing tornadoes. Men flock to Pamplona in Spain every year to be chased by bulls. Why do people risk their lives in order to have a bit of fun? To the person who loves that rush of adrenalin every time they surf the skies, Saturday morning at the local swimming pool is just for kids!

10 Talking point

Would you try parachuting? Is it actually dangerous or is it just the thought of it that's scary?

Psychologists recognise the need that people have to take risks and to escape from their work or families. When work stops on a Friday evening, do you suddenly turn into a mountain climber, a deep-sea diver, or a hang-gliding fanatic? How do you escape? What do you think of people who take risks?

11 Spoken grammar

G15 **Here are some more ways to talk about things in the future. All are common in spoken English:**

1. I've got somebody coming round.
   I've got some friends arriving from Spain tomorrow.
2. I've got to do something.
   I've got to get up really early tomorrow to take my father to the airport.
3. I'm supposed to be doing something, but . . .
   I'm supposed to be playing football on Saturday, but I've got a bit of a cold.
4. I might be doing something.
   I might be going to the coast for the weekend, but I haven't decided for sure yet.

T25 **Listen to the tape and practise saying these sentences.**

With a partner, use one of the above patterns to tell someone that:

1. A friend has arranged to come to your flat to help you with some homework on Sunday.
   . . . .
2. You've arranged to go shopping with a friend on Saturday, but you'll probably stay at home.
   . . . .
3. You've thought about going to the cinema, but you're not sure yet.
   . . . .
4. You have to do a lot of work this weekend because the deadline for your essay is Monday, and you haven't even started it yet.
   . . . .
5. Your flat is really untidy. You know you must clean it this weekend.
   . . . .
6. There's a possibility your friend, Steve, is having a party tomorrow night.
   . . . .
7. You've arranged to meet some friends on Sunday for lunch, but you don't know if you'll feel like it because you're going to a party on Saturday!
   . . . .
8. Your mother has arranged to visit your new flat on Saturday afternoon.
   . . . .

12 Role play

Have you ever had an invitation to an event like the one in the picture? Did you accept the invitation or turn it down? Can you remember what you said?

Imagine you want to invite your partner to a special event *(the wedding of a relative, a day at the races, a masked ball)*. However, your partner can't come and will make an excuse. Practise by using the example below:

Debbie and I are getting married next Saturday and we'd really like you to come to the reception in the evening.

> Oh, I'd love to, but I'm afraid I can't. I've already arranged to go away for the weekend.

That's a shame. Is there no way you could put it off?

> Well, I would if I could, but we've already booked the tickets.

Oh well, too bad. We'll save you a piece of the cake!

Do you find it easy to turn down invitations? What if you were invited to a day at the races?

13 Plan a weekend

In pairs, plan an ideal weekend. Think about whether you want to:

stay at home or go away somewhere
relax or keep busy
stay in the town or go out into the country
be on your own or with friends
eat out or at home

Now talk to another partner and tell them about your plans for your ideal weekend.

Next, plan a really cheap weekend with this new partner. When you have done this, talk to a different student and compare your plans.

Festivals

Are you interested in going to festivals such as the one shown in the pictures? It's Samhuinn (pronounced *Savin)* – an old Celtic festival, held in Edinburgh to celebrate Hallowe'en (All Souls) and the end of summer.

14 Famous futures

Can you complete these lines from famous songs? Each uses a future form. In one of the examples you will need the American spoken form of *going to – gonna*. Here are the forms you will need:

shall 'll gonna

1. We . . . . . . overcome.
2. I . . . . . . tell you what I want; what I really, really want.
3. She . . . . . be coming round the mountain when she comes.
4. Everything's . . . . . . be all right.

Find some more song lyrics which include the future forms.

Here are four famous quotations each using a future form. Which is your favourite?

"When I was young, I was told, 'You'll see when you're fifty.' I am fifty and I haven't seen a thing!" *Erik Satie*

"Old men are dangerous. It doesn't matter to them what is going to happen to the world." *George Bernard Shaw*

"I disapprove of what you say, but I will defend to the death your right to say it." *Voltaire*

Can you say this short poem?

Tomato Ketchup

If you do not shake the bottle,
None'll come, and then a lot'll.

Unit 4b : Party animals

, come on in. You're the first one here. The music's awful. Turn it down a bit. This is Paul. Pleased to meet you. Do you know anyone here? Who else is
you want to dance? The food's over there. I feel like a fish out of water. This is brilliant! Can I get you a drink? Who's that over there? What a lovely surprise!
, I didn't know you were coming. I'm getting tired. The night is young. Change the music! Try this, it's delicious. I feel a bit sick. Shall I call you a taxi? Com
ope you got his phone number? Thanks for inviting me. No, I've never been to Ulan Bator. What'll you have to drink? Oops, sorry! I'm sure it won't leave a st

1 What kind of party?

People often go to parties at the weekend. When was the last time you went to:

a fancy dress party

a dinner party

a rave

a birthday party

a farewell party

a stag night or a hen night

a family get-together

With a partner, discuss what each kind of party involves. What was the last family get-together you went to?

Which of these kinds of parties do you enjoy going to the most? And the least? Why?

Real English: A rave

A *rave* is a party with hundreds of young people and very loud dance or techno music, often held in a warehouse or other large empty building. Sometimes the venue is kept secret till a few hours before it starts so that the police will not know about it. People discover where the rave is taking place by ringing a special number or finding out via the Internet.

Real English: A stag night / a hen party

These refer to the parties usually held before two people get married. A *stag night* is when the bridegroom gets together with his male friends. A *hen night* is when the bride has a night out with her girlfriends.

2 Collocations

Before you read *Rave to the Grave*, complete the following, using the correct phrase:

led to calls for tighter laws	lose control
suffering from shock	ended in tragedy
organised crime	got out of hand

1. Our holiday in Canada was supposed to be the trip of a lifetime, but the whole thing nearly .... when our hire car went off the road in the middle of the mountains.
2. One of the problems with mind-altering drugs is that people who take them can sometimes .... and end up doing really stupid or dangerous things.
3. The demonstration was meant to be peaceful, but the whole thing .... and ended up as a full-scale riot.
4. Most murders in London are connected to ...., rather than individual criminals working alone.
5. The massacre of 15 students in America has .... on the possession of guns.
6. After the crash, three passengers were taken to hospital ....

3 While reading

On page 58, Ken and Steve talked about parties. Read the article about a rave party. Then answer these questions:

1. What happened to Bert Jones's flat?
2. Why are the police worried about rave parties?
3. Were all the party-goers aware of what had happened?

RAVE TO THE GRAVE

A rave party nearly ended in tragedy last night, when over one hundred people fell through the floor of the 4th-floor flat they were dancing in and into the flat below. Amazingly, no-one was killed, although seven people were taken to hospital suffering from shock. The party was organised by a group called Tribal Spiral, and was held in a deserted flat on a housing estate in East London. It is believed that the extremely high volume of the techno music being played weakened the structure of the floor.

Bert Jones, aged 64, who lives in the 3rd-floor flat below, said "I must admit I hadn't really noticed the party going on. I'm a bit hard of hearing, and I didn't have my hearing aid in, but I could feel the vibrations from somewhere. I just thought it must be kids messing around upstairs somewhere. Then, the next thing I knew, there was an almighty crash in the living room, so I ran in and the place was full of dust and plaster and people screaming. I just couldn't believe my eyes. I got the shock of my life, I can tell you. Now I'm waiting for the council to send someone round to fix things."

The incident follows a number of complaints about techno parties all over the capital, and will undoubtedly lead to calls for tighter anti-rave laws. A spokesman for the Metropolitan Police said, "Things are getting out of hand, and obviously what worries us the most is that where you have rave parties, you have drugs, and where you have drugs, you're bound to come up against organised crime."

David Goodyear, a Stepney ambulanceman, claimed that many of the party-goers had failed to notice the floor had collapsed. Most of the young people just carried on dancing – a fact he put down to the mind-altering effects of Ecstasy and other so-called 'dance drugs'.

4 Comprehension check

Without looking back at the text, try to correct the following false statements:

1. The party was held in Tribal Spiral's flat.
2. Dancing weakened the structure of the floor.
3. Bert Jones lives in the flat above.
4. Bert is fixing his flat himself.
5. This is the first complaint there's been about techno parties in London.
6. The dancing stopped when the floor collapsed.

5 Talking point

What's the noisiest party you've ever been to?
Why do you think young people take drugs?
Is your country 'hard' or 'soft' on drug-taking?
Is organised crime a problem in your country?

6 Just

G16 **In the text Bert said, *"I just thought it must be kids messing around."* With a partner, discuss what difference the word** just **makes in the following:**

I thought it was kids messing around.
I'm going to watch TV tonight.

I just thought it was kids messing around.
I'm just going to watch TV tonight.

T26 **Look at these natural uses of 'just'. Listen to them on tape and practise saying them.**

1. I don't usually have much for breakfast – just a bit of toast and some coffee.
2. I don't really go shopping that often. Usually just once a month.
3. It won't take long – just a few minutes.
4. I'm just going to ring my parents.
5. Just a minute, and I'll check for you.
6. Hello, John here. I'm just getting off the train. I'll be at your place in five minutes. OK?

What is the situation in no. 6?

Add just **in the correct place in each of the following sentences:**

1. There's nothing to worry about. It's a dog barking.
2. I won't be a minute. I'm going to the loo.
3. Who's that at the door? Oh, it's William!
4. I tried to ring you on my mobile after the plane landed.
5. There's nothing seriously wrong with you, Mr Brown. It's old age – nothing else!
6. I'll be a minute or two.
7. We're going to have lunch.
8. I don't feel like much to eat – a sandwich and a cup of coffee.

Tell your partner three things you're just going to do **this weekend.**
Who's doing the *least* interesting thing?

7 I just couldn't wait.

In the following expressions just is used for emphasis and has the same meaning as *really*. Use these fixed expressions to complete the situations below:

a. I just couldn't make up my mind.
b. I just couldn't bear it any longer.
c. I just couldn't wait.
d. I just couldn't resist them.
e. I just couldn't believe my eyes.

1. Sorry I've started without you, but I was expecting you at five. I got so hungry that . . . . There's still a little bit of chicken left if you want it.
2. When I saw what he'd done to his hair, ... ! I mean, it was bright pink and green!
3. Did you manage to get some shoes? > Oh, it was awful, it really was. I went into dozens of shoe-shops and tried on I don't know how many, but . . . . So in the end, I didn't buy anything!

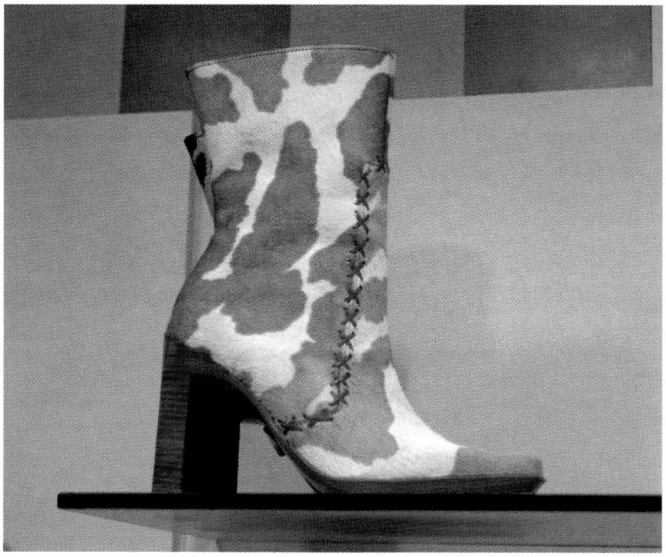

4. The meeting was supposed to run from 9 till 6, but after a couple of hours it got so boring . . . . So, I made my excuses and left.
5. I know I'm supposed to be on a diet, but the cakes all looked so delicious that . . . . Oh well, I just won't eat all day tomorrow now!

Say the expressions several times until you can say them naturally.

8 Talking point

Have you ever been in a situation where you just couldn't believe your eyes?

When was the last time you had to admit to someone that you just couldn't resist something?

When was the last time you just couldn't make up your mind? What about?

When was the last time you got so bored by something that you just couldn't bear it any longer?

Have you ever been so annoyed by somebody that you just couldn't bear it any longer and had to say something? What did you say? How did they feel? Did it make you feel better?

9 Planning a party

You are going to have a party. Put the following in order of importance:

lots of food
loud fast music
really slow music
lots of your friends
some new people
lots of different kinds of things to drink
somewhere with atmosphere

Now compare your order with a partner and try to agree.

Planning expressions

Re-order the jumbled conversation below about organising a party. The first one is correct.

a. Right, I'll bring some music if you sort out the food. How does that sound?
b. Brilliant. I'm looking forward to it already.
c. Yeah, OK, no problem. I'll try and bring some crisps and things like that. What about the invites?
d. Well, to be honest, I'd rather organise the music, if it's OK with you. Couldn't you do the food?
e. Oh, I'll do those. I'll be seeing most people at school this week, so that'll be easy.

Now underline the useful expressions above.

Real English: the invites
The normal word is *invitations. Invites* is common in informal speech.

10 Role play

You and your partner have got £100 to organise a party for some friends. Plan it together. Here are some of the questions you will need to discuss:

What kind of party do you want to have?
When are you going to have it and where?
What do you think you'll need to buy?
How many people are you going to invite?
Will your party have a theme?

Now walk around the class and invite as many people to your party as possible. Use the following expression:

We're having a party on Friday night! Would you like to come along?

When you are asked to someone else's party, make sure you ask the following questions:

Whereabouts is it?
When's a good time to turn up?
Should I bring anything?

If you have already accepted an invitation to another party on the same night, make sure you turn down the new invitation using an expression from page 62.

11 Talking point

When you are invited to a party at a friend's, what do you normally take as a present? What present would you give in these situations?

A friend is getting married.
It's your best friend's 21st birthday.
A friend is moving into a new flat.

12 Restaurant jokes

T27 **Which of the three jokes below do you like best? Why?**

1. This restaurant I went to with my boss was so fancy and posh that before you could use the finger bowls you had to go and wash your hands!
2. It's a nice restaurant, but the problem with it is, it's so crowded that no-one goes there any more!
3. A man goes into a café and says, "I want a sausage burnt to a crisp on one side, but uncooked in the middle, some really greasy bacon and a fried egg with a rock-hard yolk, all topped off with some cold baked beans, please." The manager stares at him as if he's crazy and says, "Oh, come off it! I can't cook a meal like that!" "I don't see why not," says the man, "you managed it OK yesterday!"

Now practise telling these jokes, thinking about the stresses, the linking and the pausing.

Real English: A man goes into a café and says ...
The use of the present simple makes the story sound more immediate and lively. This is a common way to tell a story in informal spoken English. You will learn more about this in unit 6.

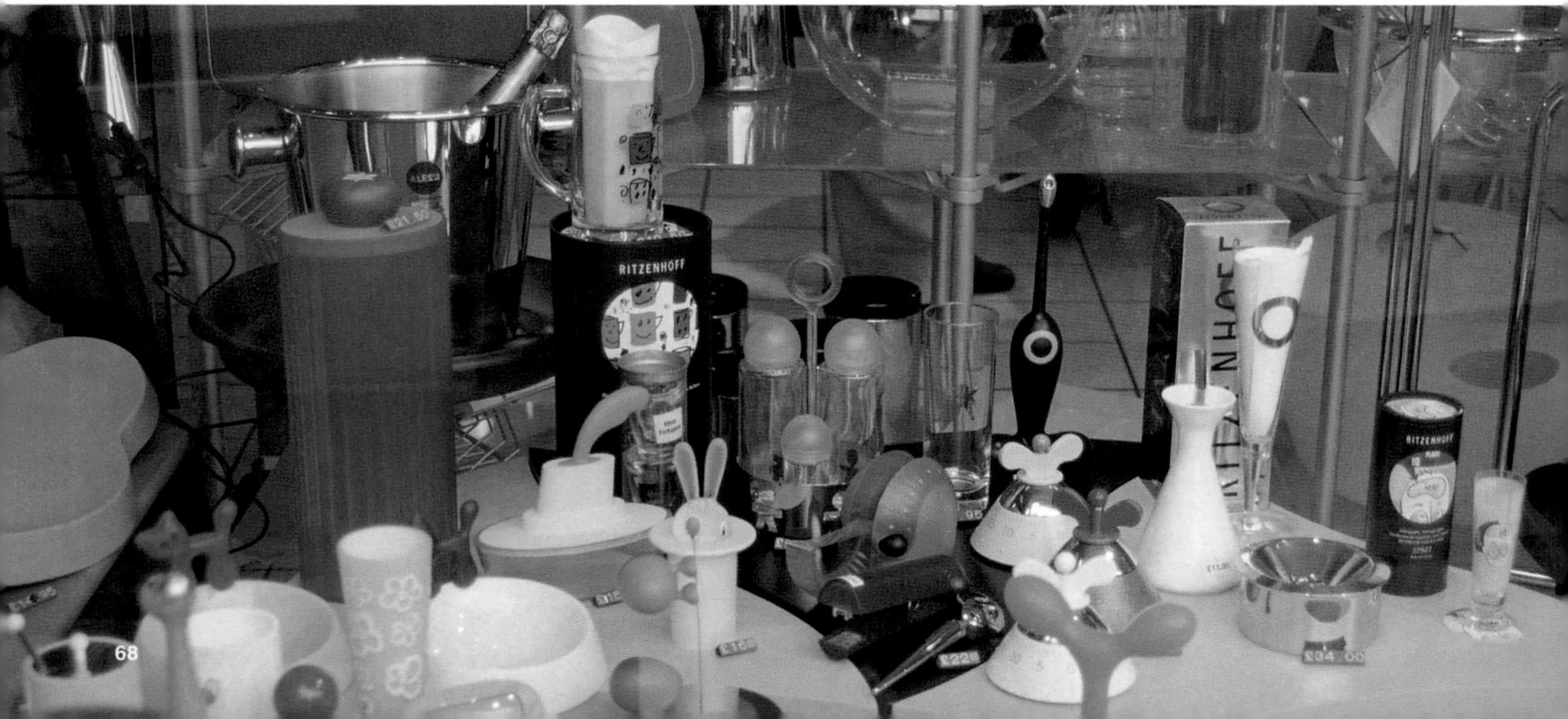

Vocabulary

Do and make

The people at the rave were *making a lot of noise*. Do and make are easy to confuse and different in different languages. Fill in the correct form of do or make in the following:

1. We must . . . . . . a decision by tomorrow at the latest.
2. Don't . . . . . . a noise or you'll wake her up.
3. Can you . . . . . . the shopping later if you've got time?
4. He's . . . . . . enough money so he can afford to retire.
5. I've . . . . . . an appointment at the dentist's first thing in the morning.
6. I wouldn't take those pills if I were you. They won't . . . . . . you any good.
7. They've . . . . . . a huge profit this year.
8. Can you wait just a minute? I've got to . . . . . . an important phone call.
9. So who's going to . . . . . . the washing-up, then?
10. When you get to the station, just . . . . . . your own way round to my place. It's only two minutes away.
11. What does your dad . . . . . . for a living?
12. At some time in our life we all . . . . . . something wrong, and we all . . . . . . mistakes!

Now go back and underline the expressions with do and make. Learn the complete expressions.

What a party!

Do you know the different meanings of the word party? Fill in the following words, then underline all the expressions using party:

farewell	birthday	leader
political	house-warming	search

1. The twins are 10 next week. We're having a . . . . party down at McDonalds!
2. We moved into our new flat on Sunday and we're having a . . . . party next Saturday.
3. When the couple didn't arrive back at their hotel, a . . . . party went out onto the mountain, but they turned up safe and sound.
4. The Prime Minister has two jobs – to run the country and to be party . . . .
5. After working at Boots for 40 years, I was given a wonderful . . . . party.
6. You'll never catch me joining a . . . . party.

Idioms

Steve used the expression no rest for the wicked at the end of his conversation with Ken on page 58. It means *"some people have got to do all the work"*. Complete these common sayings:

1. Long time no . . . . . . !	choosers
2. Talk of the . . . . . . !	joking
3. Beggars can't be . . . . . . !	me
4. Rather you than . . . . . . !	see
5. There's no time like the . . . . . . !	devil
6. You must be . . . . . . !	present

Use the correct expression in these situations:

7. Hello, Jack, ... !
   > I know. I haven't seen you for ages.
8. When are we going to plan the party?
   > Well, there's . . . . , is there?
9. We're going to the opera tonight.
   > Opera? . . . . ! I can't think of anything more boring!
10. I think Jane's just a bit annoyed because of what happened earlier.
   > Oh, ... ! Here she comes now. Let's ask her about it.
11. Look, the cheapest flight leaves at midnight and gets in at four in the morning.
   > Let's take it! . . . . !
12. I was wondering if you could lend me £50 till next Friday.
   > . . . . ! I'm still waiting for the £5 I lent you last week!

Verb + noun collocations

Use the correct form of these verbs to complete the sentences. Then underline the collocations:

get	set	take	tell
stand	give	see	have

1. Did you . . . . . . a good time at the party?
2. I can't . . . . . . the point of . . . . . . drugs.
3. When I saw her in hospital, I . . . . . . a terrible shock!
4. I'll . . . . . . you a ring later this evening.
5. Can you . . . . . . the difference between butter and margarine?
6. I can't . . . . . . people who always complain!
7. I've never . . . . . . foot in a pub in my life!

Review : Units 3 and 4

1 Tenses

Choose the correct form:

1. Before I left home, I haven't/hadn't been getting on very well with my parents.
2. I'd/I'll die if that happened to me.
3. What are you up to tonight?
   > I'm meeting/I'll meet some friends.
4. So how come you decided to go to the doctor?
   > Well, I didn't feel/I hadn't been feeling well for ages, so it seemed like the right thing to do.
5. If he does that one more time, I'll/I'd scream!
6. We weren't/hadn't been getting on very well for ages, so we decided to end the relationship.
7. We'll go/We're going to the cinema tonight. Do you want to come with us?
8. If I'm/I were you, I'd be really upset about it!
9. Will you/Are you going to tell me when it's 5 o'clock, please?

2 Expressions

The following common expressions all occurred in units 3 and 4. Use them in the sentences below:

a. make up my mind
b. I haven't got a clue.
c. I just felt like it.
d. That's a good question.
e. You must be joking!
f. I would if I could

1. Why did you go and have all your hair cut off?
   > I don't know. . . . .
2. Are you ready to leave, then?
   > . . . . I've only just started getting ready.
3. Can you give me a hand to move this table?
   > No, sorry. . . . ., but I've got to rush. I'm late for work.
4. Do you know Louise's address, John?
   > No, ... But you could try asking Sharon.
5. So, how long have you been doing t'ai chi for, then?
   > . . . . I'd have to think about it really.
6. Did you buy anything in the end?
   > No, nothing. I just couldn't . . . . what I wanted.

3 Multiple choice

Choose the correct alternative:

1. How come (a) you bought such an old car?
   (b) did you buy such an old car?
2. Did you manage (a) finding those shoes?
   (b) to find those shoes?
3. It was really (a) much more better than mine.
   (b) much better than mine.
4. I really enjoy (a) living here.
   (b) to live here.
5. I was really fed up (a) with sitting around all day.
   (b) to sit around all day.
6. I'm going (a) on a day-trip to Bath.
   (b) out for a day-trip to Bath.
7. I'm supposed (a) playing tennis.
   (b) to be playing tennis.
8. Don't worry. (a) It's just a simple mistake.
   (b) It just is a simple mistake.

4 Conversation

Put the jumbled conversation below into the correct order. The first line is correct.

a. So, what are you up to this weekend?
b. I don't know. I haven't got a clue. I suppose it depends how good my Greek gets.
c. Don't you think it'd get really boring after a while?
d. Studying? Oh right, your Greek course. How come you decided to start that?
e. I'm going away to Wales. Would you like to come?
f. It couldn't be more boring than being stuck in front of a computer all day!
g. Oh, I'd love to, but I'm afraid I can't. I've got to do some studying.
h. Well, I suppose it was because I've always wanted to live and work on a Greek island.
i. I know what you mean. I'm half-blind already. So, you think you'll get a job out there, then?

1 a	2	3	4	5	6	7	8	9

5 Collocations

Match the verbs on the left with the best collocations on the right:

1. watch	a. smoking
2. make	b. your cigarette out
3. go out	c. really early
4. stop	d. a photograph
5. go	e. too much TV
6. take	f. for a meal
7. get up	g. at home
8. put	h. a big decision
9. stay	i. everywhere for something
10. look	j. on a date

6 Idioms

Make complete idioms by matching the numbers on the left with the letters on the right:

1. It's a real weight	....	a. plain sailing.
2. No rest	....	b. me mad.
3. After that it was	....	c. be choosers.
4. It'd drive	....	d. the devil.
5. Long time	....	e. off my shoulders.
6. Talk of	....	f. for the wicked.
7. Beggars can't	....	g. than me.
8. Rather you	....	h. no see.

7 Real English

Match 1 – 6 with the follow-up comments in a – f below:

1. Hi, I'm here to see Mrs. Duncan.
2. I'm going to go and study in Edinburgh for a year.
3. It's so expensive here in London, isn't it?
4. What are you up to this weekend?
5. Doing anything tonight?
6. Did you get an invite to Ann's party next Saturday?

a. Tell me about it! I've already spent most of the money I came with!
b. Good for you! You'll have a great time.
c. No, I didn't even know she was having one!
d. Yes, I am, actually. I'm going round to Jane's.
e. OK, but actually she's a Ms – not a Mrs!
f. I'm going to my cottage in the country on Friday night.

8 Vocabulary quiz

Answer the following 20 questions with a partner. Then compare your answers with another pair. Who got most answers right?

1. If there's no sign of someone, does that mean that you can't find them anywhere or that they haven't sent you a letter?
2. When you move into a new flat, do you hold a home-warming or a house-warming party for your friends?
3. Could you be arrested for lighting up on a plane?
4. If you spent the weekend just messing around, did you get very dirty or did you not do very much?
5. If you're fined for something, are you happy about it?
6. I went round to a friend's. I went round to a friend's place. Are they both possible?
7. When you go to the dentist's, do you make an appointment or a date with him?
8. If you don't like, for example, eating frogs, would you say: I wouldn't eat a frog if you paid me or I wouldn't eat a frog if you asked me?
9. If you and some friends go to a nice little French place, what are you going to do?
10. If you're a heavy smoker, does it mean you're fat or that you smoke too much?
11. What is the difference between going shopping and doing the shopping?
12. Does a plane touch down at the beginning, in the middle, or at the end of a flight?
13. If something drags on, does it happen really quickly or take forever?
14. If you can be on board a plane, can you be on board a boat?
15. Which is the the odd one out and why? birthday party, office party, political party.
16. Are your relations the same as your relatives?
17. Do you go on a day-trip or have a day-trip?
18. You play tennis on one and you might end up in one if you're arrested. What is it?
19. Is a cosy room large or small?
20. Where do you work if you are one of the cabin crew?

Unit 5a : Last night

, yeah. What did you get up to last night? You went out where? It's not really my sort of place. What a bore! Who did you say you bumped into? I bet you've n
en there? We didn't get in till 2 in the morning! What was it like? Oh did you? I went round to a friend's place. You'd've enjoyed yourself. It was the best night
n. You're not going to have another early night, are you? You must be exhausted. Believe it or not, I'm too old for that sort of thing! It was unforgettable. I was
at's the last time you'll catch me there! It was a rip-off. The food was awful! It's THE place to be. The music was out of this world. You should've come. We ha

1 Lifestyle

What sort of lifestyle do you lead? Do you go out every evening or are you the stay-at-home type?

Read these descriptions of what some people did last night.

1. I went out for a walk around town.
2. I rang my sister.
3. I watched the semi-final on TV.
4. I just had a quiet night at home.
5. I went to my evening class.
6. I finished painting the kitchen.
7. I had an early night.
8. I visited my neighbour in hospital.
9. I tried to find a cheap flight on the Internet.
10. I went to the laundrette.

Which of these things do you do? Which do you never do?

T28 **Listen to four people talking about what they did last night. When you have decided what they did, tick the correct number in the list above.**

2 What's the difference?

Which of these pairs of sentences are different in meaning? What is the difference?

1. a. Good evening!
   b. Good night!
2. a. Isn't it a lovely evening?
   b. Isn't it a lovely night?
3. a. What did you do yesterday evening?
   b. What did you do last night?
4. a. I had an early night.
   b. I went to bed early.
5. a. I met some friends.
   b. I met up with some friends.
6. a. I met an old friend.
   b. I bumped into an old friend.
7. a. I went for a walk around town.
   b. I wandered around town.
8. a. We went out for a drink.
   b. We went out drinking.
9. a. I spent the evening at John's place.
   b. I spent the night at John's place.
10. a. We had a meal together.
    b. We went out for a meal together.

Real English: an early night and a late night

If you decide to *have an early night,* it means that you go to bed early. If you *have a late night,* it means that you don't go to bed until very late.

3 While you listen

T29 Rose and Lucy are having breakfast in the kitchen of the flat they share. Listen to them talking about what they did last night.

As you listen, try to answer the following questions:

1. What did Rose and Lucy do after work ?
2. What time did they go to bed?

Listen again and try to fill in the gaps in the conversation.

4 Talking point

Have you ever been 'chatted up' by someone much younger than you? What happened?

What's the worst club, disco, or party you've ever been to? What made it so bad?

How often do you eat foreign food? What's your favourite? Do you ever feel you watch a bit too much TV and that you should go out a bit more instead?

Real English: I bet he hadn't even started shaving.

It is very common for friends to make comments to each other starting *I bet ...* . For example:

I bet John's going to ask Angie to the party!
I bet you're wishing you'd gone!
I bet their car will break down!

We say *I bet ...* when we are fairly sure that what we are saying is true.

Real English: get a cab

This is correct spoken English for a *taxi*. For example:

You get a cab. I'll walk.

The Worst Disco in Town!

Lucy: Hey, Rose, there's a letter for you.

Rose: Thanks. You must've got in late last night. I didn't even hear you come in – and . . . . after one.

Lucy: I did, actually, yes. I went and met some old friends from college that I hadn't seen for ages.

Rose: Oh, ...? That must've been nice.

Lucy: Yes, we had a drink and a chat and caught up with all the gossip. You know what it's like.

Rose: Uh-huh.

Lucy: Then we had . . . . and then another drink and then we . . . . going on to this awful disco in town.

Rose: Oh, did you? Which one? Not 'Stardust'! No, surely not 'Stardust'?

Lucy: I'm afraid it was, actually – and it was really terrible, just full of kids and the music was so loud . . . . It was like being back at school all over again. Kids of 14 acting as if they were 18!

Rose: I could've told you that!

Lucy: This boy came up to me – you know, bottle of beer in his hand, acting all macho, and asked me to dance! I bet he hadn't even started shaving!

Rose: And did you?

Lucy: What? Dance with him? . . . .! Then I told him I was 35!

Rose: You're so cruel.

Lucy: Well, I just figured it was better he found out . . . . that I was old enough to be his mum!

Rose: I thought you were supposed to be there talking to old friends.

Lucy: I was, but there was so much noise, you couldn't really have a proper conversation. And then to top it all, I missed the last train home and had to get a cab and . . . . three!

Rose: Didn't you? You must be feeling exhausted this morning, then.

Lucy: Yeah, I could do with another hour or two in bed, that's for sure. . . . ., what about you? How was your night?

Rose: Oh, it was OK. I just did a bit of shopping on my way home, cooked myself some ramen noodles.

Lucy: Cooked yourself . . . . ?

Rose: Ramen noodles, you know, just Japanese noodles.

Lucy: Oh, OK.

Rose: They're really quick and easy, and then I just did a bit of tidying-up, you know, nothing amazing or anything, read for a bit, watched . . . . – some film – you know the kind of thing that's on late on Channel 4. Actually, I was so tired, I fell asleep in the middle of it!

Lucy: Oh, don't! You're making me feel even more exhausted!

5 Responding

T30 Look at the following common ways of responding to what someone says. Then listen to the tape and practise saying the expressions in colour.

Auxiliary question **+ follow-up question**

I met our old English teacher on the train last night.
> Oh, did you? How is she?
She's fine, she's working at another school now, teaching younger kids.

Auxiliary question **+ follow-up comment**

Hey – great news! I've just passed my driving test!
> Oh, have you? Congratulations. You must be really pleased.
Yes, it's excellent. Now all I need is the money for a car.

G17 First add the correct auxiliary questions. For example: Can you? Have you?

Then add one of these questions or comments:

a. Who do you play for?
b. How was it?
c. Say 'Hello' from me.
d. Have you sorted everything out yet?
e. Keep away from me, then.
f. Where's it on?
g. So when are you going to invite me round for dinner, then?
h. Anywhere particular in mind?

1. I'm a pretty good cook, believe it or not.
   > . . . . ? . . . .
2. I've just come back from Paris.
   > . . . . ? . . . .
3. I had a fight with my boyfriend yesterday.
   > . . . . ? . . . .
4. I was thinking of going to the circus this weekend.
   > . . . . ? . . . .
5. I think I'm getting the flu.
   > . . . . ? . . . .
6. I usually play football on Saturdays.
   > . . . . ? . . . .
7. Eventually, I'd like to end up living overseas.
   > . . . . ? . . . .
8. I'm going to see Marco tonight.
   > . . . . ? . . . .

Talking about you

Complete the following sentence starters in ways that are true for you. If you can, think of things which are interesting or unusual.

I can . . . .
I'd really love to . . . .
Believe it or not, I've never . . . .
. . . .
When I was younger, I once . . . .
. . . .
Last night I . . . .

Now tell a partner what you've written. Your partner should respond first by using an auxiliary question and then by adding a follow-up question or comment. Try to develop these conversations for as long as you can.

6 Collocations with *get*

There are many collocations using get. **Use these words and expressions to complete the sentences:**

surprise	bus
upset	wet
a job	a call
something to eat	money
my hair cut	lost

1. I got . . . . last night. Do you like it? I think it's a bit too short at the back myself.
2. I tried to get some . . . . from the cash machine last night but it wasn't working.
3. I got . . . . from an old friend of mine last night. I hadn't spoken to her for ages, so that was nice.
4. I was really hungry so I popped out to get . . . .
5. I got really . . . . last night watching TV. I watched that documentary about Hiroshima.
6. I've never seen rain like it – I got really . . . . . . on the way home last night.
7. I got a real . . . . last night. An old school friend of mine turned up out of the blue!
8. Hey, you won't believe it. I've finally got . . . . I start next Monday.
9. My car broke down, so I had to get the last . . . . home.
10. I walked around town a bit, but ended up getting . . . . I had to ask someone where I was!

Go back and underline the *get*-expressions.

You can use get **with all of the following words. Use them to say something true about yourself or people you know.**

annoyed	angry	upset
better	mad	worried
tired	married	sleepy
well paid	lazy	pregnant

When was the last time you:

had to get a taxi home?
got in really late?
got stuck in traffic?
got stopped by the police?

7 Did / had / went

Here are three ways of talking about what you did last night.

1. I did a bit of reading.
   my homework.
2. I had a drink with some friends.
   a big argument with my mum.
3. I went to see a movie.
   for a walk.

Add did, had, **or** went **to each of the following. The first two are done for you.**

1. I *went* out for a walk.
2. I just *went* straight home.
3. I . . . . to bed about 12.
4. I . . . . a bit of exercise.
5. I . . . . a terrible night.
6. I . . . . into college and . . . . a bit of work.
7. I just . . . . a bit of cleaning round the house.
8. I . . . . dinner with my parents.
9. I . . . . a bit of cooking.
10. I . . . . a cup of coffee when I got in.
11. I . . . . some reading for college.
12. I . . . . my washing.
13. I . . . . a chat with my next-door neighbour.
14. I . . . . shopping in town.
15. I . . . . a bit of shopping in town.
16. I . . . . a really great evening.
17. I . . . . a shower/a bath.
18. I . . . . to see some friends of mine.
19. I . . . . some drawing.
20. I . . . . round to a friend's.

Check your answers and then practise saying the above expressions. Find examples of other collocations using did, have **and** went **in the dialogue on page 73 and underline them.**

When was the last time you:

had a chat with your next-door neighbour?
went round to a friend's?
had a terrible night?

Work in pairs using ideas from this exercise to ask and answer questions.

8 Role play

Work in pairs taking turns to be one of the people below. Choose 4 expressions from exercise 7 to tell your partner what you did last night.

Marcia works during the day, and studies at night. She has two kids she has to look after.

Dave loves parties. He likes keeping fit. He's very creative and sociable. He travels a lot.

Tara doesn't like going out much. She reads a lot. She sees a lot of her parents and has a small dog.

9 You did what last night?

T31 **When someone says something in a conversation that you don't understand, it is not enough to say simply that you don't understand.**

Here are some typical ways of making it clear exactly what you don't understand:

I surfed the net last night.
> You did what last night?
Surfed the net – played around on the Internet.

I went on holiday to Phuket last year.
> You went where?
Phuket. It's a beach resort in Thailand.

Listen to the tape and then practise the above conversations with a partner.

Now write similar questions in the gaps below to make it clear exactly what you don't understand.

1. My car cost over two grand.
   > . . . . ?
   Over two grand, two thousand pounds.
2. I had dinner in Bellini's last night.
   > . . . . ?
   In Bellini's, that new Italian place.
3. I down-loaded this great article last night.
   > . . . . ?
   I down-loaded an article, you know, copied it off the Internet.
4. I arrived here on Boxing Day.
   > . . . . ?
   On Boxing Day, you know, the day after Christmas, December the 26th.
5. I went bungee jumping last year in Canada.
   > . . . . ?
   Bungee jumping, you know, when you jump from a bridge with elastic round your legs.
6. This shirt cost me eighty quid.
   > . . . .
   Eighty quid, you know, eighty pounds.
7. I found a baby wren in my garden today.
   > . . . .
   A baby wren. It must've fallen out of its nest.
8. We went to Alton Towers at the weekend.
   >. . . . .
   To Alton Towers. It's a kind of theme park, like Disneyland, but much smaller.

Compare your answers with your partner, then practise the above conversations in pairs.

10 I didn't . . . until . . . !

G18 **In the conversation on page 73, Lucy says:**

I didn't get in until three.

Why didn't she say *I got in at three?*

Complete the following sentences by choosing the most appropriate of the two choices:

1. I had to work late so a) I got home at 7.
   b) I didn't get home until 7.
2. The traffic on the way was really heavy, so
   a) I didn't get there until 9.
   b) I got there at 9.
3. We managed to get the bus OK, so
   a) we were there by 9.
   b) we weren't there until 9.
4. I was a late-starter.
   a) I didn't have a girlfriend until I was 21.
   b) I had a girlfriend when I was 21.
5. I just had a fairly quiet night.
   a) I didn't get to bed until 11.
   b) I went to bed at 11.
6. There were three standing ovations. The concert a) finished at 11:30.
   b) didn't finish until 11:30.
7. I'm not too bad at English, considering
   a) I didn't start studying until I was 18.
   b) I started studying when I was 18.
8. I was so busy that
   a) I had breakfast at midday.
   b) I didn't have breakfast until midday.

Can you explain your choice in each example?

Discuss

With a partner, answer the following questions. Try to use I didn't . . . until . . . . **Give reasons for your answers.**

a. What time did you get in last night?
b. When did you have your first boy/girlfriend?
c. What time did you go to bed last night?
d. When did you start studying English?

Real English: My car cost over two grand.

In informal spoken English *a grand* is one thousand pounds. In example 6 in exercise 9 *eighty quid* is informal British English for *eighty pounds*.

11 Linking ideas

G19 On page 73 Lucy talked about the disco:

It was so loud, I could hardly hear myself think.

This is a common way of linking two ideas:

I was very tired.
I fell asleep in the middle of the film.
> I was so tired, I fell asleep in the middle of it.

Match the two parts of these sentences:

1. It was so cold,
2. I was so exhausted,
3. I was so hungry,
4. It was so hot,
5. His conversation was so dull,
6. I was so angry,
7. I was so worried,
8. The film was so bad,

a. I could've killed him!
b. I rang the police.
c. I could hardly breathe.
d. I walked out halfway through.
e. I just went straight to bed as soon as I got in.
f. I could hardly stop myself from yawning.
g. my hands felt like they were going to fall off.
h. I could've carried on eating all night!

T32 Say all these sentences, making sure you stress *so*.

More conversations

Then with a partner, complete the conversations below using ideas of your own.

So, how was that club you went to?
> Terrible! The music was so loud, I just had to leave.

1. So what was that film like you saw last night?
> Well, to be honest, it was so bad, . . .
2. What was the food like in that French place you went to?
> Really good. It was so delicious, . . .
3. So did you do anything special last night?
> No, I was so exhausted, I . . .
4. So how did your meeting go last night?
> Terrible, it was so . . . . . , I . . .
5. So did you sort everything out with your boss yesterday?
> No, I got so . . . . , I . . .
6. So did you pass your driving test?
> No, I'm afraid not. I was so . . . . , I . . .

12 Role play

There's a thief in the class!

At 8pm last night, a terrible crime was committed – your teacher's car was stolen from the school car park. The police suspect two students from this class.

1. The class decides which two students are most likely to have committed the crime. The pair of suspects leave the room to prepare their story.

(Where were you when the crime happened? Who were you with? What were you doing? All the details are important!)

2. The rest of the class prepare to interview the two students.

(What will you ask them?)

3. Student 1 comes back into the room alone and is interviewed by the class. When the interview is finished, student 2 comes in to be interviewed.

4. When both students have been interviewed, the class vote. Are they both guilty? Is only one guilty? What should happen to them? Decide on a suitable punishment!

Unit 5b : Relationships

y. Where've you been all my life? He's old enough to be your father! I only like people with money. Looks don't matter to me. He's a bit of a lad if you ask me. Yo
believable! You'd never catch me going out with someone who wears red socks! I think I'm in love. Excuse me, would you like to come home and see my stamp c
t up. I really go for Scandinavians. Are you trying to chat me up because if you are, you can get lost! We've decided to go our separate ways. Go jump in
s, he is a bit of a nerd. I prefer older men. I'm not prejudiced of course. It's all over. I don't find him attractive at all. I don't know what you see in her. Congratu

1 Judging by appearances

G20 Decide which of the following statements you would make about the young people in the picture below:

She looks really nice.
She looks a bit sad.
She looks old enough to be at university.

He looks like a doctor or something.
He looks like a real creep.
He looks like a bit of a nerd.

He looks as if he's about to collapse.
She looks as if she's just won the lottery.
She looks as if she's been up all night.

Which of these structures:

a. is followed by a noun?
b. is followed by an adjective?
c. is followed by a statement ?

Which of the people appeals most / least to you personally? Why?

Real English: a real creep / a bit of a nerd

A *creep* is a very negative word to describe someone (usually male) very peculiar who makes you feel uncomfortable. A *nerd* is a negative word to describe someone (usually male) who is considered boring and unfashionable!

2 What turns you on?

Which of the following are most important for you in a partner or friend? Give each of the following ideas a score (1 – 5): 1 means you think it is not important; 5 is very important.

money	__
sense of humour	__
age	__
looks	__
nationality	__
dress sense	__
intelligence	__
cooking ability	__
honesty	__
religion	__

Compare your answers with your partner and explain your choices.

3 Prepositions

Before you read the text, try to fill in the missing prepositions from these sentences. Check your answers after you've read the text.

1. It was awful when I had to break the news .... my brother of our grandmother's death.
2. My girlfriend's a belly-dancer. I was really worried that my parents wouldn't approve .... her.
3. I've been going out .... my boyfriend for almost six years now.
4. I've never really been interested .... boys of my own age. They always seem a bit childish.
5. Personally, I don't really go .... blondes. I much prefer brunettes.
6. He kept on asking me all these really personal questions, so I just told him it was none .... his business!
7. It took the children a long time to come to terms .... the death of their rabbit.

4 While reading

In the conversation on page 73, Lucy jokes about dancing with a boy who was half her age. Read this article about another unlikely couple who found love in a club. When you have read it, answer these questions:

1. Why was Jamie Brodlin worried about introducing his new girlfriend to his parents?
2. How did they meet?
3. How do his parents get on with Jane now they've met her?

OLD ENOUGH TO BE HIS GRAN!

Teenager Jamie Brodlin simply didn't know how to break the news to his parents. Like all normal 17-year-olds, he was keen for his parents to meet and approve of his new girlfriend – the only problem was that his new love was old enough to be his gran!

Jamie has been going out with 58-year-old divorcee, Jane Fisher, since love blossomed one night last June when Jamie went out clubbing with three friends. Jamie claims he's never been interested in girls his own age. "To be honest with you, I don't normally go for girls my own age. I tend to find them a little bit immature," he said, and went instead for Mrs. Fisher, who caught his eye across the crowded dance floor – working in the cloakroom!

"I don't know what it was about her," Jamie said, "but there was just something really warm and appealing about the way she moved and the way she hung the coats up, so I went up and started chatting. My mates just couldn't believe it, but I told them it was none of their business."

Jane claims that at first she thought Jamie was just drunk. "I thought he was just some lad with a few too many beers inside him who was doing it all for a bet, and it was only later I realised just how mature and sensible Jamie really is."

The story has a happy ending, as Jamie's parents have now met and come to terms with Jane – and even have her round for the evening when Jamie's out with his friends!

5 Comprehension check

Decide whether the following statements about the text are true (T) or false (F):

1. Jamie Brodlin fell in love with his grandmother.
2. Jamie finds girls his own age a bit childish.
3. He first saw Jane on the other side of the disco dance floor.
4. When he first started chatting to her, Jane just thought Jamie was drunk.
5. Jamie's friends weren't at all surprised.
6. Jamie's parents now accept the fact he's dating someone old enough to be his grandmother.

6 Word check

Find words from the text to complete the following sentences:

1. Ever since my mum and dad split up, my mum has always hated being called a . . . . She'd much rather just be called 'single'.
2. She was really shy when she first joined this class, but she really seems to have . . . .
3. Excuse me, but is there somewhere I can leave my coat?
   > Yes, there's a . . . . just at the top of the stairs.
4. I don't know about you, but personally I don't find that kind of man very . . . . He's a bit too tall for me.
5. He's a typical . . . . , you know, out for a good time with his mates.
6. He's the . . . . one in our family, you know, careful with his money, always does the right thing.

Real English: I tend to find them ...

Jamie said, "I *tend to* find them a bit immature." Notice the difference between these sentences:

Women live longer than men.
Women tend to live longer than men.

If you add *tend to* to an opinion, it makes you sound less dogmatic and opinionated. It makes general statements sound more tentative. For example:

I tend to get up earlier in the summer.

Can you make any similar statements about your habits or opinions, using *tend to?*

7 Stages of a relationship

Decide in which order you think the following would probably occur. Use a dictionary or ask your teacher to help you with any vocabulary you are not sure of.

a. My wife/husband and I are separated.
b. I'm getting married next week.
c. We've just got engaged.
d. I'm going out with him/her.
e. My marriage is on the rocks.
f. We're having marriage guidance counselling.
g. I proposed to her/him last night.
h. We're in the process of getting divorced.

Now compare your order with your partner and explain your choices.

8 Talking point

Have you ever gone out with anyone much older or younger than yourself?
How do you feel about relationships where there's a large age difference?
How would your parents and friends react if you started going out with someone much older or younger than you?
How would you feel about marrying a divorcee ? Why?
How do you know when you're in love ?
Would you consider marrying someone if there was a big age difference? What do you think of the following relationships?

1. a man of 50 and a girl of 18
   a woman of 50 and a boy of 18
2. a man of 25 and a girl of 18
   a woman of 25 and a man of 18
3. a man of 80 and a woman of 30
   a woman of 80 and a man of 30

How would you complete these statements?

I wouldn't get involved with anyone who . . .
I'd never marry someone who . . .

Can you think of any famous people who have had relationships with people much older or younger than themselves?

9 Descriptive adjectives

First decide if the following adjectives describe character or appearance or both. Then mark them P or N, depending on whether you think they are positive or negative.

muscular	pushy	plain	forward
warm	quiet	skinny	down-to-earth
flirty	sexy	macho	unpredictable
dishy	mature	cuddly	hairy

Character	Appearance	Both

With your partner, look at these photographs and try to agree which of the adjectives above you would use to describe which people.

Now describe someone else in your class to your partner using some of the adjectives above. See if they can guess who you're talking about.

10 Chat-up lines

If you chat somebody up, **you talk to them in a friendly way to show that you're attracted to them. "Chat-up lines" are openings that people use when they want to chat you up.**

Decide which of the following you think are the best and worst chat-up lines. Compare your answers with a partner.

1. Do you come here often?
2. Someone call heaven – I think they're missing an angel.
3. What's a nice girl/guy like you doing in a place like this?
4. Are you here by yourself?
5. Excuse me, but have you got a light?
6. Can I get you a drink?
7. Has anyone ever told you you've got really lovely eyes?
8. What are you doing afterwards?

Has anyone ever tried to use any of these chat-up lines or similar versions in your own language on you? Have you ever used any yourself? Did they work?

Can you think of any other chat-up lines you've heard or used?

Real English: dishy

If you find someone *dishy*, you find them physically attractive. Some dictionaries say that this is a rather old-fashioned word, but many young British people in their twenties use it, particularly women.

Partner shopping

You are a busy executive with little free time on your hands. You are single. You are looking for a partner, but where do you start? The obvious answer is your local supermarket. That's where you go once a week to stock up on everything you need for the coming week, so why not use it to find a partner?

There's nothing new in that, you might say. You might already be one of those single guys who hang around the washing powder lane, looking as if you've never washed a shirt in your life, hoping that the woman of your dreams will take pity on you and explain the difference between soap powder and fabric softener.

Or are you the innocent blonde who picks up a passionfruit and asks that tall dark handsome guy you've been following since your eyes met over the skimmed milk if he's ever tried one?

The British supermarket chain, Asda, recently invented 'singles nights', recognising the fact that their stores were one of the best places in town to meet a partner. It's certainly the warmest and cheapest! But the prize for marketing brilliance must go to another chain, Sainsbury's. They have imported an idea from the Japanese which looks as if it might catch on. As you enter the store you take a 'love bleeper'. You key in your likes and dislikes – a 25-year-old brunette of medium height who is into rock music, or maybe what you're after is a bodybuilder who likes quiet evenings in front of the TV. If you come close to another shopper who is looking for someone like you, both bleepers will start bleeping and flashing at each other.

Crazy? Maybe! But for people living in big cities, working late every night, this idea may not be as silly as it sounds. Where DO you go to meet people? If it works, just think how romantic it'll sound when you tell your children that you met their mum over the vegetable counter!

11 Talking point

Where did the 'love bleeper' idea come from originally?

Where did you meet your partner? Would you take a love bleeper if you went to a store with that system? What would you say to the person whose bleeper bleeped at you?

Is this a sad story for sad people? Or is it the way forward in the modern world?

12 Expressions with modals

G21 Complete the fixed expressions in the situations below by adding these modal verbs:

might can must
could couldn't should

1. I used my best chat-up line on her, and then she went and told me she was married!
   > I . . . . 've told you that. I thought it was common knowledge.
2. Paddy's must be one of the best clubs in town.
   > You . . . . . . say that again! What a night!
3. The food there was terrible – again!
   > Well, you . . . . . .'ve known better after what happened last time.
4. Does Rob ever invite you round to his place?
   > You . . . . . . be joking! Rob never invites anyone round to his place.
5. I went for a walk with my parents yesterday afternoon, down by the river.
   > Oh, that . . . . . .'ve been nice. You had some lovely weather for it.
6. So, did you have a good chat with Steve last night?
   > Not really, no. It was so loud in the pub, I . . . . . . hardly hear myself think!
7. Did you see Jamie trying to chat up the cloakroom attendant last night?
   > Yes, I know. I just . . . . . . believe it. She's old enough to be his grandmother.
8. We climbed over the fence and went for a swim in their pool last night.
   > You . . . . . . be mad doing that! They've got an alsatian and a rottweiler!
9. My husband forgot my birthday – again!
   > You never know. He might be planning to surprise you later.
   Yes, right! And pigs . . . . . . fly!

Complete the 9 expressions used above:

1. . . . . been nice.
2. . . . . say that again!
3. . . . . be joking!
4. . . . . be mad!
5. . . . . believe it!
6. . . . . told you that.
7. . . . . hardly hear myself think!
8. . . . . known better!
9. Pigs . . . . !

Grammar in context

With a partner, choose which of the 9 expressions above is the best response to the following:

1. We spent the whole day on the beach yesterday.
2. Can you believe they wouldn't let me in because I was wearing jeans?
3. There were so many kids there yesterday, weren't there?
4. That guy Mike we met last night is a bit of a nerd, don't you think?
5. So what was that exhibition you went to last week like? Any good?

I could do with ...

Look at another useful modal verb expression from the conversation between Rose and Lucy.

Rose: You must be feeling exhausted this morning, then.
Lucy: Yeah, I could do with another hour or two in bed, that's for sure.

Complete the following by adding I could do with **and one of these expressions:**

a. a bit more time e. a break
b. more money f. a good night's sleep
c. something to eat g. a lie-in
d. some help h. a holiday

1. Is anyone free? . . . . This thing's really heavy.
2. Hey, can we pop in here for a snack? I didn't get a chance to have anything earlier. . . . .
3. I'm so tired staring at this computer screen. . . . .
4. I haven't quite finished it yet. . . . . , to be honest.
5. I've been up to my ears in work this month. . . . . , I can tell you!
6. I've been out every night this week. . . . . tomorrow, that's for sure.
7. I'm pretty tired. . . . . tonight, if possible.
8. I'm pretty happy at work, but . . . . I mean, I always end up broke by the end of the month.

Tell your partner some things that you could really do with at the moment.

13 Your dream partner

Have some fun! If you could order your ideal partner from The Ideal Partner Mail Order Company, what would you send off for?

Height
He/she would be about . . . . tall.

Weight
He/she would weigh no more than . . . .

Hair
His/her hair would be . . . . . .
I would / would not mind if he/she was bald.
As for body hair, ...

Eyes
He/she must have . . . . . . eyes.
He/she must / mustn't wear glasses.

Feet
I wouldn't want anyone who took shoes bigger than size . . . . . .

Car
It would be absolutely essential that he/she had his/her own car and it would have to be a . . . . .

Money
His/her bank balance would / would not be important to me.

Compare your answers with another student. Which of the pictures opposite do you prefer?

14 Why aren't you married?

Here are some amusing replies to the question which older people love to ask younger people who are not yet married. Which is your favourite?

1. Because you haven't asked yet.
2. Because I love being asked that question.
3. Because I'm waiting till I'm your age.
4. Because I just love singles bars.
5. Why don't you get lost?
6. Because I'm married to my career.
7. Why aren't you thin?
8. Because my parents would have a heart attack.
9. I suppose I'm just lucky.

Have you ever been asked this question? What do you reply?

Vocabulary

Problem words

With a partner, discuss the differences in meaning between the words in colour below:

a. I had a chat with her.
I had a talk with her.
b. We gossiped about the boss.
We talked about work.
c. I did the washing-up.
I did the washing.
d. I went to a disco.
We ended up going to a disco.
e. I missed the last bus home.
I really missed her when she was in Spain.
f. I went out last night after work.
I left work last night about 5.

Now choose the best whole sentences from a-f above to complete the following:

1. Yes, Mr. Fairhurst, ... about it. I'm sure Eve won't be late again.
2. I bumped into Marie yesterday, which was nice. about, you know, nothing much, but it was nice to see her.
3. I had a drink with Bill last week. . . . . and nothing else all evening!
4. Some of us went for a drink after work the other day. It was awful. for ages. I'm glad he wasn't there!
5. I haven't got anything to wear tomorrow. It really is time . . . .
6. Just look at all those dirty dishes. It's time . . . .
7. I had a crazy evening. I met some old friends and we went out for dinner and then eventually . . . .
8. My legs are killing me this morning! . . . . and didn't stop dancing all night!
9. I'm really annoyed. I didn't get home until 2 last night. . . . .
10. Jane came back last week. . . . .
11. and just went straight home.
12. I should have known better. . . . . with a few people from my department and I didn't get in till 3am. I feel terrible.

Compound adjectives

Make compound adjectives by matching the words below:

1. good-	a. going
2. easy-	b. confident
3. curly-	c. looking
4. self-	d. haired
5. open-	e. dressed
6. smartly-	f. minded
7. football-	g. conscious
8. self-	h. mad

Now mark each adjective P (personality) or A (appearance).

Complete the following sentences by adding the best compound adjective:

1. He's a typical fourteen-year-old boy – wants to be a professional footballer. He's . . . .
2. She always looks very professional. She's always very . . . .
3. Claudia's OK, but she's a bit shy, a bit . . . . if you know what I mean.
4. My parents travel a lot, so they're pretty . . . . about people from other cultures.
5. Mike seems very sure of himself, very . . . .
6. The man you need to speak to is Mr Philby – the . . . . man with the glasses.
7. You'll like Alison. She's nice – very laid-back, very . . . .
8. And her boyfriend Mark is nice too. And he's very . . . . He could be a model.

Now complete the following sentences in ways that are true for you, using compound adjectives:

I wouldn't want to go out with anyone who was . . . .
My ideal partner would be . . . .
and . . . .

Supermarket vocabulary

Use these six words which describe different areas in a British supermarket:

toiletries	meat	dairy
delicatessen	poultry	soft

1. Fresh cream is in the . . . . produce section.
2. Lemonade is with the other . . . . drinks.
3. Ask for fresh olives at the . . . . counter.
4. Lamb chops are in the . . . . section.
5. Shampoo and stuff like that is in . . . . .
6. Chicken, duck, and quail are in the . . . . section.

learning advice

Is there anything wrong with a slight foreign accent? No!

You are learning English as a foreign language. There is nothing wrong with a Spanish learner speaking English with a Spanish accent, or a German student speaking with a German accent – providing people can easily understand you.

If your accent is too strong, you need to listen carefully to more natural English and your accent will improve.

One of the best ways of improving your pronunciation is to learn how to say complete expressions. If you learn the pronunciation of the expression when you learn the meaning, your English will sound more natural. But don't worry about a slight accent.

Unit 6a : Telling stories

ve I ever told you about the time I got locked in the loo of a jumbo? You're having me on, aren't you? You'll never believe what happened to me this morning. It's
y well for you to laugh but you wouldn't have liked it. Once upon a time, there were three bears. Do you think I was born yesterday? Did you hear what happer
Now I've heard everything! So, to cut a long story short. I don't believe a word of what you're saying. You must be joking! A spider in her ear! Anyw
angest thing that's ever happened to me. If you believe that, you'll believe anything. It's the truth. Really? Really! You know, between you and me, I'd say it w

1 Every picture tells a story

It is a common saying in English that every picture tells a story. What do you think the stories are behind the pictures on this page?

2 While you listen

T33 **Diane and Cathy are taking the underground across London, chatting as they go. Listen to Diane talking about a strange thing that happened to her. As you listen, try and answer the following questions:**

1. Where and when did this happen to Diane?
2. What was the problem? What happened in the end?

Listen again and try to fill in the gaps in the conversation.

Real English: pinch his wallet

If you *pinch* something, you steal it. *Pinch* is a very informal word.

Real English: Yeah

Yeah means *yes.* In speech it is usually unstressed and is the normal way of saying *yes*. It is standard in both British and American English.

3 Talking point

Have you ever not recognised someone you knew?

Do you ever ignore people you know? In what situations?

What is the strangest or most interesting thing that has ever happened to you while you were travelling?

Hair today, gone tomorrow!

Cathy: So, we've got to take this one and then change at Cannon Street, right?

Diane: Yes, that's it. Hey, ... what happened with me and my dad on the underground last year?

Cathy: No, go on, what?

Diane: Well, ... , I decided to get all my hair cut off, right? I always used to have really, really long hair – ever since I was about 14 or 15, you know – way down past my shoulders – parted in the middle like curtains. So, ... , about a week after I had it all cut off, you know – really short – and I looked quite different.

Cathy: Yeah, I bet.

Diane: So, anyway, ... home on the tube, and I was half asleep because it was 5 or 6 o'clock and I was just standing there, ... – and little did I know that my dad was actually coming back from a business trip abroad, passing through London on the underground to get his train back to Durham. And . . . . ? He got into the same carriage as me! The doors closed behind him. So there I am, standing there face-to-face with my own father! I don't recognise him at first, but then I think, "Ah, that's my dad," and, of course, he's obviously only seen me with really long hair for the last ten years, and so . . . . there, staring at him and he . . . . . . on glancing at me nervously, thinking, "Who's this lunatic staring at me?" and I'm thinking – you know, it's the strangest feeling not being recognised by your own dad – so I just stood there thinking, "Well, ... just get off at the next stop without telling him, or . . . . risk giving him a nervous breakdown and a heart attack by saying, "Hello Dad?" But, anyway, ... I went, "Hello Dad" and he went, "Diane!" and then said how he was getting really worried because he thought I was a pick-pocket or a drug addict . . . . who'd been getting ready to pinch his wallet or something – and, um, yeah, that was a pretty strange and funny thing.

Cathy: Yeah, *really* strange.

4 Hairstyles

Match the following to the pictures:

a. He's got spiky hair.
b. She's got curly hair.
c. She's got a fringe.
d. He's got dreadlocks.
e. She's got dyed red hair.
f. She's got pigtails.
g. She's got hair extensions.
h. He's got short back and sides.

Have you ever thought of changing your hairstyle, dyeing your hair, bleaching it blond?

Have you ever had a really bad, unusual or different haircut? How did people react to it?

5 Vocabulary

Diane used two special words to describe how she and her father looked at each other – glancing **and** staring. **Can you explain the differences in meaning between the following words? Use them in these situations:**

caught sight of	peered	winked
stared	look	glanced
seen	watched	glared

1. I felt really uncomfortable on the bus. A very strange-looking man kept looking at me. He just . . . . . . and . . . . . . It was really weird.
2. I rang the bell several times, but there was no response. I . . . . . in through the letterbox and could see someone in the kitchen.
3. I'll need time to look through these papers in more detail. I've just . . . . . at them and they seem fine, but I need more time to study them.
4. Have you . . . . . today's papers yet?
5. I was so worried about someone stealing my motorbike, I stayed up all night and . . . . . it.
6. Just. . . . . at that car! It must have cost the best part of £100,000!
7. When I saw that boy trying to steal a Mars bar, I just . . . . . at him until he put it back.
8. When we left Tokyo, I just . . . . Mount Fuji for a second or two before the plane turned in the other direction.
9. I knew Ed was pulling my leg when he . . . . . . at me!

Real English: Ed was pulling my leg.
If someone pulls your leg, they are joking.

6 Story-telling expressions

T34 Fill in the gaps using the following words, then listen to the tape to check your answers:

well	go on	so
really	you're joking	anyway

A: Did I tell you about what happened to me in France last year?

B: No, I don't think you did. . . . .

A: . . . . , I was on holiday with my parents in this little village near the sea, and we ran out of French money.

B: . . . . ? That's awful.

A: Yes, ... we went into town to find a cash machine – which we did, no trouble. . . . . , when we put the card in the machine, it just started spitting out loads and loads of money.

B: . . . . ! So did you keep it?

A: Of course we did! Wouldn't you?

Matching

Match the expressions above to the following meanings:

1. I'm starting my story now.
2. I find that very surprising.
3. I'm very interested in what you're saying.
4. Please continue your story.
5. I'm returning to the main part of my story now.
6. I'm now telling you the result.

Can you find examples of any of the expressions in Diane and Cathy's conversation on page 88?

7 Talking point

If you had been the person using the cash machine when the money started coming out of it, what would you have done – kept it and said nothing or told the bank?

Have you ever found money or something valuable and kept it?

What would you do if you found any of the following?

1. a camera with a film in it with 35 out of the 36 pictures used
2. a £5 note
3. a lottery ticket which then won £100,000
4. a really nice CD walkman

8 Short stories

Here are three stories. Put them into the correct order.

Story 1

1. but luckily, there was a little bit of grass there and I landed on it and I was OK.
2. and I try and miss it but I hit it and I'm flying through the air and I'm thinking, "This is the end,"
3. and then all of a sudden this car drove right out in front of me
4. Well, on Thursday I was riding home on my bicycle

The correct order is . . . .

Story 2

1. when suddenly the whole thing crashed,
2. I used to write computer games for this big company. One day, I was almost at the end of a really difficult job
3. Anyway, when I re-opened the file, it was all still there. I couldn't believe my luck.
4. so I re-started it and thought, "I bet I've lost the whole thing."

The correct order is . . . .

Story 3

1. At the check-in they asked to see her passport
2. and she suddenly remembered she'd left it at home,
3. Once, this friend of mine was coming back from Germany, where she used to live.
4. and so in the end she had to go all the way back to Berlin.

The correct order is . . . .

Go back and underline the expressions which link the parts of the story together.

Then take turns telling each of these stories, adding your own extra information. Try to use some of the expressions from exercise 6.

9 Telling a story

G22 **Look at the pictures opposite and try to imagine the stories. The expressions below will help you tell the stories. Work with a partner. Use one expression from each group and plan how to tell each story.**

1. Introducing your story

Did I ever tell you about the time I ...
I must've told you about the time I ...
Did I ever tell you about this friend of mine who ...

2. Giving background details

A few years ago, when this friend of mine was ...
Last August when my family was on holiday in ...

3. Introducing the problem

When all of a sudden ...
Then suddenly ...

4. How the problem was solved

Well, what happened in the end was ...
Eventually ...
Luckily ...

5. Finishing off the story

It was one of the funniest/silliest/strangest/worst things that's ever happened to me!
Looking back on it, it was all very exciting/interesting/strange/upsetting.
It seems funny now, but it didn't seem like that at the time!

Now change partners and tell one of the stories again. Your partner should try to respond with the expressions in exercise 6.

10 Talking point

What have the main stories been in your local paper recently?
Are most of the stories about crime or are they about good news?
If you were the editor of your local paper, which two of the following stories would you be interested in for tonight's edition?

1. My parrot tells the time!
2. Famous footballer opens new supermarket
3. Local boy bungee jumps from Eiffel Tower
4. Local girl to marry Hollywood star
5. Headmaster shaves head for charity
6. Factory to close – 50 jobs disappear

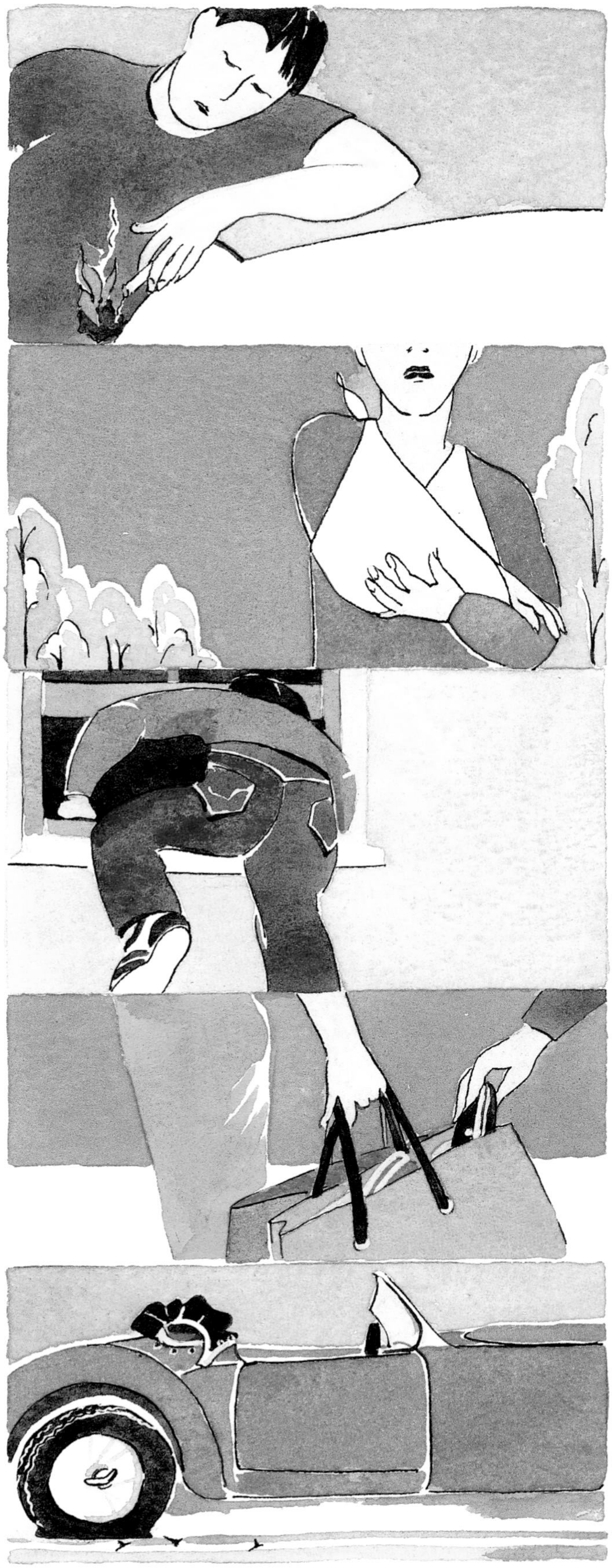

11 *-ing* clauses

Grammar in context

G23 In the conversation on page 88 Diane says:

I was just standing there – minding my own business.

Notice that she did *not* say:

I was standing there. I was minding my own business.

Cross out the words which are not needed in the following:

1. I saw a man. He was breaking into a car.
2. Two firemen died. They were trying to get a child out of the blazing flat.
3. The car broke down. It was going up the hill.
4. He had a heart attack. He was playing golf.
5. I was standing outside the bank. I was waiting for a bus.
6. The police caught them. They were trying to break into the shop.
7. We caught sight of the Queen. She was driving past on the way to the funeral.
8. We had to wait ten minutes. We were standing outside in the pouring rain.
9. Some children were in the shop. They were stealing sweets.

Look back at the conversation on page 88 and complete the following:

10. It was 5 or 6 o'clock and I was just standing there, ...
11. My dad was actually coming back from a business trip abroad, ...
12. He keeps on glancing at me, ...

Grammar activity

With a partner, complete the following sentences by adding as many *-ing* clauses as you can.

There was this really strange-looking guy, . . .
I was rushing around madly, . . .
On Thursday I was driving along, . . .
So there we were, in this fancy restaurant, . . .
My uncle was sitting there in the bar, . . .
There was this huge crowd outside the parliament building, . . . and . . .

Now report some of your sentences to the whole class and see who has made the funniest examples.

Pronunciation

T35 Listen to the tape and notice where the speaker pauses:

There was this great big dog, sitting there . . . barking at me.

Listen to the following short sections of speech and mark the pauses.

1. It was 5 or 6 o'clock and I was just standing there, minding my own business.
2. My dad was actually coming back from a business trip abroad, passing through London.
3. He keeps on glancing at me, thinking, "Who's this lunatic staring at me?"
4. I was dancing about in the street, acting like a fool.
5. I was lying there on the ground, screaming in pain.

Now listen again and underline the strongest stress like this:

There was this great big <u>dog</u>, <u>si</u>tting there, <u>bar</u>king at me.

Practise saying the above, stressing the correct syllables and pausing in the right places. Then do the same with examples 1 – 12 in the Grammar in Context exercise opposite.

Grammar check

Notice that this -ing structure is often used with the past continuous. Go back and underline all the past continuous forms in the exercises on this page.

Here are some more typical examples. Fill in the correct verb:

trying	packing	sunbathing
minding	doing	waiting

1. I was just standing on the corner, ... for a friend.
2. I was just having a coffee, ... my own business.
3. We were just getting ready to go, ... our things and saying our goodbyes.

But other tenses are sometimes used:

4. Why are you just standing there, ... nothing?
5. We lay on the beach most days, ...
6. You're always coming in to my office, ... to borrow something or other!

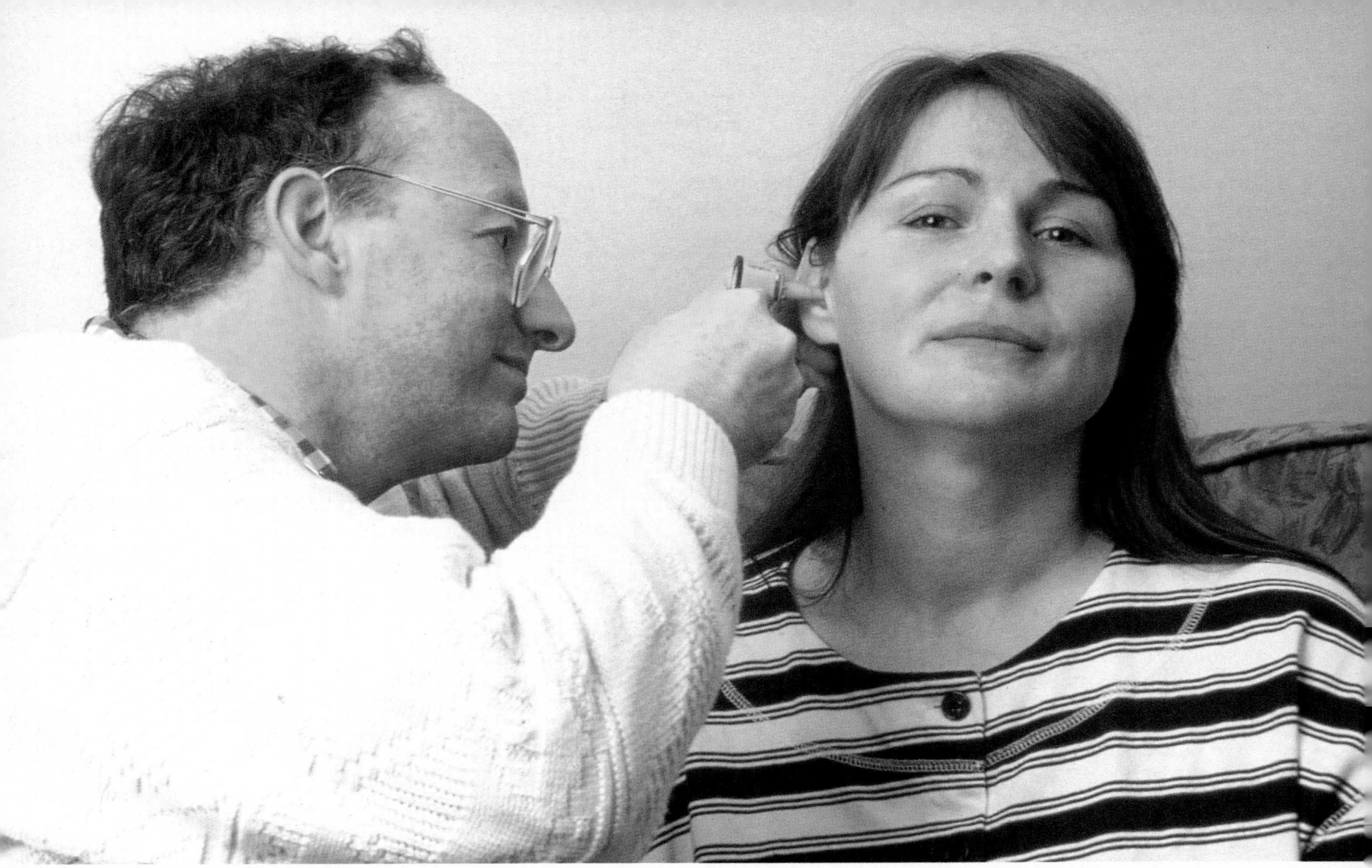

Spider woman

Have you heard the story of the woman who dried her cat in the microwave after it had got wet – or the one about the woman who opened a bag of prepared salad and out popped a fully-grown frog? Whether they are true or not, we love telling each other scary stories. Unfortunately, the story that follows is definitely true.

Recently, a woman living in Kent in southern England went to her doctor. For days she hadn't been able to sleep because of noises in her ear. The doctor told her that this was not unusual. Lots of people have noises in their ears. However, when he looked into her ear, he got the shock of his life. He could see legs and something moving. It was a large spider! The woman was absolutely terrified of spiders! The doctor was able to remove it quickly and set it free.

When speaking to a colleague a few days later, the doctor mentioned that that was the first time he had ever found a spider living in someone's ear. His colleague suggested that the spider was probably looking for somewhere warm in order to lay its eggs.

12 Talking point

What would you do if you found the following?

1. a spider in your bath
2. a mouse in your bedroom
3. a snake in your kitchen
4. a caterpillar in your salad in a restaurant
5. a cockroach in your hotel bathroom
6. a spider in a friend's hair (she's terrified of all insects)

13 Idiomatic language

Colourful expressions are a common feature of story telling, and help to make stories more interesting. As you study this page, try to think what these expressions would be in your own language.

Comparisons

We use strong comparisons to emphasise what we are saying. For example:

It's a great bike. It goes like a bomb!
He's got a great appetite. He eats like a horse!

Use these expressions to complete the sentences below:

a. like clockwork
b. like a chimney
c. like a house on fire
d. like a lunatic
e. like dirt
f. like death warmed up
g. like a fish
h. like a log

1. I used to have this friend who drank . . .
2. This guy was driving along . . .
3. He's horrible to his wife. He treats her . . .
4. When I saw myself in the mirror, I looked . . .
5. My granddad used to smoke . . .
6. The tube system in Tokyo runs . . .
7. I was so exhausted that I slept . . .
8. My sister and I get on . . .

With a partner, check how many of these comparisons you can remember. Cover the list and test each other.

Tell your partner about anybody you know who:

smokes like a . . .	drives like a . . .
eats like a . . .	looks like . . . in the mornings

Have you ever heard any of the following expressions? Can you guess what they mean?

I've got a memory like a sieve.
I felt like a fish out of water.
She spends money like water.

When was the last time you slept like a log ? Have you ever met anybody who you immediately got on with like a house on fire?

Exaggerating

In Diane's story about her father not recognising her on the tube she uses exaggeration in the following way:

> . . . so I just stood there thinking, "Well, shall I just get off at the next stop without telling him, or shall I risk giving him a nervous breakdown and a heart attack by saying, 'Hello Dad'?" . . .

What do you think she really means here?

In English, it is very common to exaggerate by talking about illnesses, death, killing, and so on. Complete the sentences by adding the correct word from the list below.

die	death	died
killing	murder	dying

1. I'm . . . . . . for a coffee.
2. She gets away with . . . .
3. My feet are . . . . . . me!
4. It's . . . . . . trying to get him to do anything.
5. I nearly . . . . . . when he told me that!
6. I nearly . . . . . . laughing.
7. I'm sick to . . . . . . of it.
8. I'd . . . . . . if anybody else found out.
9. If he does it again, I'll . . . . . . him.

With a partner, discuss what you think the common exaggerations above actually mean.

Now add one of the sentences in 1-9 above at the end of each of the following:

a. I used to be really into dance music, but now. . .
b. I can't wait to get these new shoes off and get into a nice hot bath.
c. I can't wait for the break.
d. That film was so brilliant. It was so funny . . .
e. And then he said I'd been accepted for the team.
f. Only you know it's a wig.
g. Dad's a bit too easy-going with her.
h. I asked him time and time again to fix it, but . . .
i. That's the second time he's thrown his rubbish over into OUR garden.

Do you have similar expressions in your language? Are there any phrases above you wouldn't feel comfortable using? Why?

Unit 6b : Difficult to believe

bsolutely incredible. I wouldn't have believed it. I've no idea how he got away with it. It was kind of weird. What a funny story. What was he doing there anywa
a lot of stories, but that beats them all. That's incredible! That couldn't happen here. What were the parents thinking about? Boys will be boys! I wouldn't ha
dn't have believed it if I hadn't seen it with my own eyes. It was amazing, utterly amazing. You should have seen the mess it made. Is that all it cost? He was
ke down and we were miles from anywhere! You must be joking! You'll never believe who I bumped into the other day. Not THE Darryl Hocking? You aren't, a

1 He used to be so nice!

With a partner, think of three naughty things that children sometimes do. Add them to this list:

1. fight with their brothers or sisters
2. watch videos they shouldn't
3. experiment with cigarettes
4. ....
5. ....
6. ....

On your own, decide which of the above are the most and which the least serious.

Compare your answers with your partner, and explain your choices.

Did you ever do any of the things on your list? Do you know any children who do?

Have you heard the saying 'Boys will be boys'? Does your language have an equivalent?

2 Collocations

Before you read the text, try to make collocations by matching these words:

1. blockbuster	a. spree
2. spending	b. card
3. chauffeur-driven	c. attraction
4. security	d. movie
5. theme	e. newspaper
6. credit	f. guard
7. daily	g. car
8. magnetic	h. park

Skim through the text on the next page to check your answers. Then discuss the meaning of the collocations.

3 While reading

Answer these questions after you have read the text about Lamine.

1. Who did Lamine go to Disneyland Paris with?
2. How did he spend his time there?
3. How did his little adventure end?

RUNAWAY SPENDS £7,000 ON DISNEY SPREE

It was like something out of a blockbuster children's movie. A boy of 12 went on a 10-day spending spree at Disney's theme park outside Paris, treating other children to free rides, hiring a chauffeur-driven car and sleeping in a £300-a-night hotel.

The Parisian runaway, identified only by his first name, Lamine, spent more than £7,000 until the theme park's security guards finally notified the police of his unusual behaviour.

Like Peter Kerry, the 14-year-old schoolboy who has travelled the world on his father's stolen passport and credit card, Lamine is a serial runaway. Unlike Peter Kerry, however, he has a magnetic attraction to one place: this is the third time he has run away to Disneyland Paris – also known as Euro Disney.

Lamine took with him 70,000 French francs (£10,000), which his parents had in cash at their home, according to the daily paper, *Le Parisien,* yesterday. When he was caught, he had just £3,000 left.

As an alternative to Disneyland Paris's fun, he also hired a six-door, chauffeur-driven limousine one day to drive him to Parc Astérix, another theme park, north of the French capital.

4 Comprehension check

Decide whether the following statements are true (T) or false (F).

1. Lamine starred in a blockbuster children's movie.
2. He spent a lot of money at Disney's Paris theme park.
3. Lamine went round Euro Disney in a taxi.
4. The police warned security guards about Lamine's behaviour.
5. Lamine stole his father's passport.
6. This is the first time Lamine has ever run away from home.
7. His parents had left a lot of money lying around the house.

5 Word check

Find words from the text to complete the following sentences.

1. Just because you've won £1,000, don't go on a spending . . . . and waste the lot!
2. I didn't have enough cash on me, so I used my . . . .
3. After these latest murders, everyone's terrified that perhaps there's a . . . . . . killer on the loose.
4. Is there a bank near here? I've run out of . . . . . .
5. It was great in the States, because we . . . . . . a jeep and were able to explore off road.

6 Talking point

Why do you think it took Lamine's parents so long to find him?
Why do you think his parents had so much money lying around?
Have you ever been to a theme park? What was it like? How do you feel about them?
Why do you think theme parks like Disneyland are so popular?

7 Role play

In pairs, prepare one of the following situations for two or three minutes before you have the conversations.

1. Lamine and a policeman

Lamine has just been taken to the police station nearest to Disneyland Paris. The policeman asks him where he got the money from, what he has done with it, where his parents are, why he is not at home, and so on.

2. Lamine and his father / mother

The parents ask all the questions which parents would ask in this situation!

3. Lamine and his best friend

Lamine uses his mobile phone to call his best friend to tell him what he has been doing for the past 10 days.

8 Past simple / continuous

G24 **Form logical sentences by matching the numbers on the left with the letters on the right.**

1. She was just sitting there, reading,
2. Just as I was leaving the house,
3. It was raining really heavily as I was leaving,
4. I was living in Italy
5. I was just going home
6. Just as I went into my daughter's school,
7. While we were trying to decide where to go,
8. I resigned from my job on Friday

a. I remembered the tickets were on my bed.
b. so I grabbed an umbrella.
c. when the big Mafia trials were happening.
d. when this guy suddenly started talking to her.
e. I won this fabulous holiday to Jamaica!
f. and found a better one on Saturday!
g. she came running up to me, crying.
h. when my boss rang and told me I was going to Washington!

Underline the past verb forms in each sentence.

Grammar discussion

One sentence in each of the groups of three below is wrong. Why?

What is the difference in meaning between the other two sentences?

1a. We were cleaning the carpet when we were finding the diamond.
1b. We got the system checked out because we were finding lots of problems with it.
1c. We got the system checked out because we found lots of problems with it.
2a. I was driving through town when I got stopped by this police car.
2b. I was driving through town when I was getting stopped by this police car.
2c. I was driving through town when I realised I was getting really tired.
3a. I was coming home on the tube when I suddenly bumped into an old friend.
3b. I came home on the tube when I suddenly bumped into an old friend.
3c. I came home on the tube when I missed the last bus.

Compare your answers with a partner, then look at the Grammar Introduction on page 176.

Grammar check

Put the correct forms of the verbs into each of the following gaps.

1. As I was on my way back from France, my car . . . . *(break down)*
2. When I . . . . home last night, I bumped into an old friend of mine. *(walk)*
3. My mother was tidying my room up when she . . . . the letter. *(see)*
4. We . . . . along the beach when we suddenly saw a body in the sea. *(walk)*
5. I . . . . . . of writing to her when the next thing I knew she turned up on my doorstep. *(think)*
6. I was talking to a friend on the phone when my dad . . . . rushing into my room. *(come)*
7. You can imagine how angry he was when he . . . . how much they were charging him. *(find out)*
8. Oh, it was so stupid! I . . . . up some water when I knocked it all over myself. *(boil)*

When the clock struck 12 on 31st December 1999, where were you and what were you doing?

9 Tall stories

Here are four 'tall stories' – stories which are probably not true, but people enjoy telling them. Sometimes they are called urban myths. Read them and decide whether you think they really happened or not.

Safety first!

Did you hear about the plane which crashed somewhere in South America as it was coming in to land?

Apparently, it was fitted with a device which warns the pilot that he is approaching the ground – a Ground Warning Alarm (GWA) system. Some pilots find this warning irritating so they switch it off.

When the black box was examined, the crash was blamed on pilot error. The decision had been easy to reach. When the plane had been coming in to land, the GWA had gone off, telling the pilot he was too close to the ground. On the tape the pilot can be heard saying, "Shut up, you stupid machine!" Then you hear the sound of the crash.

True story or myth?

What a rat!

Then there was the story of the couple who were in Thailand on holiday. The morning after they arrived, they found a thin little cat sitting on their balcony. They immediately fell in love with it. They cleaned it and fed it. By the time they were ready to leave, they couldn't bear to be parted from it.

They arranged for the cat to come home with them. Waiting at home was their pet poodle. The poodle and the cat seemed to get on together very well, so the couple decided to go out for dinner. When they got back, they found their sitting room covered in poodle hair and the dog halfway down the cat's throat!

It turned out the cat was not a cat, but an enormous Thai water rat!

True story or myth?

Drowned in a drain

A man from Wakefield in Yorkshire went out one night for a few drinks at his local pub. He left his car in the street near the pub. When he decided to go home, he went out to his car, took out the keys, and then accidentally dropped them down a drain in the road.

He could see the keys down the drain on top of some leaves. So, he managed to lift the drain cover, but the key was too far down for him to reach. He lay down in order to reach them.

Suddenly, he fell into the drain head first. Just as he did that it started to rain heavily. Nobody heard his cries for help. The next morning he was found drowned, his head down the drain, his legs sticking up in the air.

True story or myth?

Sunk by flying cow

A few years ago, the crew of a Japanese fishing boat were rescued from the wreckage of their boat in the Sea of Japan. They said that their boat had been sunk by a cow falling out of the sky. Nobody believed them.

A few weeks later the Russian Air Force admitted that the crew of one of their planes had stolen a cow in Siberia and put it into the plane's cargo hold.

At 30,000 feet the cow started to run around the plane out of control. The crew decided there was only one thing they could do. So, they opened the cargo door and the cow jumped out, landing on top of the Japanese fishing boat.

True story or myth?

Read one of these stories again at home. You will be asked to tell it to the class at the next lesson. If you like this kind of story, they are all on the Web. Find them under 'urban myths'. Bring one in to class!

10 Being vague

Different techniques

When talking about things that have happened to us, it is common to use vague or approximate language. Choose the best definition for each of the following examples:

1. There must've been about 30 or 40 people there.
   (a) Either 30 or 40 people.
   (b) Between 25 and 45 people.
2. He was sort of smiling at me.
   (a) It was a particular kind of smile.
   (b) It wasn't exactly a smile, but it was more like a smile than anything else.
3. His skin had turned a weird blueish colour and he'd stopped breathing.
   (a) It was bright blue.
   (b) It wasn't exactly blue, but it was more blue than any other colour.
4. There must have been 500-odd people there.
   (a) The 500 people were very strange.
   (b) There were approximately 500 people.
5. And the policeman looked at me and said, "Is this your car?" you know, "blah, blah, blah."
   (a) And some other things I didn't understand.
   (b) I'm sure you can imagine what else he said, and you don't need me to tell you.
6. It must have been built about 1985 or so.
   (a) It was built in 1985.
   (b) It could have been 1984 or 1986.
7. It cost two hundred and something pounds.
   (a) Just a little more than two hundred pounds.
   (b) Almost three hundred pounds.
8. And I spoke to that man who works in the office there, you know, what's his name, and he told me . . .
   (a) I can't remember his name, but I'm sure you know who I mean.
   (b) Please tell me his name.

Real English: sort of / kind of

It was *kind of* expensive-looking.
She was *sort of* annoyed with me.

Sort of and *kind of* are both very common in spoken English. They are often used when you cannot find the right word to express what you mean. Some people do not like these phrases, but they are extremely common even in educated speech.

... or something / ... or anything

G25 **Look at these two examples:**

My dad thought I was a pick-pocket or a drug addict or something.
There was no hot water or showers or anything!

Phrases with or something / or anything are common in spoken English when we want to be vague. Complete the following sentences using these expressions:

or something like that
food or anything
showers or anything
a bit of wire or something
a hammer or something

1. He managed to get the lock to work by using . . . .
2. The campsite was horrible. There were no proper toilets or . . . .
3. They must have broken into the car with . . . . They did a lot of damage.
4. I didn't really see the registration number, but I'm sure it started TKP . . . .
5. We flew on one of those budget airlines. There were no drinks or . . . .

-ish

Adding -ish to an adjective or number is a common way of being less precise:

He's about forty-ish.
Her hair is a sort of reddish brown.

Complete the following using these words:

seven-ish	yellow-ish	purple-ish
long-ish	tall-ish	sixty-ish

1. He's not retired yet, but I'm sure he's about . . . .
2. When you get malaria, your skin turns a sort of . . . . . colour.
3. I think we'll have to get the train about . . . . . . to get there in time for 8.
4. Although it was red wine, it was a kind of deep . . . . . colour.
5. Eva's the one with . . . . . dark hair.
6. You'll recognise him. He's a sort of . . . . . . version of Charlie Chaplin without the moustache.

11 Stories, tales and myths

All cultures have their own folk tales. Many cultures share the same stories – sometimes with small differences. A child growing up in Britain will know the following stories:

Cinderella
Sleeping Beauty
Snow White and the Seven Dwarves
Little Red Riding Hood
Babes in the Wood

What are the names of these stories in your culture?

With a partner try to remember what happens in these stories. Choose one and tell it to the rest of the class.

Very often these stories contain a moral – a lesson about life. Can you say what the moral of each story is in one sentence?

12 The birds and the bees!

T36 **Here's a joke which you can practise telling each other in pairs, then in front of the whole class. Take a vote on who is the best at telling the joke. Remember how important it is to think about pausing and stress if you really want the joke to work.**

My little boy came in the other day with a really serious look on his face and said, "Dad, do you mind if I ask you a question? Where do I come from?" I'd been dreading this question for ages, but, like a good father, I sat him down and gently told him all about the birds and the bees. When I'd finished, he was very quiet. He then got up and went, "Thank you, Dad," and headed for the door. I said, "So what made you ask me?" and he turned around and said, "I just wanted to know because Bobby next door says HE comes from Manchester!"

13 And finally

Think of something really interesting or funny or scary or embarrassing that has happened to you and then tell your story to some other students in the class. Try and use what you have learned in this unit.

Try and remember some of the stories you hear and tell them to other people in your class. Start like this : "You'll never believe what happened to (name of person in class). Well, . . ."

Vocabulary

Trip, tour, travel etc

Use these words to complete the situations:

trip tour travel
journey flight travelling

1. What time is their . . . . . . supposed to be getting in now?
   > About six-thirty, I think. It's already been delayed an hour!
2. What a . . . . . . ! 12 hours on a plane, then six hours on a freezing cold train.
3. I always try and . . . . . . light, if I can.
4. When I graduated, I worked for a bit and then went . . . . . . for a year.
5. I was thinking of going on a day-. . . . . . to Brighton this Saturday. Do you fancy coming?
6. He's away on a business . . . . . . , I'm afraid. Try again on Monday.
7. I never . . . . . . by bus, if I can help it. I much prefer just cycling or walking.
8. I spent a couple of months . . . . . . round Peru.
9. I can't believe my parents are planning to go on a . . . . . . to Disneyland when they retire!
10. There's a coach-. . . . . . of the city this afternoon. Do you fancy going?
11. Once you land, have you got a long . . . . . . ahead of you before you get home?
12. While I was in Granada in Spain, we went on this guided . . . . . . round the Alhambra, which was really interesting.

Different kinds of stories

Complete the sentences below with these words. Then underline the complete expressions.

bedtime old hard-luck
inside tall love

1. The story of Romeo and Juliet must be one of the world's greatest . . . . stories.
2. I ended up sitting beside this guy who'd just got divorced and lost his job. I spent the whole six-hour flight listening to his . . . . story.
3. The lift's broken down again!
   > The same . . . . story, then!
4. The kids say they won't go to sleep unless you go up and read them their . . . . story.
5. You're a friend of Jane's. Nobody understands why she's leaving. Come on, you must know the . . . . story!
6. Jason told everyone at work that he'd won £10,000, but then managed to leave it in a taxi!
   > I wouldn't believe a word he says. It sounds like another one of his . . . . stories.

Slang

In the conversation you heard *pinch his wallet*. Match the slang words on the left with their equivalents on the right:

1. Chuck it to me.	a. lost his temper
2. Have you got a fag?	b. stolen
3. They went out boozing.	c. throw
4. My bicycle's been nicked.	d. sell
5. I've decided to flog the car.	e. drinking
6. It only cost ten quid.	f. cigarette
7. He's a really nice bloke.	g. pounds
8. He flipped his lid.	h. man

Always be careful with slang. You may think you know what a slang word means, but sometimes it has an extra meaning. In the examples in this exercise boozing means drinking in order to get drunk. This is a dangerous area in all languages and you should always check with a teacher before using slang.

Phrasal verbs with *get*

1. Match the parts of the sentences below:

1. I'll get round to	a. my work.
2. I'm getting behind with	b. it sooner or later.
3. Can we get together	c. to discuss it?

Which sentences from above complete these?

4. I keep forgetting to write to Julia but . . .
5. You know that report I asked you to write . . .
6. I've been ill quite a lot recently and . . .

2. Do the same with these:

1. Right. Let's get down to	a. until 3am.
2. I didn't get in	b. well with her.
3. I get on really	c. business.

Which sentences from above complete these?

4. Is everybody here? Good . . .
5. I'm so tired this morning . . .
6. I do like Cathy . . .

Review : Units 5 and 6

1 Tenses

Choose the correct form:

1. Oh, you stayed in Bahia? That must be/must've been lovely.
2. I was breaking/I broke my leg skiing.
3. Would it be OK if I was leaving/left an hour early today?
4. I was walking down the road when suddenly a woman came up/was coming up to me and started/was starting screaming.
5. I phoned you last night at about 9-ish.
   > Oh sorry, I was cooking/I cooked, so I didn't answer/wasn't answering it.
6. I watched/was watching TV when the lights just suddenly went/were going out.
7. Were you living/Did you live in Paris when Princess Diana died/was dying.
8. Did you manage to see the first performance?
   > No, I wasn't arriving/didn't arrive until after they'd finished.

2 Multiple choice

Choose the more natural alternative:

1. I had an argument with my flatmate last night.
   > Oh, (a) had you? What about?
   (b) did you? What about?
2. I'm exhausted this morning.
   (a) I got in at four in the morning!
   (b) I didn't get in until four in the morning!
3. This traffic's absolutely awful, isn't it?
   > (a) You can say that again!
   > (b) You could say that again!
4. I'm going parachuting this weekend.
   > (a) You mustn't be serious!
   > (b) You can't be serious!
5. I was lying by the pool,
   (a) I was sunbathing.
   (b) sunbathing.
6. I arrived at (a) sort of nine o'clock.
   (b) about nine-ish.
7. (a) He was sort of just standing there.
   (b) He was about just standing there.
8. I do drink wine and beer, but I never touch vodka or whisky (a) or something like that.
   (b) or anything like that.

3 Expressions

The following common expressions all occurred in units 5-6. Use them in the sentences below:

a. sick to death of
b. or something like that
c. You must be mad!
d. when all of a sudden
e. You went WHERE?
f. You can say that again!

1. I went to Burkina Faso last year.
   > . . . . last year?
   Burkina Faso, in West Africa.
2. It's freezing outside, isn't it?
   > . . . . ! I had to wear two pullovers when I went out.
3. I was just walking down the road . . . . these two guys came running up to me and accused me of stealing their car!
4. You paid two grand for a 1985 Renault with rust everywhere! . . . . !
5. What does her boyfriend do for a living?
   > I think he's a lawyer . . . .
6. Shall we eat out tonight? I'm . . . . cooking!

4 Collocations

Match the verbs on the left with the best collocations on the right:

mind	1.	like a chimney
smoke	2.	into an old friend
spend	3.	your own business
go	4.	at my watch
do	5.	exhausted
glance	6.	something to eat
bump	7.	out for a quick run
feel	8.	a bit of washing-up
catch up	9.	the evening round at Dave's
get	10.	with some gossip

5 Conversation

Put the jumbled conversation below into the correct order. The first line is correct.

a. So when did you find out Dave had bought a dog?

b. That sounds terrible. He must be mad!

c. It's a he. Dave wants to call him Arsenal.

d. I bet you couldn't believe it! Is it a he or a she?

e. He IS mad! And what's worse, it's a boxer or something, and the stupid animal barked all night long!

f. You know – Arsenal – after the football team.

g. Well, I told him – you've got to choose! It's either Arsenal or me! One of us will have to go!

h. He wants to call him what?

i. Did it? You'll end up getting divorced!

j. Last night. I didn't get in until eleven, and there it was, just sitting there.

1 a	2	3	4	5	6	7	8	9	10

6 Real English

Match 1-8 with the follow-up comments in a-h:

1. What's your brother like?
2. Do you love him?
3. Are you OK? You look dreadful.
4. It hurt like hell when he pulled the tooth out.
5. I heard someone pinched your bag.
6. Did you do anything special yesterday after work?
7. I tend to go to bed earlier in the winter.
8. I heard the house cost your sister a fortune.

a. Yes, I bet it did! Rather you than me.

b. Yes, it was over eighty grand!

c. He's a bit of a nerd, actually.

d. Kind of, I suppose.

e. No, I just went straight home and had an early night.

f. Yes. I'm really annoyed about it!

g. Yes, I'm OK. I just had a bit of a late night, that's all.

h. Yes, so do I.

7 Idioms

Make complete idioms by matching the numbers on the left with the letters on the right:

1. I nearly	a. a log.
2. I slept like	b. a fish.
3. I could hardly	c. on the rocks!
4. I'm dying for	d. a lunatic.
5. He drinks like	e. might fly!
6. Pigs	f. died laughing.
7. He was driving like	g. a coffee.
8. My marriage is	h. hear myself think!

8 Vocabulary quiz

Answer the following 20 questions with a partner. Then compare your answers with another pair. Who got most answers right?

1. If you wanted to show someone you were angry with them, would you stare at them, glare at them or glance at them?
2. Do you go on a spending spree or go to one?
3. Is a sensible person someone who understands their friends' feelings or someone able to make good decisions?
4. If you're going out with someone, what two meanings could this have?
5. If you bump into an old friend, does it hurt?
6. Do you go to a theme park or go on one?
7. Is a divorcee someone who is divorced or someone who is getting divorced?
8. If you propose to someone, what is the question you ask?
9. If you run out of money, do you have none or a lot?
10. If you've flogged your car, what have you done to it?
11. If you're tired, do you go asleep or fall asleep?
12. If you don't have any clean clothes to wear, would you do the washing-up or the washing?
13. If someone tries to chat you up, do they just want to talk to you?
14. If I say That's none of your business, what kind of question have you just asked me?
15. Is someone who kills a lot of people over a period of time a serious killer or a serial killer?
16. Do you surf the net or the beach?
17. Are lads young men or young women?
18. Is a blockbuster a kind of tool or a film?
19. If you go to a club, do you leave your coat in the cloakroom or the bathroom?
20. If you find someone appealing, do you like them or not?

Unit 7a : Old friends

, hello Liz, how are you? Don't you remember me? What a lovely surprise! I haven't seen you for ages. You haven't changed a bit. What are you up to these d
ally? Not a lot. I've been travelling. Oh, that reminds me. I windsurfed across the Atlantic, which was nice. I keep meaning to do that myself. Do you still reme
w could I forget! You're looking well. It must be ten years. I've completely forgotten your name. I bumped into Frank this morning. Well, I'd better be going. M
ely to see you again. Give my regards to Jill. You don't look a day older! Do you remember when we first met? We've lost touch. Keep in touch. We've got tw

1 Ten questions

Imagine you are attending a reunion of all your old friends from secondary school. Here are some of the things you might want to say:

1. Hello, Carrie, how are you?
2. I haven't seen you for ages.
3. You haven't changed one bit.
4. You look exactly the same! Not one day older!
5. What've you been doing for the past (10) years?
6. What're you doing now?
7. Are you married? What does your husband/ wife do?
8. Have you got a family?
9. Are you still (afraid of spiders)? Do you still (play tennis)?
10. Where do you live now?

First, work alone and decide how you would respond to these questions and comments.

Then talk to other students in the class and find out what you have all been doing.

2 I haven't seen you for ages

Who is your oldest friend? When did you first meet?

Can you think of someone you haven't met for a long time?

The pictures show some friends who haven't seen each other for a long time. What do you think they are saying to each other?

Work with a partner and prepare the opening of a conversation for the people in one of the pictures.

3 While you listen

T37 **Sharon and Barry are friends who live in the same area. They've bumped into each other in the street, and are catching up with each other's news. Listen to them talking about what they've both been up to.**

As you listen, try to answer these questions:

1. What's Barry been up to?
2. What's Sharon been up to?

Listen again and try to fill in the gaps in the conversation.

Real English: Long time, no see!
This is an informal expression, used between friends, meaning *I haven't seen you for a long time.*

Real English: I actually thought it was excellent.
Actually is used like this when we want to stress something we see as a fact, and which is different from what the other person expected. For example:

That jacket must've cost you a lot.
> Well, it was actually quite cheap.

4 Talking point

Has there been an exhibition or concert that caused a big fuss in your country? Why was it so controversial?

What makes you go *Yuk?*

Long time, no see!

Sharon: Barry! Hi, how are you? I haven't seen you for ages.
Barry: Hello Sharon. Long time, no see.
Sharon: I know. So how're you doing?
Barry: I'm all right, thanks. And you?
Sharon: Yeah, not too bad. So, what've you been up to since I last saw you?
Barry: Not a lot – working mostly – . . . . really long hours this week, getting really fed up with it, you know.
Sharon: Really?
Barry: Yeah, but I went down to Kent last weekend, for my grandma's birthday party.
Sharon: Oh, how old was she?
Barry: 85. It was really great. We . . . . this lovely meal and then we . . . . a walk along the beach. It was good to get out of the city.
Sharon: I bet. I . . . . have a weekend away myself.
Barry: I know. You get to the point where you really need it, don't you? If you don't get out of London from time to time, it starts driving you crazy, you know. . . . . , what about you? . . . . ?
Sharon: Well, on Sunday morning I . . . . that exhibition at the Royal Academy.
Barry: Oh yes, the one there's been . . . . about – dead sheep and pictures of toilet rolls and things.
Sharon: Yeah, my friend Angela – she's at art school – she kept nagging me to go and see it, so I went.
Barry: And what did you think of it? . . . . ?
Sharon: Oh, I . . . . thought it was excellent, really good and challenging. There's only one thing that made you go 'yuk!' – the dead sheep. I think it's meant to shock you, though. Anyway, after that, I . . . . and saw a friend of mine, Richard, for a bit and then we went up to Camden market to do a bit of shopping.
Barry: Oh yeah, it's nice up there on a Sunday, isn't it?
Sharon: Yeah, it's great. And then I . . . . at my mum's, which was nice.
Barry: Oh, that sounds good.
Sharon: Yeah, and apart from that, ... things for college, really.
Barry: Uh-huh, still being a good student, then. Oh look, there's my bus into town. . . . . I'll see you soon, then. Bye.
Sharon: Yeah, OK, bye.

5 Pronunciation

T38 **Listen to the intonation pattern of this line from the conversation:**

How are you? I haven't seen you for ages.

Practise the following which have similar patterns:

1. How are you? We haven't spoken for weeks.
2. How are you? We haven't had a chat for ages.
3. How are they? I haven't seen them for months.
4. How is he? I hear he's just got back.
5. How is she? I haven't seen her for ages.
6. How's your dad? I haven't seen him for years.
7. How is she? I heard she's had a boy.
8. How much was it? I heard it cost a fortune.

6 Vocabulary

In the conversation Barry talked about getting to the point where you need time off. **There are lots of expressions with** point. **Complete these sentences with the correct verb:**

get see make

1. Do you think you could . . . . . . to the point, please?
2. Please . . . . . . a point of being early.
3. I just don't . . . . . . the point of complaining.
4. If you don't . . . . . . your point strongly, people will just ignore what you're trying to say.

Now add the following adjectives:

high turning strong sore

5. The real . . . . . . point in my life was when I was told ten years ago that I only had three months to live.
6. One of Mary's . . . . . . points is the fact that she never gets annoyed with anyone.
7. Don't talk to Bill about his divorce. It's still a very . . . . . . point with him.
8. I think the . . . . . . point of my trip to Africa was standing at the Victoria Falls.

Now add these common expressions:

on the point of there's no point

9. Jane's working in Greece for a month, so . . . . trying to ring her.
10. I was . . . . leaving when the phone rang.

What are the strong and weak points **of your English – grammar? pronunciation? vocabulary?**

7 Short negative answers

Look at this question and answer from the conversation on page 105:

What've you been up to since I last saw you?
> Not a lot.

The six questions below can be answered in two different ways. Match the questions with the sets of answers:

1. So have you seen much of Derek recently?
2. So what was the play like?
3. So you're spending all Saturday working, then?
4. So what've you been up to?
5. How was your grandmother, then?
6. So you do the housework, do you?

A. Not too bad, as a matter of fact.
Not that good, actually.

B. Not if I can help it.
Not likely!

C. Not a lot, really.
Not that much, really.

Practise saying each answer.

Can you translate the expressions with not **into your own language?**

Did you notice that the two answers in A are opposite in meaning, but the two answers in B and in C are similar in meaning?

What's the question?

Now work in pairs to make questions for the following answers:

1. . . . . ?
Not a lot. I've just been working.

2. . . . . ?
Not that good, actually. It was quite boring.

3. . . . . ?
Not too bad, actually, but I've still got a bit of a cold.

4. . . . . ?
No, not all that often. They live a bit too far away.

With a partner, answer the questions you have made in a positive way. For example:

So have you seen much of Derek lately?
> Yes, quite a bit/quite a lot, actually.

8 Talking about the past 1

Past simple / present perfect

G26 Match up the following sentences and their meanings:

1. I worked with Pete for ten years.
2. I've worked with Pete for ten years.
   a. and I still do.
   b. but now I don't.
3. We were married for a long time.
4. We've been married for a long time.
   a. and we still are.
   b. but that was a long time ago.
5. I lived in Madrid for 20 years.
6. I've lived in Madrid for 20 years.
   a. but then I moved to Barcelona.
   b. and I wouldn't live anywhere else.
7. I believed in God for a long time.
8. I've always believed in God.
   a. but I don't any more.
   b. and I still do.

Notice that all examples of the present perfect look back on the past from the present. **See the Grammar Introduction on page 176.**

Grammar in context

The past simple and the present perfect give us two ways of looking at the past:

I saw you on TV last night.
I know who you are. I've seen you on TV.

Complete the following sentences using either the present perfect simple or the past simple with the verbs given. Where there is no mention of time, we usually use the present perfect.

1. Last Saturday night, I just . . . . at home and did nothing. *(stay)*
2. Guess what! I . . . . going to a gym. *(start)*
3. I . . . . round to a friend's last Friday. *(go)*
4. I . . . . and . . . . my front room all day Sunday. *(stay in, paint)*
5. I . . . . to Manchester last year. *(move)*
6. We . . . . a really great time in Paris at the rugby final at the weekend. *(have)*
7. We . . . . a holiday in the Seychelles. *(book)*
8. I . . . . . . and . . . . . . *Screamers* last night. *(go, see)*
9. I . . . . at six flats now and not one has been suitable for a young family. *(look)*

Follow-up comments

Once we've said what we've been doing, we often describe what it was like. Add the best comment from below to the sentences in the exercise above:

a. I don't think we'll ever find the right place.
b. It was a bit of a drag, but it looks great now.
c. I'm really enjoying it. I feel a lot fitter than I did.
d. What a match! And it was great to get away from the kids as well.
e. It was really good to see him again.
f. I'm glad I did. I love the North of England.
g. It wasn't as shocking as I thought it would be.
h. It's somewhere we've always wanted to go.
i. It was great! It's been a while since I did absolutely nothing!

Time expressions

Try each of the following time expressions with these two structures. Which go with which?

1. I lived in America . . .
2. I've lived in America . . .

a. during the war	d. for too long now!
b. since 1995	e. when I was young
c. a few years ago	f. since I was 30

3. I rang you . . .
4. I've been trying to ring you . . .

a. earlier today	d. since I saw you last
b. for the last hour	e. since last weekend
c. last week	f. last Thursday

Now complete this:

Numbers . . . and . . . are the past simple.
Number . . . is the present perfect simple.
Number . . . is the present perfect continuous.

Real English: It was a bit of a drag.
This means that something is irritating or boring:
My car's still not right.
> *What a drag!* You must be getting fed up with it.

9 Talking about the past 2

G27 You arranged to meet a friend at seven o'clock. He finally arrives at eight. Which do you say to him – a or b? Explain your choice.

a. Where on earth have you been? I've been waiting here for an hour.
b. Where on earth have you been? I've waited here for an hour.

The next example is very strange. Correct it.

I'm afraid I can't go. I've been breaking my arm.

Which of these sentences sound OK?

1a. You look as if you've been crying. What's the matter?
1b. You look as if you've cried. What's the matter?
2a. Hey! I've been finding your passport.
2b. Hey! I've found your passport.

Adverbs with the present perfect

Look at these common adverbs which are often used with the present perfect:

just almost never completely

Discuss which is the most *likely* in the following:

1. I've . . . . . . been to Siberia.
2. I've . . . . . . bumped into Harry on the tube.
3. I've . . . . . . finished. Give me two minutes.
4. I've . . . . . . forgotten your name.
5. I've . . . . . . got to the end of the book.
6. I've . . . . . . had an idea.
7. He's . . . . . . had an original idea in his life!
8. I've . . . . . . seen something really funny.
9. She's . . . . . . got over the death of her son.
10. I've . . . . . . seen anything so funny.

10 Present perfect collocations

Some verb forms occur very often with the same expressions. Choose the correct expression to complete these present perfect sentences:

1. I've been at college	for the past three years. since the last three years.
2. I've been travelling	about Africa. around Africa.
3. I've been studying	for a doctor. to become a doctor.
4. I've been abroad	studying. for studying.
5. I've been working	as a volunteer in Africa. as volunteer in Africa.
6. I've been on a course	to better my English. to improve my English.
7. I've been away	since two months. since Christmas.
8. I've been ill	for the past fortnight. since the past fortnight.

11 Grammar in use

1. **Think of somewhere unusual you've been to. Ask a partner:** *Have you ever been to ...?*
2. **Think of an unusual kind of food you've eaten. Ask a partner:** *Have you ever eaten ...?*
3. **Think of a great film you've seen recently. Ask a partner:** *Have you seen ...?*

1066 all over again!

Hastings is famous in everyone's mind as the place where William the Conqueror landed from France in 1066. 933 years later Paul Warburton could not believe his ears when he helped a French windsurfer land on that famous beach. The Frenchman had not just come back from a quick sail round the bay. He had set out five hours earlier from Cherbourg, intending to land at Brighton, 30 miles to the west.

François Letourneau, a nineteen-year-old sailing instructor, said that strong westerly winds had blown him off course. The English Channel is one of the busiest shipping lanes in the world and he had taken his life in his hands sailing the 120 miles alone without any kind of support vessel. He even admitted that when he had felt a bit tired halfway across, he had stopped and had a cigarette! He had been carrying his cigarettes and a lighter in a waterproof bag.

Mr Warburton took François home and gave him something to eat and some dry clothes, before taking him to Portsmouth to buy him his return ticket on the ferry back to Cherbourg. The one thing François had forgotten to pack was money for the return journey. He had planned to return to France on his windsurfer the same day!

12 Talking point

What would you have said to the windsurfer when he told you his story?

Do you think it is fair that people like that put other people's lives at risk?

Would you ban mountain-climbing because very often it is the rescuers who die? What about a huge tax on windsurfers and yachts to pay for the coast guard and lifeboat services?

What is the most dangerous thing you have ever done?

13 Adverbials

G28 **We often want to talk about how long we did something for and why we did it.**

Time expressions	Reasons
for the evening	to finish off some things
for a few minutes	for a friend's wedding
for the weekend	for a big conference
for a few hours	to pick up some aspirins
for a week	to have dinner with him and his family

Complete each of the following sentences by using a time and a reason expression from above.

1. I only popped into the chemist's .... and I ended up getting a parking ticket!
2. I went to work on Saturday just .... that I hadn't got done during the week.
3. I went to Brussels .... It was interesting , but it was very hard work, and I really missed my family after a few days.
4. I went round to Pascal's .... He'd made this thing with prawns and ginger.
5. I went down to the country .... By Sunday evening we were absolutely exhausted.

Think of three things you've done recently. Try to add two adverbial expressions to each, as above.

Compare your answers with your partner. Who has done the most interesting things?

14 Oh, that reminds me!

When people are talking about what they have been doing, it often reminds us of things which we have thought of doing ourselves. Look at the highlighted expressions in the following examples:

I went with some friends and saw *Love Conquers All* last Wednesday.
> Oh, yeah. I keep meaning to go and see that myself. What was it like?
Oh, it was OK, but nothing special, really.

I went round to see my mum on Sunday.
> Oh, that reminds me . . . I must phone my mum tonight. I always try to ring her once a week.
Yeah, parents get upset if you don't keep in touch, don't they?

T39 **Now match up the following two-line conversations, then underline the important expressions.**

1. I visited Alan in hospital last Friday to see how he was getting on.
2. I spent all day Sunday catching up on all my mail.
3. I went and saw that musical, *Chicago*, last week.
4. I went round to Mike and Sue's the other day to see that new car they've been telling everyone about.
5. I went down to Bristol for the weekend a couple of weeks ago.
6. I just stayed in last night and watched TV. There's a great thing on on Fridays at the moment about Antarctica.

a. Oh, that reminds me. I must record that new thing on Channel Four tonight. It's meant to be really funny.

b. Oh, really. I've been thinking about having a weekend away myself. Were you camping or what?

c. Oh, that reminds me. I must send in my passport application.

d. Oh, did you? I keep meaning to go and see him myself. How was he?

e. Oh, that reminds me. I must give them a call. I haven't spoken to them for ages.

f. Oh, I've been meaning to go and see that for ages. Was it as good as everybody says?

15 Pair work

Practise reading the conversations in exercise 14 aloud with your partner. Try to add a third response, as in this example:

I visited Alan in hospital last Friday to see how he was getting on.
> Oh, did you? I keep meaning to go and see him myself. How was he?
Not bad. You should go and see him. I'm sure he'd love to see you.

Work in pairs and have similar conversations with these ideas:

1. buy a birthday card for my brother
2. phone my parents
3. pay my telephone bill
4. book my summer holiday
5. send in my application form
6. have my hair cut

16 Adding a comment

G29 **When we talk about the things we've been doing, we usually follow facts with comments. For example:**

I went to a friend's wedding last week, which was really nice.
There was a power cut on Saturday, which meant I couldn't use my computer.

Try to think of comments for the following:

1. It was pouring with rain on Sunday, which meant . . . .
2. I went to visit a whisky distillery, which was . . .
3. Mieko and Keiko came over for a meal, which was . . .
4. I went to see *Tosca* at the opera last night, which was . . .
5. I missed the train this morning, which meant . . .
6. I failed my exam, which meant . . .

Think of two things you've done recently, and tell your partner about them. Be sure to add comments starting with which.

17 Talking point

There is a TV programme in Britain called 'Surprise Surprise'. If you want to get in touch with someone you haven't seen for a long time, you contact this programme and they try to put you back in touch – and film the meeting! Some people think this is a very good idea; some think it is a dreadful idea. What do you think?
If you were the programme's producer, which two of these stories would you be interested in?

Bob's story

When I was in the army, I was very friendly with a chap called Tom Ramsay from Leeds. We lost touch when we left. I would love to meet him again to talk about all the things we went through together.

Jill's story

When I was a young girl of 15, I had a baby. My parents forced me to have it adopted. All I know is that she was born on 14th March 1975 and the people who adopted her lived in York. I would love to meet her. I think about her every day of my life.

Jim's story

I'm now 85. When I was a young lad of 15, I spent a summer working on a farm in Kent, picking fruit. I fell in love with a girl called Irene Smithson. She came from Canterbury. At the end of that beautiful summer, we went our separate ways and never met again. My wife died last year. I would love to meet Irene again. I have three children and 12 grandchildren.

Hugh's story

I'm 25 and single. I live in Birmingham. Last month, I spent the weekend in London with some friends. On the Saturday night, I met a fabulous girl called Melanie Brown at a disco. We danced together all night and talked for hours. We just seemed to click. The trouble was she had a boyfriend who was abroad on business that weekend. She gave me her telephone number, but I've lost it. I'm desperate to see her again. I know she had a flat in Notting Hill Gate. But that's all I know – except that she had huge brown eyes.

Unit 7b : Art

d £500 for it. Do you call that art? It's a masterpiece. I did it myself. A pickled sheep! I really recommend it. What's it supposed to be? They all look the sa
ll. So, what exactly is cubism? Me? Draw? What do you think of this one? It's not really my cup of tea. So, you'd recommend it, then. I'd give it a miss if I wer
only a collection of old bits of cars. Sounds interesting. It's got so much detail. I painted this when I was depressed. I just love bright colours. I prefer a
you really? Dali and stuff like that. I like landscapes. Monet's my favourite. It must be a fake. I like art, but I'm not arty. I do a bit of pottery in my spare time.

1 Talking point

Do you ever go to exhibitions? What kind? Has your home town got an art gallery? When was the last time you went to it?

What is the best exhibition you have ever been to?

What are the names of the major galleries in London, Paris, New York, St Petersburg and Madrid?

The pictures on this page are 'Jeanne Hebuterne' by Amedeo Modigliani and 'Plums, apricots in a bowl' by J. Van Hulsdonck. Do you like them? Can you say why?

Have you ever painted or sculpted or drawn? Has any of your work ever been exhibited – perhaps at school?

2 Before reading

After you have matched these words with their meanings, look them up in your dictionary to check that you fully understand them.

1. suspend
2. container
3. controversial
4. motive
5. consent
6. protester
7. pickled
8. formaldehyde

a. permission
b. very likely to cause an argument or protest
c. hang
d. reason for doing something (often criminal)
e. a bottle, can, jar or similar thing
f. a liquid used to preserve things
g. a person who disagrees in a public way
h. preserved (often in vinegar)

ART ATTACK

A man almost destroyed a work of art, worth £25,000, in a London art gallery yesterday. The work of art consisted of a glass container with a dead sheep suspended in formaldehyde.

The protester poured black ink into the case while it was on display at the Serpentine Gallery. Gallery staff were shocked as they saw the protester run away after first changing the name of the work to 'Black Sheep'.

The controversial work was originally called 'Away from the Flock'. It was the latest in a long line of animals pickled by famous British artist Damien Hirst. Neither the police nor gallery staff could think of a motive for the attack, other than the fact that it might be a protest about its controversial nature.

Hirst spent last night emptying the case and cleaning the animal in the hope that it might be repaired. Hirst said recently of the sculpture "I don't think it's shocking. It gets people interested in art. The worst thing is if someone just walks through a gallery without seeing anything." However, he went on to say, "People can't come in and mess about with exhibits without the artist's consent. But it could have been worse. Someone could have come in with a hammer."

Hirst has stated that he intends to pickle his grandmother in formaldehyde when she dies, but only if she gives her consent!

3 Comprehension check

Decide whether the following statements about the article are true (T) or false (F):

1. The sheep was inside a glass case in the gallery.
2. The gallery staff changed the name of the work to 'Black Sheep'.
3. Damien Hirst has put a lot of other dead animals in formaldehyde.
4. The police do not know why the man attacked Hirst's work.
5. The sculpture was totally destroyed.
6. Hirst says his grandmother wants to be pickled when she dies.

4 Recommending

T40 **Put the following jumbled conversations into the correct order:**

Conversation 1

a. Yes, you should go and see it.
b. So you'd recommend it then?
c. Quite good actually, the photos were really great, quite amazing – some of them.
d. Oh, really? It sounds quite interesting. What was it like?
e. I went and saw an exhibition at the Hayward Gallery earlier in the week.
f. It was a collection of photos from the first lunar landing.
g. Oh, did you? What was it?

1	2	3	4	5	6	7

Conversation 2

a. So you wouldn't recommend it then?
b. Oh, it was this collection of Flemish paintings from the seventeenth century.
c. Oh, did you? Which one's that again?
d. Well, I didn't think much of it myself. It was all a bit dull, you know.
e. No, I'd give it a miss, if I were you – unless you really like that sort of thing, of course.
f. Oh really? What was it like?
g. I went and saw that new exhibition at the National Gallery the other day.

1	2	3	4	5	6	7

Now practise both conversations with a partner, making sure you sound enthusiastic or not, as appropriate.

Recommending expressions

When we talk about an exhibition we've been to, we usually say whether we think it was worth seeing or not. Re-order the following to make fixed recommending expressions:

1. you're OK It's sort if into thing that of.
   . . . .
2. a must It's.
   . . . .
3. recommend really I it.
   . . . .
4. you give if were miss a I'd it I.
   . . . .
5. visit well It's a worth.
   . . . .
6. entrance not It's the fee worth.
   . . . .
7. It's my tea cup of really not.
   . . . .

T41 **Listen to the tape and check your answers. Which expressions recommend an exhibition? Which do not?**

5 Talking point

Would you ever do something like the protester did? In what circumstances?
Some of Hirst's other famous works contain a glass case full of maggots, a dead shark in formaldehyde and a cow cut in half and placed in two glass cases. Would you go and see an exhibition containing these works?
Do you think art should try to shock?

6 Pronunciation

T42 **Listen to the different ways the is pronounced in the following sentence:**

I went and saw that new exhibition at the National Gallery the other day.

Now decide how the will be pronounced in the following:

1. It's the first gallery I've been to.
2. Hirst spent last night emptying the case and cleaning the animal.
3. I loved the Indian sculpture exhibition. I really liked the way things were displayed.
4. The only thing I didn't like was the dead sheep.

Do you know why the is pronounced in these two different ways?

7 Vocabulary

Below are eight ways of describing paintings. Check that you understand them, using a dictionary if necessary. Use them to complete the sentences below:

a. portrait	e. detailed
b. landscape	f. traditional
c. still life	g. original
d. abstract	h. colourful

1. I think his work is very individual, very . . . . I've never seen anything else like it.
2. I've just been to a . . . . exhibition – it's something I've tried to do myself, but my apples always look like peaches!
3. We've got a . . . . of my great-grandfather at home. He was a general in the army.
4. Renaissance paintings were always very . . . . You could see all the stitches on the clothes.
5. His most famous . . . . was a picture of the scenery around his home in Provence.
6. I don't actually like much modern art. I much prefer more . . . . things.
7. I don't like paintings that are all greys and browns. I like really . . . . things. You know, lots of bright greens and reds and yellows.
8. I don't understand her work at all. It's just too . . . . for me.

8 Talking point

Try to use the language in exercise 7 to describe the works of art opposite and also those on page 112. The top picture is 'Brittany Landscape' by Henry Moret. The bottom picture is 'Room Construction' by Liubov Popova.

Then describe each work of art to your partner and see if they can guess which one you are talking about. Your partner may choose to disagree with your descriptions.

Postscript

In the end, the protester who poured ink into Hirst's work had to pay £1,000 to help restore it to its original condition. He turned out to be an unemployed artist who was inspired by Hirst's work and thought that it would be all right to react to the work in the way he did! Was he right to do what he did?

9 Talking point

Here are 6 examples of things you might go and see. Do you find any of them offensive – morally? politically?

1. A display of Egyptian mummies.
2. An exhibition of the body of a man found frozen in the Alps after hundreds of years.
3. A zoo with lions and tigers in cages.
4. A museum in Britain displaying statues taken from Greece 200 years ago.
5. A science museum with human foetuses preserved in formaldehyde.
6. An exhibition about some of the most famous murderers in history.

Would you ban any of them?

Would you be happy taking your children or your younger brothers or sisters to them all?

What do you think of the example of street art below?

10 Art joke

T43 **Read through the joke below and guess how it ends. Compare your ending with a partner. Then listen to the tape.**

When I was in Italy last year, I stumbled across this lovely little gallery by a canal, so I went inside and had a look around and ended up buying this old landscape.

When I got it home, I took it up to a big auction house in London to get it valued. I asked the dealer there what he thought of it and he said, "Well, the good news is it's a Pandino, from his Venice period, but I'm afraid the bad news is that . . . . !"

(Answer on page 192)

Vocabulary

Relationships

Which adjective collocates most strongly with which noun?

a. my next-door	friend
b. a chance	neighbour
c. a close	relative
d. a distant	acquaintance

Use these expressions in the following sentences:

1. We're having trouble with our . . . .'s cat.
2. A . . . . is turning up tomorrow from Canada. He's a cousin I've never met.
3. Gill and I have been . . . . since we were at school.
4. I can't even remember her second name. She's only . . . . I met a couple of years ago on a plane.

Phrasal verbs with *out*

In this unit we met sell out of **and** turn out to be. **Use the following verbs in the gaps and then go back and underline the phrasal verbs.**

kicked	fell	sold	stands
make	tired	turned	worn

1. I'm sorry there's none left. We've completely . . . . out of the small ones.
2. I didn't like Molly at first, but she . . . . out to be one of the nicest people you could ever hope to meet.
3. These boots are . . . . out. I'll need a new pair before we go on holiday.
4. Joe and I used to be really good friends, but we . . . . out a few years ago after he never paid back the £250 I lent him to buy a car.
5. I need a rest. All this walking has really . . . . me out.
6. Could you speak up a bit, please? I can't quite . . . . out what you're saying.
7. Alan was . . . . out of the team. He was always late for training.
8. Beckham . . . . out as the best player in the team. He's head and shoulders above everyone else.

Art movements

Here are the English words for some major periods in the world of art. First mark the strong stress, then match them up with the correct artist from the period:

1. Impressionism	a. Pablo Picasso
2. Cubism	b. Leonardo da Vinci
3. Art Nouveau	c. Salvador Dali
4. Surrealism	d. Claude Monet
5. The Renaissance	e. Antonio Gaudi

Places of work

In this unit you read of art galleries, museums, whisky distilleries. Match up the two halves of the following places of work:

1. shopping	a. surgery
2. doctor's	b. store
3. town	c. studio
4. carpet	d. hall
5. car	e. mall
6. ship	f. factory
7. design	g. plant
8. department	h. yard

Expressions with *get*

In this unit you met the expression get to the point. Get **is a very common verb in English.**

Here are 8 things you can get. **Use them to complete the situations below:**

a. the impression	e. 5 years
b. shock	f. my father
c. some sleep	g. the bus
d. a doctor	h. the flu

1. I'm leaving now to get . . . . from the airport. He's landing in half an hour.
2. I really got a terrible . . . . when I saw Mary after all those years. She looked really old.
3. That guy got . . . . for knocking down one of our neighbours' children. He was driving when he was drunk.
4. Quick, get . . . . ! She's stopped breathing!
5. Sorry, I've been working non-stop for 18 hours. I need to get . . . .
6. I think I'm getting . . . . I feel awful.
7. Let's get . . . . There's never a taxi when you need one.
8. Do you get . . . . that Claire is bored with her job?

learning advice

How are you organising and storing all the new words and expressions which you are learning?

It is very important that you keep some kind of notebook which you use on a daily basis to store new language.

Your notebook should be organised into several sections so that you can find what you have put in later.

This is something you can do yourself – especially if you have a looseleaf notebook. Possible sections are:

- **phrasal verbs**
- **expressions with common verbs such as *get***
- **adjective + noun collocations**
- **verb + noun collocations**
- **expressions with prepositions such as *in***
- **topics such as *travel, holidays, health***

You can decide for yourself what sections you want. The most important thing is that your notebook is organised.

Unit 8a : Describing things

olutely brilliant! But the acting was horrendous. A bit like Paris, only smaller. It's not exactly Shakespeare, is it? That must've been lovely. Didn't you find it borir
lent for my taste. To be or not to be? Don't ask me. What's it like? Any good? Not bad considering the price. A bit like you but better looking. Nothing special
the top if you ask me. Star fruit? I've never eaten one. He's not exactly Superman, is he? Loved the food. Didn't you think it was a bit bland? It's a great city.
t place to visit – although I wouldn't want to live there. It was very disappointing, considering how much it cost. Sort of reddish with blonde bits. I wish you'd be

1 So what was it like?

Do you understand the meaning of these common adjectives?

1. It was horrendous.
2. It was a bit bland.
3. It was wonderful.
4. It was a bit over the top.
5. It was nothing special.
6. It was very ordinary.
7. It was a bit disappointing.
8. It was really brilliant.

T44 Underline the main stressed syllable in each expression and then practise saying them. Which would you use to describe:

1. A play or performance you enjoyed a lot. (two expressions)
2. A bottle of expensive wine which wasn't as good as you expected. (three expressions)
3. Food which didn't really taste of anything. (one expression)

T45 Check your answers by listening to the three conversations on tape.

Now use the expressions to describe the pictures. How many other ways can you describe them?

2 While you listen

T46 Paul and Mick are two friends chatting over a coffee. Listen to them talking about the films they have seen recently. While you listen, try to answer these questions:

1. Which films are they talking about?
2. What do they think of them?

Listen again and try to fill in the gaps.

Real English: It's not exactly Shakespeare.

This mildly sarcastic remark is typical in informal conversation between people who know each other. Do you understand what the following remarks refer to?

He's not exactly Superman, is he?
It's not exactly a Picasso, is it?

Do you say things like that in your language?

Real English: over the top

Over the top means 'exaggerated or extravagant in some way'. It could refer to someone's dress or behaviour or the amount of food or drink at a party. For example:

Didn't you think their house is a bit over the top?

I thought 10 Rolls Royces at the wedding was a bit over the top.

Sometimes we say *OTT* instead. For example:

It was a bit OTT!

3 Talking point

Which film would you rather go to – *Titanic* or *Bomb Alert 2?*

What's the most over the top film you've ever seen?

Not exactly Shakespeare!

Paul: Guess what I went and saw last night – *Titanic* – it's on again this week at the Duke of York's.

Mick: Oh, yeah. I saw that when it first came out. What did you think of it? . . . . ?

Paul: Oh, it was great. I really enjoyed it. I thought the special effects were amazing, and the acting was brilliant. It's one of those films where, you know, when I first heard about how much money they'd spent on it, ... , but it was really great. It was a bit like one of those old disaster movies, you know, like *Towering Inferno* or *Earthquake*, ...

Mick: Really? I'm surprised. I thought the acting was a bit wooden myself, and the dialogue was just awful. . . . . you actually thought it was worth the money they'd spent on it. I mean, ... the whole thing just a little bit over the top?

Paul: Oh, no. . . . . I thought it was brilliant.

Mick: But the acting was horrendous!

Paul: Well, I know it's . . . . Shakespeare, but it's not meant to be, is it? I'll tell you something weird though, there was this guy sitting next to us who snored all the way through the film!

Mick: Really? That . . . . really annoying. How could anybody actually sleep through all that noise!

Paul: I don't know – just dead tired, I suppose.

Mick: Yeah, I guess so, but really though, ... it was all just a bit too sentimental?

Paul: . . . . , but I honestly didn't. I really thought it was all done just right. It was so romantic.

Mick: Oh well, each to his own. Have you seen *Bomb Alert 2* yet?

Paul: No, I haven't even heard of it. . . . . ?

Mick: Um, Jean-Paul van Klam, he's great in it and, um, that woman from *Kamikaze*, you know who I mean. Remember? She was Turtle-woman too, ... I must . . . . she wasn't very good in that.

Paul: Oh, her. So what's it like? . . . . ?

Mick: Yeah, it's great – if you like blood all over the place and that sort of thing.

Paul: Oh, it doesn't really sound like . . . . , actually. I think I'll give it a miss.

4 Negative questions

Mick asked Didn't you think **it was all just a bit too sentimental? Negative questions can express an indirect opinion or surprise.**

Do you like cheese? (normal question)
Don't you like cheese? (I'm surprised)

What did you think of it? (normal question)
Didn't you think it was really boring? (*I* did)

Negative questions are often followed by the verbs find **and** think:

1. **Don't / Didn't you find it + adjective**

I really like living out here in the country.
> Oh, really. Don't you find it a bit boring?
No, not at all. It's great.

2. **Don't / Didn't you think it + verb**

I'm going to see *Dogs of War* tonight.
> Oh really. Don't you think it looks really violent?
Yes, a bit, but then I like that kind of thing.

T47 **Listen to these examples on tape and practise them with a partner.**

Grammar in context

Complete the following with negative questions:

1. I really like watching films with subtitles.
> Really? .... them hard to read?
2. I really loved that Italian actress.
> Did you? .... she over-acted a bit?
3. Did you see that Chinese film last night?
> Yes, ... it was a bit slow?
4. I thought that last scene was a bit slow.
> Yes, it was a bit, but .... it was really romantic?
5. I thought the plot was a bit too predictable.
> Did you? .... it quite funny, though?
6. I thought that lead actor was brilliant in it.
> Really? .... him a bit too much like Robert De Niro?
7. *Titanic* won loads of Oscars, didn't it?
> I know. .... it's a bit over-rated?
8. It was rubbish, but at least it was funny rubbish!
> Did you think so? .... it was just silly and typical of late-night cable TV?

With a partner, practise the above conversations.

Grammar role play

Imagine your partner lives in the biggest city in the country. While you make a list of four or five negative things about living there, your partner should make a list of the positive things. Then have conversations like this:

You:	Don't you find Tokyo just a bit too big and crazy?
Your partner:	Yes, I know what you mean, but I love the night life.
You:	You must be mad! I can't stand it.

5 Talking point

In the conversation Mick said the film was a bit too sentimental. A similar common pattern is:

It's a bit too (romantic) for my taste.

Tell a partner about a film you have seen, but did not like very much. Criticise it. Use the following or a word of your own:

It was a bit too	violent slow predictable far-fetched sentimental romantic clever	for my taste.

If something is *far-fetched,* it is very difficult to believe.

6 Pronunciation

In the conversation Mick said:

That must've been really annoying.

T48 **In the following, try to say** must've, could've, might've, should've, couldn't've **naturally:**

1. There must've been a mistake.
2. It must've arrived while I was away.
3. You should've told her.
4. It might've helped.
5. You must've been very upset.
6. It must've been very upsetting.
7. It could've been John.
8. You should've reported it to the police.
9. It could've been very serious.
10. I should've known better! I must've been mad!
11. It couldn't've happened to a nicer person.
12. It couldn't've been serious.

7 Comparing

G30 One way of describing something is to compare it with something else. For example:

So what was that fashion show you went to like?
> Oh, all right, I suppose. It was a bit like last year's really, but not as good.

Here are some more common expressions for comparing.

It was a bit like .... but not as good/nice.
but there's a lot less/more people there.
only a lot louder/quieter/more beautiful.
only there's more/not as many cars on the road there.

Describing things

Match the numbers on the left with the letters on the right to make complete descriptions.

1. What's Indonesian food like?
   > Delicious. A bit like Thai food, I suppose,
2. What was Lizzie's party like, then?
   > Oh, it was OK, a bit like her last one,
3. So what's New Zealand like, then?
   > A bit like Ireland, really,
4. So, what's Nick and Beth's flat like, then?
   > I suppose it's a bit like ours, really,
5. What's snowboarding? I've never heard of it.
   > Snowboarding? Well, it's a bit like skiing,
6. So, what's Graham's sister like, then?
   > Well, actually, she's a bit like him,
7. What's your new laptop like?
   > It's the same as my old one,
8. So, what're the Spiders like, then?
   > They're OK, they're a bit like the Beatles,

a. only the kitchen's not as big.
b. but there's more sheep.
c. only a bit more modern-sounding.
d. only a lot faster.
e. but a little bit less spicy.
f. only a lot more difficult, really.
g. but there weren't as many people as I'd expected.
h. only she's easier to get along with, I suppose.

Now describe the things in these pictures:

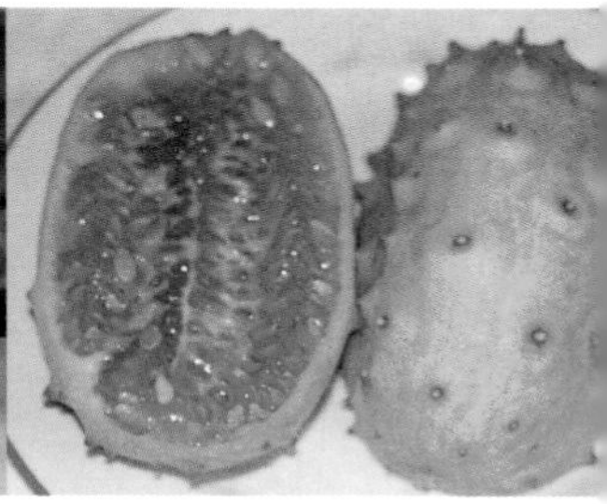

Now describe the following things in a similar way:

1. a film you have seen
2. a big city you know
3. a café, restaurant or club you know
4. a drink
5. a band you like
6. a vegetable
7. a piece of furniture
8. a new television programme

Read your descriptions to a different partner. Can they guess what you are describing? For example:

O.K. It's an alcoholic drink which is a bit like whisky or vodka, but it's made from rice.
> Oh, it must be that stuff they drink in Japan. What do you call it? Oh yeah, sake.
That's it. Have you ever tried it?

8 *Must* for guessing

G31 We often make guesses about something. Here are two ways of doing this using must:

must be

Have I told you yet? We've finally moved into our new house.
> Oh really? It must be really nice to have a bit more space at last.

must've been

I grew up in a small village near Ludlow.
> Oh, that must've been wonderful. It must've been a bit of a shock when you first moved to Birmingham then.

Grammar check

Add must be or must've been in the following sentences:

1. Sally's new boyfriend has a foreign accent. I think he . . . . French.
2. The car won't start. The battery . . . . dead.
3. I'm not sure where Pete went to school. I think it . . . . somewhere in Wales, judging from something he said the other day about Cardiff.
4. Well, if this pen's not yours, it . . . . mine!
5. I'm tired. Surely it . . . . time to go home?
6. Bali . . . . wonderful! Are you planning to go back?
7. Just look at those poor people. It . . . . dreadful having no money and no food.
8. Two years ago we paid £30 a night. I should think it . . . . at least £40 now.
9. Did you see that police car? It . . . . doing over a hundred.

Real English: doing over a hundred

This means the car was going at over a hundred miles an hour. For example:
You can't do more than 30 in town.
We did an average of 70 on the motorway.

Grammar in context

Use must or must've to respond in these situations:

1. My brother and his wife have actually got eleven kids now.
   > Eleven! . . . .
2. We stayed in this huge twenty-storey hotel.
   > Oh, one of those places! . . . .
3. I usually cycle into work, if it's not raining.
   > Oh really? . . . .
4. I got up at 5, just as the sun was coming up, and went for a walk along by the river.
   > Wonderful! . . . .
5. I like my job, but I have to work a six-day week every week!
   > Every week? . . . .
6. The plane was delayed 48 hours! Can you imagine what it was like?
   > 48 hours! . . . .
7. Did you hear that over 200 people were killed in that crash?
   > I know. . . . .
8. Every year we have our annual sales meeting at a beautiful castle in the Scottish Highlands.
   > Really? . . . .

Compare your responses with a partner, then practise the conversations in pairs.

9 Talking point

Tell a partner about two interesting things you have done or seen. Your partner should respond with a comment using must be / must've been. For example:

I spent a week in Hong Kong, which was great.
> Wow! That must've been interesting. I've always wanted to go there. It sounds like an amazing place.

Where do you think these places are?

To be or not to be

You may never have read a play by Shakespeare. You may never even have seen one in the theatre or even a film of one. But if English is your mother tongue, you cannot open your mouth without quoting something he has written. Quotations from his plays are part of modern everyday English.

Everyone knows that "To be or not to be, that is the question" comes from Hamlet, but when someone says "Neither a borrower nor a lender be", they are probably unaware that they are also quoting from the same play.

Below are some very common quotations with one word missing. Can you complete them?

All of Shakespeare's plays have been translated into many other languages. This means that quotations like the ones below have been translated and are now part of other languages, too.

Why do quotations become famous? The answer must be because it says something which everyone knows is true and it says it in an original and interesting way. Shakespeare did this better than most writers.

1. I must be . . . . only to be kind. (Hamlet)
2. Something . . . . this way comes. (Macbeth)
3. What's in a . . . . ? (Romeo and Juliet)
4. If . . . . be the food of love, play on. (Twelfth Night)
5. There is method in his . . . . (Hamlet)
6. All that glitters is not . . . . (The Merchant of Venice)
7. To thine own . . . . be true. (Hamlet)
8. The course of true . . . . never did run smooth. (A Midsummer's Night's Dream)

(The answers are on page 192)

a. cruel
b. name
c. self
d. love
e. wicked
f. music
g. gold
h. madness

10 Talking point

Who is the most famous writer in your language?
Have you ever been to a Shakespeare play in your own country?
Did you have to study any of his plays at school? Can you answer these questions?

1. When did Shakespeare live?
2. Where was he born?
3. What was his wife's name?
4. Can you name a Shakespeare play which has been turned into an opera?
5. Which Shakespeare play was the basis for a famous Broadway musical?

11 Asking linked questions

T49 We sometimes ask two questions at the same time. For example:

So what's that new film like? Any good?
> Yes, it's great – if you like Hugh Grant.

What was Malta like? Was it hot?
> Yes, it was really lovely. We were never out of the water.

Write similar questions to suggest these answers. The first one has been done for you.

1. *What's his house like? Is it big?*
   > Yes, it's huge. It's got four bedrooms and an enormous garden.
2. . . . . ? . . . . ?
   > No, it wasn't, actually. It was really boring. In fact, I didn't even finish reading it.
3. . . . . ? . . . . ?
   > Yes, very much. My boss is really nice and it's quite well paid, really.
4. . . . . ? . . . . ?
   > Yes, it WAS quite warm, but not as hot as the last time we went.
5. . . . . ? . . . . ?
   > Yes, I think it's great. The third track is brilliant.
6. . . . . ? . . . . ?
   > No, we lost three-one. It was just terrible. I can't believe it.

Check with a partner to see if you have similar questions. Then listen to the model answers on the tape and practise saying them.

Pair work

Now ask your partner two linked questions about the following:

a. the weather on their last holiday
b. their job
c. their house or flat
d. how they get on with their parents
e. how they are
f. their day yesterday

12 Conjunctions

G32 Look at the following examples of although, considering **and** in spite of:

I quite like her new shoes – although I think the heels are just a bit too high.
I quite like her new shoes – considering how cheap they were.
I quite like her new shoes – in spite of the flashy designer label.

Grammar in context

Use although **or** considering **in the following:**

1. Talking about a new CD.

a. I think the whole CD is really good – . . . . how many changes the band's had since their last one.
b. I think the third track's the best – . . . . I quite like that song called 'Dolphins' too.
c. I think it's a great CD – . . . . it's still not as good as their first album.
d. I think it's really great – . . . . how different it is from what they usually do.

2. Talking about a trip

a. The trip was great – . . . . the mosquitoes were a bit of a problem at night!
b. I really enjoyed the flight in the end – . . . . how nervous I was before we took off.
c. I had a really brilliant time – . . . . I probably wouldn't go back.
d. We had a great trip, ... how little it cost!

Now use although **or** in spite of:

3. Talking about buying a watch

a. I reckon this one's got to be the best buy, ... I know I shouldn't really spend more than £100 on a watch.
b. I think this one just looks nicer – . . . . . . being a lot cheaper than the others.
c. I'd go for that digital one, ... the strap. You can always get that changed later.
d. I think the Rolex one's the nicest, ... it is going to nearly bankrupt me!

Make three questions you'd like to ask a partner with this pattern:

So what's . . . . like?

Now take turns asking and answering these questions. Try to describe things in as much detail as you can, using as much of the language in this unit as possible.

Unit 8b : Films and television

d then someone sat down right in front of me. The ending was brilliant. Pass the popcorn. Shh! Has it got subtitles? I loved every minute of it. Where's the remot
d I've heard it's really good. Who's in it? That was rubbish! Is there anything good on tonight? Sport, sport and more sport. Typical Hollywood stuff. I prefer
n't you? Surely, you're not going to watch THAT are you? You must go and see it. What's it about? It's on cable. They bleeped out all the F-words. The spec
re amazing. Leonardo who? Turn it off. There's too much sex and violence on TV these days. Have you seen his latest? I prefer the adverts. They're more en

1 What kind of film is it?

Do you recognise any of the films shown in these pictures? Have you seen any of them? What were they like?

Match the descriptions of films to the pictures.

1. It's a kind of sci-fi thing.
2. It's a costume drama.
3. It's a typical Hollywood action movie.
4. It's a horror movie.
5. It's a comedy.
6. It's a real weepie.

Can you think of other examples for each kind of film?

What kind of films do you like most? Why?

Are there any kinds of films that you really can't stand?

2 Film vocabulary

Complete each of the following gaps by adding one of the words given:

banned	stars	director
dubbed	cut	special effects

1. My favourite . . . . is Hitchcock. There's never been anyone else like him.
2. The government thought the film might corrupt people, so they . . . . it.
3. Have you ever seen *Mean Streets?* It . . . . Robert De Niro and Harvey Keitel.
4. I thought that the . . . . in *Jurassic Park* were amazing.
5. When they showed *Robocop* on TV, they . . . . about fifteen minutes out of it, because it was so violent.
6. I prefer to see foreign films in their original versions with subtitles, rather than . . . .

soundtrack	set	scene
dialogue	plot	ending

7. The thing I love about that film is that the . . . . is just so sharp and witty. I laughed at almost every line.
8. I loved the . . . . so much that I went out and bought the CD the next day.
9. I loved all the twists and turns in the . . . . . , and the way it only made sense right at the very end.
10. I liked most of it, although I did think that the . . . . was just a bit too sentimental.
11. It looks amazing. It's . . . . in New York in the year 2050.
12. My favourite . . . . in the whole film is the bit where the aliens finally come out of the spaceship.

3 Talking point

Do you prefer foreign films to be dubbed or have subtitles?

What are the best special effects you have ever seen in a film?

Do you have a favourite film soundtrack?

Do you go to the cinema to see a new film when it comes out or wait till it comes out on video?

4 Before you read

First, check you understand the words in the left hand column by matching them with the meanings on the right:

1. offend	a. a small number of people
2. a decade	b. cut down the number
3. attract complaints	c. up-to-date, modern
4. censor	d. worried about something
5. ruined	e. a period of 10 years
6. the TV version	f. completely destroyed
7. minority	g. specially made for TV
8. concerned	h. upset someone badly
9. reduce	i. cut out offensive bits
10. current	j. stimulate complaints

Do you think film censorship is a good thing? Give an example.

Did your parents ever stop you watching anything on TV? What ? Why?

Have you ever seen *Robocop?* What did you think of it?

5 While reading

In the conversation in unit 8a, Mick said he loved violent films full of blood. Read this article about what happened when a film like this was shown on British TV. When you have read it, answer these questions:

1. Why did the TV version of *Robocop* offend so many people?
2. What effect did the censoring of the film have?
3. Who is Michael Winner and how did he feel about all the complaints?
4. Who is Mary Whitehouse and how did she feel?

TV ROBOCOP NOT VIOLENT ENOUGH FOR VIEWERS

Robocop, the sci-fi movie best remembered for its comic-book violence, is still offending viewers a decade after its original release. Audiences watching it on TV have been shocked by polite language and annoyed that it was not violent enough.

The film, shown last Saturday night at 10.05pm, attracted more complaints than any other film this year. Hundreds of angry viewers called local television stations saying that the TV version had been censored so much that the film had been ruined. The strong public reaction has even led TV executives to consider putting back some of the bad language and violence when it is shown again.

One executive commented that "one can't help but notice we've taken too much out of a film like *Robocop*. Maybe we've gone a bit too far this time."

The British TV version of the film is a classic example of over the top censorship, with the F-word over-dubbed and the violence so reduced that at times it's hard to follow the plot.

Michael Winner, *Robocop's* director, said that he was pleased people were making their voices heard. He had become tired of hearing so much noise from what he called the very small 'moral minority'.

However, Mrs Mary Whitehouse, head of the National Viewers' and Listeners' Association, stated, "People that make these kind of complaints are only concerned about their own interests rather than the good of society as a whole. Anybody who can't give up a little bit of film in order to reduce the current climate of violence should not be taken seriously."

Real English: bad language and the F-word

Bad language is swearing.

Saying *the F-word* is a common way of avoiding saying f**k. itself. You should only use the word itself in very informal situations with people you know who are happy using it in conversation. Many people find the F-word very offensive.

6 Collocations

Complete the collocations in this summary of the text:

The TV version of *Robocop* caused a strong . . . . Many people rang their local . . . . to complain that too much violence had been cut from the film. In fact, so much had been cut, it was difficult to . . . . . . the plot. It was a classic . . . . . . of over the top censorship. Mary Whitehouse, a famous protester against violence on television, was in favour of the cuts because she objects strongly to the current . . . . . . of . . . . . . on television.

7 Talking point

Look at the following statements about films below. Decide how strongly you agree.

1 = strongly disagree
5 = totally agree

Violent films can be really offensive.
Cutting films ruins them.
Bad language should be cut out of films.
Very few people complain about violence.
Banning violent films will cut crime.
The TV version of a film should be censored more than the cinema version.

Discuss your opinions with a partner. See if the whole class can agree.
Do you agree more with Michael Winner's opinion or Mary Whitehouse's?

8 Enough

Some people thought the film was not violent enough. Enough **normally comes after adjectives:**

not violent enough

but before nouns:

not enough violence

Match up these two half-sentences with enough:

1. There isn't enough classical music on TV
2. This flat isn't big enough
3. We simply don't have enough time
4. We're not rich enough

a. for four children, two cats and a hamster.
b. for my taste.
c. to afford a week in the Maldives.
d. to go home and get back in time for the show.

Now underline the phrases with enough.

9 Past perfect

G33 **Look at these examples from the text:**

The TV version had been censored.
He had become tired of hearing so much noise.
The film had been ruined.

The past perfect is used to talk about an idea or event which happened before another event in the past. For example:

I'd passed the turn-off for Leeds before I realised.
The house had burned to the ground by the time the fire brigade got there.

What sentence comes to mind in these situations? The first one is done for you.

1. I was terrified as I put on my parachute.
   I'd never jumped out of a plane before.
2. I was feeling sick at the thought of my speech.
   . . . . in my life before!
3. I was worried about meeting Mary's parents.
   . . . . before!
4. I wasn't sure if I'd like Korean food.
   . . . . before.
5. The woman in red was his first wife.
   . . . . once before.
6. The news said thousands were dead.
   . . . . an earthquake.
7. He left without saying goodbye to me.
   . . . . an argument.
8. I was terrified as I arrived at the airport.
   . . . . before!

Can you say something true about yourself using the past perfect and the following ideas? For example:

I'd never eaten paella until I went to Spain.

1. . . . . until I went to a Chinese restaurant.
2. . . . . until I went abroad.
3. . . . . until I did my military service.
4. . . . . until I went to university.
5. . . . . until I went to Britain / America.
6. . . . . until I fell in love.

10 Film expressions

Make complete expressions to give an opinion using the endings below:

1. It's one of the best films . . . .
2. I'd really like to . . . .
3. It wasn't as good as. . . . .
4. I thought. . . . .
5. It wasn't . . . .
6. It was the first time . . . .
7. I loved. . . . .
8. It's the kind of thing that . . . .

a. it was a bit disappointing, really.
b. you either really love or really hate.
c. I'd expected, actually.
d. I've ever seen in my life.
e. every minute of it.
f. see it again.
g. I'd seen anything like that.
h. particularly good.

Now use some of the expressions to tell your partner about one of your favourite films. For example:

. . . was one of the best films I've ever seen. It was so . . . . I loved every minute of it. It starred . . . . It was about . . . . The thing I liked most about it was . . . .

11 I've heard it's really good

Re-order the conversations about films below.

Conversation 1

a. No, I haven't actually, but I've heard it's really good. Friends have told me it's worth seeing.
b. Have you seen *Day of the Dogs* yet?
c. Really? Well, I must admit it looks a bit too violent for me.
d. Yes, I'm not sure if I want to see it myself.

The correct order is . . . .

Conversation 2

a. I'm thinking of going to see that new De Niro film.
b. Well, the reviews I've seen were very good.
c. Are you? I've heard that it's terrible. Just typically Hollywood.
d. Were they? I've heard the opposite.

The correct order is . . . .

Conversation 3

a. But it's meant to be one of the best horror films ever made!
b. Is it? You're not going to watch it, are you? It's supposed to be really horrible.
c. Excellent. It sounds right up my street then.
d. *Thriller Killer* is on tonight.
e. Well, someone told me that it's the most disgusting thing they'd ever seen in their life.

The correct order is . . . .

With a partner, use the language highlighted in these conversations to talk about a new film that you would really like to see.

12 Television vocabulary

Use the following common words in the text below:

series	channel
digital	advertisements
remote	documentaries
aerials	cable

As I sit here today in front of my TV with my . . . . . . control in my hand, it's easy to forget that when I was growing up in the fifties, there was only one . . . . . . in the UK. It was BBC and it was years before we got ITV and BBC2. The main difference was that ITV had . . . . . . and BBC didn't.

During the 50s, lots of houses had television . . . . . . on their roofs, but nowadays even they are becoming a thing of the past. Things have changed so much with the arrival of . . . . . . , ... and satellite TV.

At first, the idea in the UK was that TV should be educational, so there were lots of . . . . . . , but today the channels seem to do nothing but fight to see which one gets the biggest audience for soaps such as *Neighbours, Eastenders* and *Coronation Street.*

The BBC is still one of the best companies when it comes to making serious drama . . . . . . – *Pride and Prejudice* and things like that.

Have you got satellite or cable TV? What about digital – is it really better?

Do you know anyone who doesn't have a television? Why don't they have one?

How much TV do you watch per week? What kind of thing do you normally watch? What makes you switch the television off?

13 Asking questions

Here are common questions to ask about films:

a. Who's in it?
b. What's it about?
c. Where's it on?
d. What's it like?
e. Who's it by?
f. When was it made?
g. Where's it from?
h. What kind of film is it?

Match these questions to the following answers:

1. . . . .
> Two or three years ago.
2. . . . .
> Juliette Binoche and that guy who was in *Dimples.*
3. . . . .
> Japan, but it's subtitled.
4. . . . .
> At the Odeon in Queen Street.
5. . . . .
> This guy who has a mid-life crisis and drives across America looking for his parents.
6. . . . .
> Some Italian director.
7. . . . .
> It's a cross between a traditional cop movie and a more arty kind of movie.
8. . . . .
> It's silly. I mean, it was amusing for a while, but then I just got bored by it.

Real English: some Italian director

Using *some* in example 6 in exercise 13 means that you don't know the person's name. For example:

Some woman came to the door collecting for charity.

And when you can't answer!

Re-order the following to make expressions that we use when we can't remember something.

1. Sorry, completely gone mind's blank my.
. . . .
2. Wait, minute to a come in me it'll.
. . . .
3. Wait, it's tongue my tip the on of.
. . . .
4. Sorry, my top the head can't I remember off of.
. . . .

T50 **Now practise saying these expressions.**

a. Which expression means *I'd need to look it up*?
b. Which two expressions mean *I can almost – but not quite – remember*?
c. Which expression means *I've forgotten*?

14 Pronunciation

T51 **Practise saying the questions from exercise 13. Listen to the tape, then say them again.**

In pairs, try to have your own conversations about films you have seen, using these questions.

Use the 'forgetting' expressions if you can't remember specific details.

15 Contradicting

In unit 8a we studied negative questions. Look at these two responses: the first agrees, the second disagrees or contradicts.

So don't you like horror films much?
> No, not really. or > Well, yes, I do actually, but I just find some of them a bit over the top.

T52 **Match the following two-line conversations. Then listen to them on tape. Practise them in pairs and try to sound as natural as possible.**

1. You went to see that war film? It doesn't sound like your sort of thing.
2. So it's not a British film then? I thought it was.
3. So you can't make it tonight?
4. You've never seen *Star Wars?* I can't believe it!
5. They didn't release the soundtrack, did they?
6. That never came out on video, did it?

a. Well, actually, I think they did. I think I've seen it in a second-hand record shop.
b. Yes, it did. And what's more, I've got it!
c. Yes, it is. It's British, but it was financed by an American company.
d. Well, actually, I've always liked things like that.
e. Yes, I have! I saw it ages ago. Everyone's seen it!
f. Yes, I can. I'm still coming. I'm just running a bit late, that's all.

16 Film knowledge

Here are the names of 20 of the most important people in the history of the cinema. How many have you heard of? Can you say one thing about each of the ones you know? For example:

He was the guy who made . . .
Wasn't she in . . . ?

Charlie Chaplin
Orson Welles
Alfred Hitchcock
Walt Disney
John Wayne
Sergei Eisenstein
Greta Garbo
Ingmar Bergman
James Dean
Stanley Kubrick
Sam Warner
Akira Kurosawa
Marlon Brando
Woody Allen
Marilyn Monroe
François Truffaut
Federico Fellini
Clint Eastwood
Martin Scorsese
Steven Spielberg

Is there anyone missing from this list? If so, who? Who is your favourite director? Do you have a favourite film actor?

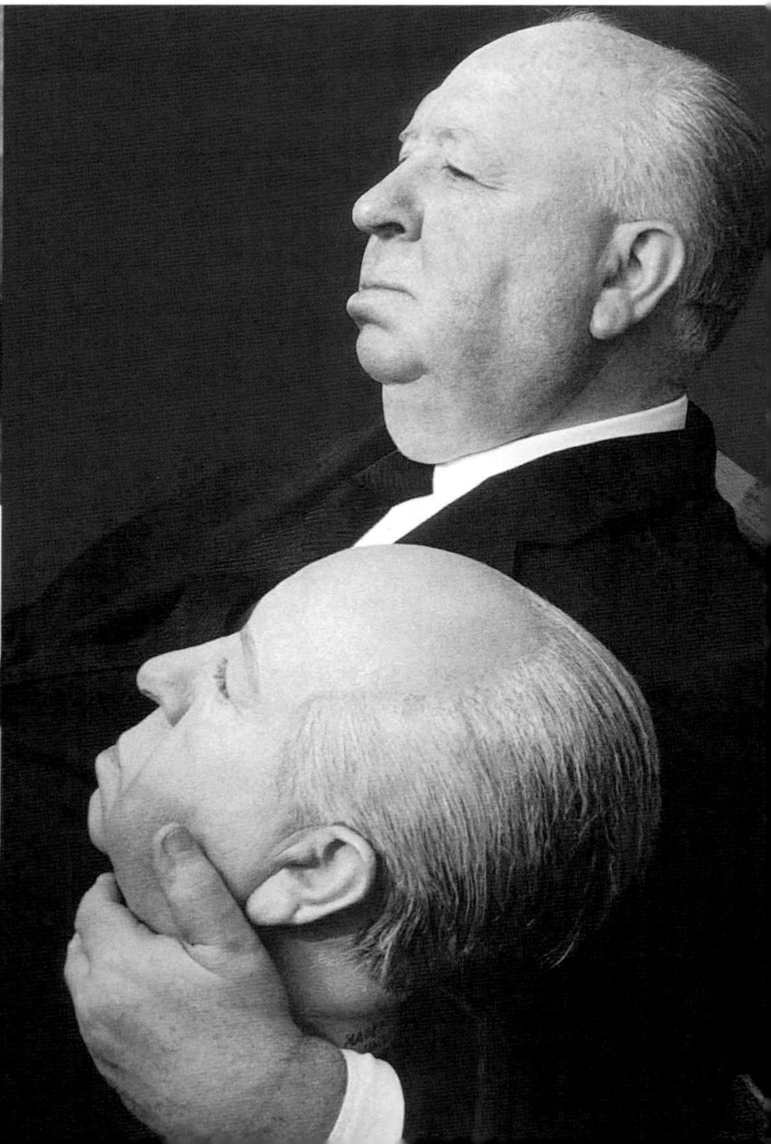

Vocabulary

Adjective collocations

A small group of adjectives collocate with other adjectives to add the idea of 'very'. For example:

dead **tired = very tired**

Complete the sentences below by adding one of the following adjectives:

cold wet tired dirty hot clear

1. I spent all weekend cleaning up my new house. It was filthy . . . .
2. It was lovely in Greece, good food, good wine, lovely beaches, boiling . . . . . . , just great really.
3. Quick, get me a towel. I'm soaking . . . . I just got caught in a downpour.
4. It was lovely in Scotland, the people were great, lovely scenery, but it was freezing . . . . .
5. You should have seen the water! It was emerald blue and crystal . . . .
6. I just flopped into bed the minute I got through the door. I mean, I was just dead . . . .

Do the above collocations remind you of any moments in your life?

Idioms

Here are more idiomatic expressions which make common adjectives stronger. Match them up, then use them in the sentences below:

brand	. . . .	sharp
razor	. . . .	asleep
dirt	. . . .	hard
stark	. . . .	easy
dead	. . . .	cheap
fast	. . . .	awake
wide	. . . .	new
rock	. . . .	naked

1. Be careful with that knife. It's . . . .
2. I got these shoes cheap in a second-hand shop, but they're almost . . . .
3. It was so embarrassing. He walked into the bathroom and saw me, ... !
4. I wish the kids would go to sleep. They're still . . . . and it's almost midnight!
5. I bought 5 bottles. They were . . . . I'll never see them at that price again!
6. Don't wake him. He's . . . .
7. I finished the crossword in a couple of minutes. It was . . . .
8. Throw that bread away! It's . . . .

Synonyms

On the left are 8 common adjectives used in this unit. Match them with the words of similar meaning on the right:

1. crazy	a. clever
2. weird	b. huge
3. horrendous	c. exhausted
4. brilliant	d. correct
5. annoying	e. strange
6. tired	f. irritating
7. right	g. mad
8. enormous	h. terrible

Which most commonly collocate with these nouns? Use a dictionary if you need to.

a. a . . . . or . . . . car crash
b. a . . . . or . . . . young composer
c. an . . . . or . . . . habit
d. a . . . . or . . . . coincidence

Adjectives

Here are 18 ways to describe something. Six mean *very good;* six mean *very bad;* six are mildly critical. Sort them into the three groups below:

terrific	horrible	awful
a bit bland	marvellous	nothing special
excellent	horrendous	on the dull side
very ordinary	dire	not very inspiring
dreadful	brilliant	superb
wonderful	terrible	a bit disappointing

Very good	Mildly critical	Very bad
. . . .	. . . .	. . . .
. . . .	. . . .	. . . .
. . . .	. . . .	. . . .
. . . .	. . . .	. . . .
. . . .	. . . .	. . . .
. . . .	. . . .	. . . .

Audiences

The article on page 128 talked of the TV audience. **Use the following words in the sentences below:**

spectators fans congregation
audience on-lookers viewers

1. The . . . . . . gave the singers a standing ovation.
2. The . . . . . . were silent as the priest came in.
3. Boy bands usually have mostly girl . . . . !
4. Lots of . . . . . . object to violence on TV.
5. Some . . . . were injured when Hakkinen crashed.
6. The police couldn't get to the crash because of all the . . . .

Review : Units 7 and 8

1 Tenses

Choose the correct verb form:

1. I've been/I went to China last year on holiday. It was great.
2. I've played tennis/I've been playing tennis twice this week.
3. Have you been staying in/stayed in quite a lot lately? I haven't seen you about.
4. I've asked/I asked him five times now, and he still hasn't done anything about it!
5. It rained the whole time we were in Wales.
   > Really? That must be/must've been horrible!
6. I've been trying/I've tried to do it all week, but I still haven't managed to get it done.
7. Did you speak/have you spoken to him before he left to go home?
8. I'm working six days a week at the moment.
   > Wow, that must be/must've been really exhausting!
9. What's happened to Mike? I haven't seen/I haven't been seeing him for ages.

2 Multiple choice

Choose the correct alternative:

1. I've worked here (a) since 5 years.
   (b) for 5 years.
2. I've (a) never been anywhere like Ios before.
   (b) never been somewhere like Ios before.
3. I went up to Glasgow
   (a) to see some friends of mine.
   (b) for to see some friends of mine.
4. I do quite like life in central London,
   (a) in spite of the fact it's so noisy!
   (b) considering it's so noisy!
5. I've been trying to understand the present perfect
   (a) since ages!
   (b) for ages!
6. We spent a couple of weeks in Hawaii,
   (a) that was nice.
   (b) which was nice.
7. Have you got a) money enough to get two?
   b) enough money to get two?
8. Some bands are a) a lot louder than others.
   b) a lot more louder than others.

3 Expressions

The following common expressions all occurred in units 7-8. Use them in the sentences below:

He's not exactly . . .
Not a lot, really.
They weren't as good as I'd expected.
That reminds me.
I haven't seen you for ages.
It's on the tip of my tongue.

1. What's the name of that place where you can get copies of your birth certificate?
   > Oh, it's um, oh. . . . . It'll come to me in a minute.
2. So what've you been up to since I saw you last?
   > . . . .
3. What's your brother like? Is he good-looking?
   > Well, let's just say . . . . the best-looking guy you've ever seen.
4. How was the band?
   > OK, I suppose, but . . . . , to be honest.
5. I'd better just give my mum a call, to say I've arrived safely.
   > Oh, ... I must remember to send MY mum a birthday card this week.
6. Hi, how are you? . . . .

4 Conversation

Put the jumbled conversation below into the correct order. The first line is correct.

a. I bumped into Richard and Judy the other day.
b. I must admit, it doesn't really sound like my sort of thing actually.
c. No, they really enjoyed it actually. They said it was a bit like Thailand, only wilder!
d. Oh really? How are they? I haven't seen them for months.
e. What did they think of it? Didn't they find it really difficult?
f. They're great. They've been travelling around India and have just got back.

1 a	2	3	4	5	6

5 Collocations

Match the verbs on the left with the best collocations on the right:

1. send	a. a point of doing something
2. dub	b. 20 minutes out of a movie
3. get	c. and see an exhibition
4. love	d. to the point
5. star	e. in an application form
6. go	f. in a movie
7. make	g. every minute of it
8. cut	h. a film into a foreign language

6 Idioms

Match up the following to make idioms:

1. It's not really	a. seeing.
2. It drives	b. up my street.
3. I'd give it	c. in a minute.
4. It's not worth	d. my cup of tea.
5. It sounds right	e. completely blank!
6. My mind's gone	f. off the top of my head.
7. I can't remember	g. a miss, if I were you.
8. It'll come to me	h. me crazy!

7 *For* and *since*

Put *for* or *since* into the spaces below:

1. Hello Mark, I haven't seen you . . . . ages.
2. I haven't seen Rachel . . . . I left college.
3. Late again! I've been here . . . . ten o'clock.
4. I've loved swimming . . . . as long as I can remember.
5. I've been working here . . . . last summer.
6. You've been going out with Chris . . . . quite a while now, haven't you?
7. I've known Charlie . . . . we were teenagers.
8. I haven't been to an art gallery . . . . years.

8 Real English

Match 1-7 with the follow-up comments in a-g:

1. Hi, Dave. How are you?
2. How's things at work? OK?
3. What are his paintings like? Any good?
4. Did you see that car?
5. Don't you find him a bit on the slow side?
6. Who was that at the door?
7. Where's Nigel gone for his holiday? Anywhere good?

a. Well, we've actually been incredibly busy just lately.
b. Yeah. It must've been doing about a hundred and twenty!
c. Oh, just some guy asking if we wanted any work done in the garden.
d. Well, he's not exactly Picasso, if you know what I mean!
e. Lee! Hello. Long time, no see!
f. Oh, I can't really remember. Some Greek island or other, I think.
g. Well, he's not exactly Einstein, is he!

9 Vocabulary quiz

Answer the following 20 questions with a partner. Then compare your answers with another pair. Who got most answers right?

1. If you don't see the point of something, do you need glasses?
2. Do the police look for reasons or motives for crimes?
3. Does a weepie make you cry or make you laugh?
4. Would you expect to sleep well on a bed that's rock hard?
5. Can food be a bit bland?
6. Where are sci-fi films usually set?
7. In which two places do you find stars?
8. Name two things you can pickle.
9. Do censors dub films into foreign languages?
10. Can you go and see a banned film at your local cinema?
11. If I tell you that a new film's a must, am I recommending it or not?
12. What does OTT mean?
13. When are costume dramas usually set?
14. Does an old friend have to be old?
15. If something's not really your cup of tea, does it mean you prefer coffee instead?
16. Is a plot the same as a story?
17. Do you find turning points in the road or in your life?
18. If you give someone your consent, are you stopping them from doing something?
19. Would you be happy if your TV only had one channel?
20. If something's still a sore point with someone, does it hurt them physically or emotionally?

Unit 9a : Cars and cities

. Oh no, look at the traffic. Well, that's a difficult question. When are they going to do something about it? It's a major issue. Personally, I think it's ridiculou
agree with you up to a point. What exactly is global warming anyway? That would be far better. What we need is more policemen. I know what you mean.
things are just getting worse. What we need is more sleeping policemen. This place is crazy in the summer. What sort of car have you got, then? Stop!
this was a one-way street. Sorry, officer. Was I really doing 60? It's just so crowded. Just ban all cars, full stop! It's getting impossible. If only more people us

1 Traffic survey

You are doing a survey of traffic problems in the town where you live. Here are 10 possible steps which could be taken to improve the situation.

a. install speed cameras at all accident black spots
b. increase parking fines
c. put more sleeping policemen in quiet streets
d. ban all on-street parking in the town centre
e. pedestrianise the main shopping area
f. set up more bicycle lanes
g. provide better and cheaper public transport
h. ban all cars from the town centre
i. double the number of traffic wardens
j. start a one-way system

In pairs, decide which 4 should have the highest priority, which 3 are of medium priority, and which 3 should have the lowest priority.

Real English: sleeping policemen

Sleeping policemen is the normal way in speech of referring to *speed humps* on the road, designed to slow cars down in town.

2 While you listen

T53 Chris and Claire are having coffee in a town centre café. As you listen, try to answer the following questions:

1. What traffic problems do they mention?
2. What suggestions for solving these problems do they come up with?

Listen again and try to fill in the gaps in the conversation.

Real English: I mean

I mean is very common in spoken English. It is used before we go on to make our meaning clearer. For example:

So, what was Iceland like?
> Oh, I loved the place. I mean, I wouldn't want to live there, but it's a great place for a holiday.

Real English: six penalty points

In Britain there is a system of *penalty points*. If you are caught speeding, for example, you could get 4 penalty points. If you get too many, you lose your driving licence.

3 Your view

Do you drive? Have you got a car? Do you use it in town?

Have you ever driven in Rome, Athens, London, or Paris?

What's the worst city you've ever driven in?

Have you ever been stopped by traffic police? What had you done?

More sleeping policemen!

Chris: Did you hear about that kid who was knocked down on Junction Road the other day?

Claire: Yes, it was awful, wasn't it? Still, it's . . . . , is it?

Chris: What do you mean?

Claire: Well, there are always accidents down there, aren't there, ... with the speed cars go at. And, well, basically, the crossing's in the wrong place, isn't it? I don't know why they've never moved it. I mean, ... it was exactly opposite the shops, wouldn't it?

Chris: Yes, ... They could do something to slow the traffic down, couldn't they? Maybe they could put sleeping policemen there or something like that.

Claire: Yeah, maybe – maybe one every so often would help, but . . . . really great is if they had one of those speed cameras.

Chris: Big Brother, you mean!

Claire: No, they really make a difference. You should see how they've slowed the traffic down where my parents live.

Chris: Yeah, ... I'm only against them because I got caught by one last month.

Claire: You're kidding!

Chris: No. A hundred and fifty pounds it cost me! A fine AND six penalty points!

Claire: Oh, that's terrible!

Chris: Yeah, but it was my own silly fault. I mean, I should've known better, but . . . . to what you were saying about the crossing, you're right. It would be far safer if it was closer to the shops, because that's where everybody crosses, you know. That's where most kids cross, so . . . . if it was moved down.

Claire: Yes, I think that's the root of the problem. I mean, it does seem a funny place for a crossing. And . . . . the other problem with it is the fact that lots of cars park all round there.

Chris: Yes, that does make it difficult to see, I suppose. Apparently, the car that hit that kid had just driven off from there.

Claire: Oh, really? Had it? Well, you see what I mean, then.

4 Suggestions with *if*

G34 **In the conversation on page 137, Chris and Claire talked about the pedestrian crossing. Chris said,** It would be far safer if it was closer to the shops. **Match these four suggestions below with the responses:**

1. This town's dead at night, isn't it?
2. The traffic's impossible, isn't it?
3. They've made the main car park bigger.
4. So what do you think they should do about all the homeless people sleeping rough?

a. Yes, but it'd be more useful if they built a multi-storey.

b. Absolute chaos! What would be really great is if buses were cheaper and there were more of them.

c. Well, I'm not an expert, but I think it'd be a really good idea if they spent more on trying to build flats for single people.

d. I know. It'd be far better if the shops stayed open a bit later in the evenings.

Do the same with these examples:

5. It really annoys me that they close the library for the whole of August.
6. The pollution in the High Street is really bad. I wish they'd do something about it.
7. So what do you think they should do about all the street crime?
8. I can't believe that people are still allowed to smoke on the buses.

e. I know. It'd be better if there was just a total ban on it in all public places.

f. Well, I think it'd be a really good idea if they had more police cameras around.

g. Me too! It'd be more useful if they kept it open all through the summer.

h. I know. What would be really great is if there were some way of importing fresh mountain air from Switzerland or somewhere like that!

Summary

In a-h above, there are four different 'if-sentence starters'. Write them in the spaces below.

a. ....
b. ....
c. ....
d. ....

5 Collocations

Below are some useful expressions for talking about your views on things. Choose the best collocation in each:

1. Well, that's a difficult/big question to answer.
2. I don't really have any heavy/strong views on that. What do you think about it?
3. You would've thought they'd be able to tackle/put away that problem somehow, wouldn't you?
4. I know what you mean, but that also brings/raises the question of how you could do that, doesn't it?
5. Yes, but I think that that can cause/do problems as well as solve them.
6. You'd think that it was such a large/major issue that they'd do something about it.
7. Oh well, it seems that we've got completely different/unlike views on that.
8. I think you're trying to escape/avoid the issue by saying that.

6 Personal opinions

Here are some ways of giving your opinion:

Personally,
As far as I'm concerned,

	brilliant.
	a great idea.
I think it's	not a bad idea.
	outrageous.
	ridiculous.
	mad.

Work in pairs with the above and give your opinions on:

shops staying open 24 hours a day
men in kilts
getting married at 16
legalising cannabis
one car per family
body piercing
free coffee during English lessons

7 Role play

You and your colleagues have decided it's time to meet to discuss your working conditions. You work for a very old-fashioned bank, founded in 1748. The management don't like change. Use the language from exercises 4, 5 and 6 to suggest changes to the following – which you are not happy about:

- The computer system is 10 years old and there is no network system.
- People can smoke wherever they want.
- There are no plants or pictures or anything on the walls.
- There is only one toilet for both men and women.
- Everybody has got to start at 8.30 and finish at 4.30.
- Women must wear skirts and men must wear ties.
- Private telephone calls are not allowed.
- There is nowhere to relax during breaks or lunchtime.
- You have to buy your own tea and coffee. It is not provided by the bank.

Can you think of any changes you'd like to make to the place where you work or study?

8 Disagreeing

Re-order the following to form very common sentence starters which show you disagree:

a. Well a agree I but up to point

. . . .

b. what I you but Yes know mean

. . . .

c. think Yes don't that but you

. . . .

d. don't Yes forget that but

. . . .

T54 **Listen to the tape to check your answers. Practise saying them. Then in pairs, take turns putting forward and disagreeing with the views below. Try to continue the conversations.**

1. There's too much sport on TV, isn't there?
2. The way I see it, most TV these days is just a load of rubbish.
3. I don't mind a bit of violence in a film. It's more realistic, isn't it?
4. People like footballers get paid far too much. At least, that's what I think.
5. If you really want to improve your English, the only thing to do is go and live in Britain.

Do the exercise again, but this time begin by saying Oh yes, I know what you mean **before adding why you agree.**

9 Impersonal *they*

G35 They **is common in spoken English when, for some reason, we don't know, or don't need to name, the subject. In these examples,** they **refers to the local council or the police.**

They could do something to slow the traffic down. They could create a pedestrian precinct.

With a partner, decide who they **refers to in each of the following:**

1. They're supposed to be getting tougher on car crime, aren't they?
2. They haven't taken the rubbish this week.
3. They're thinking of putting up income tax.
4. I only arrived 5 minutes after the flight closed, but they wouldn't let me through.

Discuss how life could be better, using these:

I wish they'd . . .
Wouldn't it be great if they . . .

Now discuss all the ways life could be worse:

Wouldn't it be awful if they . . .

Global Warming

There is no escaping global warming. You cannot pick up a newspaper or watch TV without hearing about this major issue. Views on it vary. There is a small number of people who think that global warming is a myth. They say that the earth's climate has been changing for as long as anyone can remember. Why worry about the changes that are happening today?

Most people, on the other hand, take the issue very seriously indeed. Scientists have shown that for the past twenty years the temperature of the earth has been increasing by 0.1ºC every ten years. As the earth gets hotter, so the Arctic and Antarctic ice caps will slowly melt. The level of the oceans will rise. A recent report says that the sea will rise by 70 metres in the next five generations.

But there will be many more changes. Certain areas of the earth will become wetter, while others will become drier. Areas which today are green and fertile will turn into deserts. Summers will become warmer. Tropical diseases such as malaria will be common in areas where today they are unknown.

Why is this happening? For many people the answer is simple – greenhouse gases are allowing more of the infra-red heat from the sun to reach us on earth. They believe the solution is also simple and lies with each one of us – stop producing greenhouse gases. In other words, stop using your car!

10 Talking point

1. Are you worried about global warming?

2. What are the effects of global warming?

3. Have you noticed any changes to the weather where you live?

How much of your country would be under water if the sea rose by 70 metres?

Are you prepared to use your car less?

11 The passive

G36 **Compare these two sentences:**

They've knocked down that old cinema.
That old cinema's been knocked down.

Do they mean the same? What is the main difference? Change the sentences below in the same way:

Present perfect

1. They've found an old bomb in the town centre.
   An old bomb. . . . .
2. They've closed the High Street.
   The High Street . . . .

Present continuous

3. They're cleaning the swimming pool today.
   The. . . . .
4. They're building a multi-storey car park.
   A . . . .

Present simple

5. They collect the rubbish on Wednesdays.
   The . . . .
6. They never clean the streets round here.
   The . . . .

Past simple

7. They closed down that restaurant last year.
   That . . . .
8. They found rats in the kitchen.
   Rats . . . .

Past continuous

9. They were still cleaning the toilets when the Queen arrived.
   The toilets . . . .
10. They were repairing the road all last week.
    The . . . .

Going to

11. They're going to build a new airport.
    A . . . .
12. They're going to improve the street lighting.
    The . . . .

Should

13. They should do something about all the litter.
    Something . . . .
14. They should provide more rubbish bins.
    More . . . .

Make sure you read the grammar commentary on the passive and study the examples given.

12 Talking point

Look at these modern pictures of Brighton. Say what each one *used to be* and then make a passive sentence about each one. For example:

It used to be a bank.
It's been turned into a video shop.

1. estate agent's > restaurant

2. insurance office > trendy bar

3. bank > fish and chip restaurant

4. public toilet > sandwich bar

Now talk about your home town and tell the others how buildings have changed and what they have been turned into.

13 Pronunciation

T55 In the conversation, Claire was talking about a pedestrian crossing. She said:

It would be far safer if it was closer to the shops.

In comparative sentences we use far and much to stress what we are saying. Say the following sentences after the tape:

1. It would be FAR safer to build a new crossing.
2. It would be MUCH better to stay at school.
3. We would be FAR better taking the plane.
4. London is MUCH more expensive than Leeds.
5. Telling him the truth would be FAR worse.
6. The oral exam is MUCH more difficult.
7. This coffee's MUCH better!
8. The weather's FAR nicer in July and August.

14 Comparatives

Use the following strong comparatives in the following sentences:

much safer	far more dangerous
much faster	far slower
much more difficult	far easier
much more expensive	far cheaper

1. Going to Paris now only takes about 3 hours. It's . . . . since the tunnel was built.
2. You can pick up a good computer for well under £1,000. They're . . . . than a few years ago.
3. You can't fly to Japan now for less than £600. It's . . . . than ten years ago.
4. Passing your driving test used to be dead easy. Today it's . . . .
5. You just turn up at the airport, buy your ticket, and hop on the next flight. It's . . . . than it used to be.
6. I need some more memory for my computer. It's now . . . . than it was a year ago.
7. Think of all those plane crashes, and wars, and hurricanes! I think the world today is a . . . . place than it was when I was young.
8. Cars today are . . . . than they used to be. You know, with air bags and seat belts.

Use strong comparatives to give your opinion on the following:

School exams today are . . . . . . than they were when I was at school.
Finding a job when you leave school is . . . . now than it was when I left school.

15 Animal idioms

A zebra crossing is a kind of pedestrian crossing where the road has black and white stripes. Use the following animals in the idiomatic expressions below:

cows	ants	goose	dogs
sheep	cat	rat	donkey

1. That night club is dreadful now. It's usually half empty. It really has gone to the . . . .
2. There's something not right about these accounts. I think I smell a . . . .
3. You've done absolutely nothing today! You can't expect to sit around while I do all the . . . . . . work.
4. Peter can't sit in one place for two minutes. He's got . . . . . . in his pants!
5. Please don't tell Mum that we're going to have a surprise party for her. And tell Jane not to let the . . . . . out of the bag either!
6. Our daughter is always watching TV instead of doing her homework. She could watch soap operas till the . . . . come home.
7. I suppose I'm the black . . . . . . of the family. I mean, I went away to New Zealand and didn't get in touch for 20 years.
8. No wonder we couldn't find the right house! You sent us on a wild . . . . . chase! You gave us the wrong address.

16 A really major issue

With a partner, decide which are the three biggest problems facing the world at the moment.

1. . . . .
2. . . . .
3. . . . .

Join another pair and ask their opinions:

So, what do you think about . . . ?
So, what're your views on . . . ?

Try and use as much of the language you have learned in this unit as possible.

Unit 9b : Annoying things

on't believe it. Dogs shouldn't be allowed in this park. It really bugs me. Calm down. I wish they wouldn't do that. I thought it was going to be free. It's a free wo
ook at that. It doesn't really bother me. Whose idea was it, anyway? BMW drivers. It really annoys me. Not again! You're a bit late, aren't you? We've run o
e. Stop going on about it. People who whistle all the time. That's the last thing I need. How was the journey? Don't ask! Mobile phones ringing on trains. There
thing you can do about it. I suppose you think that's funny. It makes my blood boil. We can't have run out of milk again! That's the second time this week! Peop

1 It really drives me mad

Tell a partner which of the things in the list below really annoy you:

1. finding public telephones always out of order when you need to use them
2. chewing gum on the pavement sticking to your shoes
3. people letting their dogs foul the pavement
4. people talking loudly in public on their mobiles
5. finding out before breakfast that you've run out of milk
6. discovering that a pair of trousers you bought have shrunk in the first wash
7. uncollected rubbish in the street

Choose the three most annoying things and discuss how to prevent them from happening.

2 While reading

Read this article about one town's solution to a sticky situation! When you've read it, answer these questions with a partner:

1. What problem is Darlington currently facing?
2. What made the council decide to take action?
3. What solution has been put forward?

A STICKY PROBLEM

A town is attempting to clear its streets of used chewing gum by providing boards where people can stick the remains. Darlington faces a £6,000-a-year bill for clearing up the sticky mess from its pavements and roads. The decision to act was made after complaints from shopkeepers, locals and visitors to the town, which last year won a 'Beautiful Britain' competition.

Up to 30 chewing gum 'parking boards' are to be put up in an area in the town centre, which recently underwent a £1-million facelift.

They will cost £3,000 to provide, are aimed at the 13-to-23 age group, regarded as the worst offenders, and will bear the messages 'Don't Gum Up Darlington', 'Chew It, Bin It' and 'Park Your Gum Here'.

The boards, to be situated at places such as sports centres and cinemas, will have a bull's-eye target so youngsters can aim at them. Keith Atkinson, head of Darlington's environmental and consumer protection department, said, "Most don't see chewing gum as litter, but we are hoping the boards will help people to start thinking that way. We've been flooded with complaints, mainly from visitors, who say gum on the streets, sticking to pavements and shoes, is both unpleasant and makes Darlington look untidy."

3 Word check

Find words from the text to complete the following sentences:

1. Where do you want this put?
   > Could you just . . . . . it up on the board there? Here's a drawing pin.
2. The whole place is in such a . . . . . that it'll take forever to get it sorted out.
3. If the police don't . . . . . soon, parking will end up becoming impossible.
4. The railway station hasn't been painted for about 50 years! It badly needs a . . . .
5. The office was . . . . . with so many applications for the job that it took almost two weeks to read through them all.

4 Comprehension check

Answer these questions on the text:

1. How much does it currently cost to clean up the mess caused by chewing gum?
2. What did the council spend £1,000,000 on?
3. How much will each board cost?
4. What is a bull's-eye?

What do you do with your used chewing gum?

Will Darlington's plan work? Why? Why not?

5 Phrasal verbs

Each of these sentences is a complaint. Form sentences by matching the two parts. Use a dictionary to check the meaning of any of the highlighted phrasal verbs you have not met before.

1. If work carries on like this, I'm going to end up
2. I don't know how they can get away with
3. It drives me mad the way she goes on about
4. The dry-cleaners have completely messed up
5. I just can't put up with

a. these people any longer. I'm calling the police.
b. my shirt! Just look at the state of it!
c. her silly little problems all the time.
d. having a nervous breakdown.
e. such awful service. It should be illegal!

Now use the correct form of these phrasal verbs in these situations:

1. If this weather doesn't get better, I'm going to .... going mad!
   If they don't do something about all these cats, the place is going to .... smelling awful!
2. I really don't think I can .... the flat being in such a state any more!
   I don't know how you can .... him treating you like that. I'd resign if I were you.
3. If I thought I could .... it, I wouldn't pay tax at all.
   She's the office golden girl. They let her .... murder!
4. I somehow spilt my coffee and managed to totally .... that essay I've been working on.
   I don't trust them, personally. I'm sure they'll .... the economy, just like the last government did.
5. She's always .... how hard life is and how little money she has to live on.
   I hate the way he's always .... how much money he's earning and how rich he is.

Look again at these examples. What follows the phrasal verbs – a verb or a noun? Pay close attention to the contexts of each example.
Does anywhere you know get away with really bad service – a restaurant, petrol station, shop? Have you ever messed up anything really important? What was the last thing you really messed up?

6 Complaining

T56 **Complete these conversations with the correct expression to complain about something.**

Complaining about a meal

they made it sound as if
And then, to top the whole thing off
It would've been OK if that was the only problem, but

Joan: How was the meal last night?
Mike: Oh, it was awful! The food wasn't very good. .... the waiters were really rude as well. ...., they tried to overcharge us. Then when we complained about it, ... it was our fault!

Complaining about a situation

I wish they wouldn't
I've got a bit of a problem with
I mean, the last thing I need

Terry: How's college going?
Julie: Not very well, actually. .... my timetable this term. .... is three lectures on a Friday. .... change the timetable every term. Last term was much better.

With a partner, practise reading the conversations above. Take turns being the first and second speaker. Make sure you try to sound annoyed when you're complaining.

7 Role play

With a partner, take turns complaining about the following situations, using expressions from exercises 5 and 6. Spend a few minutes preparing what you will say before you start.

Student A:

1. a terrible English course
2. the trouble you had trying to find a friend's house using the map they gave you
3. roadworks going on right outside your house

Student B:

1. a horrible hotel you stayed in
2. the trouble you had trying to work out how to use a new video recorder
3. a doctor who you don't feel is treating an injury you have properly

Now think of two really annoying situations from your own life that you'd like to complain about. Spend a couple of minutes planning what you're going to say. Then get things off your chest by telling your partner about these things. Use as many expressions from exercise 6 as possible.

Real English: get it off your chest

This is a common idiom which means *to tell somebody about something that is annoying or irritating you.*

8 Useful fixed expressions

Re-order the expressions in colour to complete the following mini-conversations. All of these expressions are typical responses when people are complaining to us.

1. Doesn't it bug you the way shops always charge £9.99 when you know it's really £10?
   > I must admit, ...
   like me things that really bother don't
2. Look, I'm really sorry. There's no way I can come to your party tomorrow night. I've got to work late.
   > Oh, well, don't worry. . . . .
   world not end the the it's of
3. I really thought I'd got the job. I mean, my interview went really well, and then they tell me I'm not even short-listed!
   > . . . .
   let you get down it don't
4. I've got about five bills I'm supposed to pay by the end of the month. What do they think I am? Made of money?
   > Oh well, ...
   you do nothing can about there's it

T57 **Check your answers on the tape, then practise the conversations with a partner. Try to keep the conversations going by adding further comments of your own.**

9 Talking point

Complete the sentence starters below in ways that are true for you:

1. One thing that really drives me mad is . . .
2. Doesn't it really bug you the way . . .
3. It really annoys me when people . . .
4. I don't know about you, but personally I can't stand . . .

Now walk around the class talking to some other students about the things that really annoy you. Try to use some of the fixed expressions from exercise 8 to respond to other people's complaints.

Real English: It really bugs me.

If something *bugs you,* it annoys you. For example:
It really bugs me when people don't return my pen when they borrow it.

10 Was / were going to

G37 **We often make complaints with** was / were going to **like this:**

I thought it was going to be the holiday of a lifetime, but it was a nightmare from start to finish.
I thought the hotel was going to be really romantic, but it was horrible.
The advert said we were going to have a sea view, but we had a tiny room at the back of the hotel.

With a partner, imagine you were on this holiday. Complete the following sentences using was / were going to **and the verb given.**

1. I thought . . . . in a 5-star hotel, but it turned out to be only 3-star. (stay)
2. It said there . . . . a drinks party on arrival, but there was nothing. (be)
3. It said the new swimming pool . . . . ready, but it wasn't. (be)
4. I thought the hotel . . . . a five-minute walk from the beach, but it was more like 20! (be)
5. They said every room . . . . fresh flowers every day, but we didn't see any. (have)
6. The brochure said that we . . . . new towels every day, but we only got one! (have)

You will need to use going to + a passive **in these examples:**

7. I thought we . . . . at the airport and taken to the hotel in a taxi, but we weren't. (meet)
8. I thought our towels . . . . every day, but they were only changed once. (change)
9. It said we . . . . on a moonlight cruise round the bay, but we never were. (take)

11 Your complaints

Now take a minute or two to think of things from your own experience which you thought were going to be better than they actually were. Tell a partner about them.
With a partner, take it in turns to moan about the following:

a bad haircut / hairdo you've just had	I thought it was going to be . . . ., but . . .
a diet someone told you about	I thought I was going to lose . . . ., but . . .
a second-hand car you bought	I thought it was going to . . . ., but . . .
a film you went to see	I thought . . . ., but . . .
your favourite TV show not being on	I thought . . . ., but . . .

Real English: a haircut / hairdo
Both men and women can have their hair *cut*. It is usually only women who have their hair *done*. A *hairdo* implies more than just cutting.

12 One final complaint

Are you a complainer or do you just tend to put up with things? Which of the following situations would you complain about? What would you say?

1. You get to your hotel room and discover they have given you a room at the back. You had booked a room at the front with a balcony overlooking the beach.
2. Your hotel room has a shower and you wanted one with a bath and shower.
3. Your soup has arrived at your table. It is warm, but not hot.
4. Your bill has arrived for your meal. They have overcharged you by £10.
5. Your bill has arrived for your meal. They have undercharged you by £10.
6. It is 2am. You're trying to get to sleep. Your neighbour's dog is barking. You like your neighbours.
7. It is 2am. You're trying to get to sleep. Your neighbour's dog is barking. You don't like your neighbours.
8. Someone has just lit a cigarette on the train. Smoking is not allowed in any part of the train.

Vocabulary

Fixed expressions

Complete the mini-conversations by adding the following fixed expressions:

a. It's a Catch 22 situation, isn't it?
b. Yes, and that's just the tip of the iceberg.
c. It's a bit of a mixed blessing, isn't it?
d. Yes, poor guy. It's a vicious circle, isn't it?

1. John drinks to stop himself worrying about money, and the more he drinks, the more he spends, and so on and so on.
   > . . . .
2. The thing is, I can't get a work permit unless I've got a job and I can't get a job till I've got a work permit.
   > . . . .
3. 100 people have already lost their jobs.
   > . . . . I think there's worse to come.
4. Our neighbours won half a million on the National Lottery last year, but six months later they separated and now they're divorced.
   > . . . .

Expressions with *bother*

Match the following two-line dialogues, then underline all the expressions with bother.

1. Do you fancy coming out for a quick jog?
2. I'm going to complain about that guy smoking.
3. That was really delicious. Let me wash up.
4. I think I'll try that new bar tonight.
5. Sorry to bother you, but have you got the time?
6. I was really upset by her letter.
7. I can't stand mobile phones going off in public!
8. Are you sure you don't mind giving me a lift?

a. No, it's OK. You needn't bother! I'll do it later.
b. Really? Things like that don't bother me.
c. Oh, it's no bother at all. I'm going your way.
d. Sorry, no, I haven't.
e. Oh, don't let it bother you. She didn't mean it.
f. No, I can't be bothered. I'm too tired.
g. Why bother! You'll only start an argument.
h. I wouldn't bother if I were you. It's dead.

Driving vocabulary

Complete the story below by adding the following words and expressions:

one-way	petrol
pull over	turning
U-turn	direction
headlights	brakes

Last Friday night, I was driving to a friend's when I suddenly realised I'd taken a wrong . . . . . . and I was going in completely the wrong . . . . So, I quickly did a . . . . . . to get back to the main road. Unfortunately, I'd gone down a . . . . . . street and all I could see were . . . . . . coming straight towards me, so I quickly slammed on my . . . . . . and tried to . . . . so that I could wait till the road was clear. The car suddenly stalled and I realised that I'd run out of . . . . . . ! What a nightmare!

Complete these collocations with verbs from above:

1. . . . . . . a wrong turn
2. . . . . . . in the wrong direction
3. . . . . . . a U-turn
4. . . . . . . down a one-way street
5. . . . . . . on the brakes
6. . . . . . . out of petrol

Cities

Complete the following using these words commonly used to describe cities:

shanty towns	cosmopolitan
capital	overcrowded
historic	industrial
inner city	centre

1. Is Sydney the . . . . . . of Australia?
2. Sheffield used to be nothing but factories and steel works – very . . . . . , but not any more.
3. New York's one of the most . . . . . places I've lived – every nationality under the sun!
4. There are a lot of slums in the . . . . You know, lots of tiny bedsits with no bathrooms.
5. York's a really . . . . . city – Roman ruins and the medieval walls still in good condition.
6. Thousands of the poorest people live in . . . . . .
7. The city . . . . . . shopping mall is the place to go.
8. There's 17 million people living in Jakarta. It's really . . . . . .

learning advice

How can you continue to improve your English on your own when this course is finished?

One thing is certain: if you do nothing, your English will get worse! The key is motivation.

If you really want to improve, you must actively look for English and do your best to use it.

Here are some of the things you could do:

- **Read an English language newspaper each week.**
- **Watch an English language video every week.**
- **Listen to some English on the radio (eg the BBC World Service) every day. Just have it on when you are washing the dishes or cleaning your flat.**
- **Keep a vocabulary notebook and make a note of something new every day.**
- **Find somewhere local where you can meet and talk to native speakers of English.**
- **Read English books and magazines regularly.**

Unit 10a : Your future

:. What I really want to do is marry a millionaire. It depends really. I'm happy doing what I'm doing. Basically, I just want to be happy. I haven't got a clue. I wis
s just go to Australia. He knows what he wants and he knows how to get it. I might try and learn another language. Money's always a problem. Have I got a
, I really need a change. I'm sick of my job. Just do it! I just take things as they come. How about an Internet relationship? If all else fails, yes! I'm looking all
it? The minute I've finished this course, I'm going to change the world. A safe job, a nice house, children. I'm in a rut. Who cares? The world might come to an

1 Optimistic about the future?

T58 Do you agree with the statements these people are making?

1. The world is a better place than it was 20 years ago.
2. You aren't even safe in your own home today.
3. Young people today have got a good chance of getting a well-paid job when they leave school.
4. There's no such thing as a safe job today.
5. Pollution is getting worse.
6. I feel much more confident than I used to.
7. It's harder than ever to find a good job.
8. People are more aware of environmental issues than they used to be.

Complete the following sentence by adding *a pessimist* and *an optimist*:

. . . . is someone who always thinks the glass is half-full, while . . . . always thinks it's half-empty.

Now mark the eight statements with an O or a P depending on whether you think they are optimistic or pessimistic.

2 Talking point

Tell your partner how optimistic you feel about your own future, the future of your country, or the future of the world.
The young people in this picture are protesting against the cutting down of trees. Would you?

3 While you listen

T59 Rachel and Nick, two friends both in their last year at university, are chatting over coffee. Listen to them talking about what they see themselves doing in the future. As you listen, try to complete the following sentences:

1. Nick's thinking about .... but it depends on ....
2. He'd like to .... but he probably won't have ....
3. Rachel wants to .... and ....
4. If she .... then she'll .... Otherwise, she'll probably go ....

Listen again and try to fill in the gaps in the conversation.

4 Talking point

Are you the kind of person who could just suddenly go abroad for six months, on the spur of the moment? Have you ever done anything like that?

Have any of your friends ever gone off to work in another country?

Where did they go?

Is it possible to plan too much for the future?

Real English: the Aussies

This is an affectionate term used by British people for Australians. Australia is also called *Oz* by both the Australians and others.

New Zealanders are known as *kiwis* after the name of a bird unique to that country. Australians call British people *poms* or *pommies*. Because of the close connections between the three countries, there is a lot of friendly rivalry between them – particularly connected with sport!

Now you're talking!

Rachel: So, have you had any more thoughts about what you're going to do next year, then?

Nick: Mm. I don't know, really. I mean, ... that it might be a good idea to do that art course I was telling you about, but it all depends on my results.

Rachel: So what about France? .... going to Paris a while back?

Nick: Oh, for that French course? Well, I would still like to do it, but I just don't know if I can afford it.

Rachel: Oh, I know what you mean. Money's always a problem, isn't it? I mean, ... next year is learn to drive and buy a car, but I'm not sure if I'll have the cash. ...., I'm just so sick of having to get buses everywhere.

Nick: Dreadful, aren't they? You wait half an hour and then three come along at the same time. So, you're .... just going to be staying around here, just trying to save up some money, then?

Rachel: Yes, I suppose so. It depends, really. I mean, if I can find a good job then I'll stick around, but otherwise .... eventually is going back to Glasgow.

Nick: Oh right, because you grew up there, didn't you?

Rachel: Yes, that's right, yes, so I suppose I do see myself ending up there eventually.

Nick: Yeah.

Rachel: So, ... you do this art course, what do you see yourself doing after that, in the long term?

Nick: Oh, I don't know. No idea really. I haven't thought that far ahead. I'll just .... and see what happens.

Rachel: Just listen to us, Nick! We just sound so boring! .... go off somewhere together this summer, you know, maybe – I don't know – work abroad for six months?

Nick: What? You mean picking grapes in France? That kind of thing?

Rachel: Yeah, or, I don't know – working in a hotel in Spain, or –

Nick: Or going to Australia. If the Aussies can work over here, ... go and get a job over there?

Rachel: Yeah, I'd love to do that. Where's the paper? What's the cheapest flight to Sydney?

Nick: Now you're talking!

5 Pronunciation

T60 Rachel and Nick used these responses:

I don't know, really.
It depends, really.

Did you notice how the speaker didn't pause before *really*? It is common to add really, then, **or** actually **at the end of what you are saying without pausing. Listen to these dialogues on tape. Then practise saying them.**

really

1. So, do you think you'll buy a digital TV?
   > It depends how much it costs, really.
2. Do you fancy watching the late film?
   > Well, it's more your kind of thing, really.
3. I wish you'd come and try the opera.
   > No, you go on your own. It's not my cup of tea, really.

then

4. So, what do you do for a living, then?
   > Well, actually, I'm an income tax inspector.
5. Are you just trying to save some money, then?
   > Who isn't?
6. Are you busy, then?
   > No, we're very quiet at the moment.

actually

7. So, are you going to Blackpool again this year?
   > No, we're off to Florida, actually.
8. Joe's your second husband, isn't he?
   > No, he's my third, actually.
9. Still driving this old banger, George?
   > Well, my other car's a Porsche, actually. I try not to mention it. It just makes people jealous.

Real English: What do you do for a living, then?
This use of *then* is very common in spoken English. It does not mean *not now*. It makes a question sound less direct and aggressive. For example:

So, have you got any children, then?
Are we going in your car, then?
Is Sandy coming, too, then?

It can also mean *in this situation*. For example:

I've got no Guardians left, I'm afraid.
> I'll have the Independent, then.

I think we're going to miss the ten past five.
> We'll just get the five-thirty, then.

This use of *then* is not slang or bad English. It is perfectly standard in informal speech.

6 Starting with *what*

Rachel said What I'd really like to do next year is learn to drive. ***What* can be placed at the beginning of a sentence to give special emphasis to what follows. It means *the thing that* ... .**

What I really need to do is get away for a break.
What I'd really like to do is learn to drive.
What I was thinking of doing is going abroad.

Grammar practice

Choose the best expression from above to start the sentences below:

1. Your company is sending you to Japan, so you have to start learning the language.
   What . . . .
2. You think it would be a great idea to buy a flat in the next couple of years.
   What . . . .
3. You have no money and desperately need to start saving.
   What . . . .
4. You think you would quite like to travel round India in the not-too-distant future.
   What . . . .
5. You've always wanted to start a family as soon as you get married. (next month!)
   What . . . .
6. You've had an idea – maybe go abroad for Christmas this year rather than stay at home.
   What . . . .

Grammar in context

Complete the following in ways that are true for you:

1. What I really need to do before the end of the week is . . .
2. What I'd really like to do this/next summer is . . .
3. What I was thinking of trying to do next year, if I get the chance, is . . .
4. What I'd really like to be doing in a few years' time is . . .

Now tell a partner about what you have thought of, giving more details if you can.

7 Plans for the future

Complete the following common answers to the question What are your plans for the future?

wait and see	perfectly happy
can't really	take things
change	see myself

a. I'm . . . . doing what I'm doing.
b. My plans . . . . fairly often.
c. I can't . . . . staying there for much longer.
d. I'll just have to . . . . what happens.
e. I just . . . . as they come.
f. I . . . . say yet. It all depends.

Practise saying these expressions.

Now complete the situations below by adding the most appropriate expression:

1. I'm a fairly laid-back kind of person. I mean, ... and only worry about things if and when they happen.
2. So what're you going to do once you get back to Madrid?
   > Well, I might try and get a job as a chef, but yesterday I was thinking about maybe going back to college. Ask me again in a week! . . . . , you know.
3. So how's it all going?
   > Well, to be honest, I'm really fed up at work. . . . . It sounds to me like it's time to move on.
4. So what're your plans for the future?
   > Well, right now, life's great. Maybe in a couple of years I might change my mind, but at the moment . . . .
5. So are you still off to Kenya in the spring?
   > Well, I'm not 100% sure just now, because my dad's still very ill, so . . . .
6. So how long are you going to be staying here for?
   > . . . . on my girlfriend. If things work out between us, we might think of getting married and settling down.

Do any of these expressions apply to you in your present situation? For example:

I wouldn't say, "I just take things as they come" now, but I might've done when I was 18 or 19 because I didn't have a job then, and I didn't really know what I wanted to do in the future.

8 Planning structures

What would you like to do in the future? What do you see yourself doing? Complete each of the four sentences below using two different endings:

a. my own country	e. back to university
b. abroad	f. with my girlfriend
c. a new job	g. somewhere nicer to live
d. studying	h. where I grew up

1. I might try and find
   . . . .
2. I can see myself going
   . . . .
3. I'd really like to spend a bit more time
   . . . .
4. I really want to go back to
   . . . .

Now do the same with the following:

i. reading	n. south
j. a better laptop	o. my family
k. to buy a flat	p. for a video recorder
l. house	q. sport
m. the world	r. a new car

5. It'd be good to see a bit more of
   . . . .
6. I'm thinking of moving
   . . . .
7. I'd like to start doing a bit more
   . . . .
8. If I can, I'll probably save up
   . . . .
9. I think I'm going to buy
   . . . .

How many of the sentences above are true for you?

9 A year away

In the conversation on page 151 Rachel and Nick talked about going to Australia. If you had a year free, what would you do? Do any of these appeal to you?

1. building a primary school in Bangladesh
2. working for an aid agency in Ethiopia
3. going on an expedition to the North Pole
4. working with homeless people in Manchester
5. sailing round the world
6. writing a book

10 Sentence adverbs

Here are five useful sentence adverbs. Use them to express your attitude to what comes next.

Basically Ideally Hopefully
Realistically Eventually

Match each of the meanings below with one of the adverbs:

a. I think this will happen in the end.
b. This would be the best possible result, but it might not happen.
c. I would like this to happen.
d. This will probably happen, even though I may not want it to.
e. This is my general/simple view of what will happen.

Complete the following sentences in a way that is true for you. Then compare with a partner.

1. Basically, what I'd really like to do in the future is . . . .
2. Ideally, I'd love to be able to . . . . sometime in the next few years, but realistically I'll probably . . . .
3. Next year I can see myself . . . . and after that I'll hopefully . . . .
4. Well, if I carry on doing what I'm doing now, eventually I'll . . . .
5. Well, you know that I really like . . . . , so ideally I'd like to end up . . . .

11 Finding out more

When we talk to people we know, we often try to find out more about things they've mentioned. Below are three common ways of doing this:

So what about those holiday plans you were telling me about?
> Oh, what? Estonia? It's been put on hold – because of money problems, you know.

So have you had any more thoughts about going back to your country this summer?
> Yes, I have, actually. I've already bought the tickets. We're off in August.

And are you still thinking of going back to college next year?
> Well, I might do. It all depends on whether I can find someone to look after the baby.

Write down two things that you know your partner is thinking of doing in the future.
Try to find out more by using the highlighted expressions above.

12 Chat rooms

Can you explain what a chat room is? If not, read the text below. In your own words, explain to a partner what a chat room is and how to enter one.

How would you explain what a chat room is to someone who a) doesn't own a computer b) lived 100 years ago?

MAKE FRIENDS

Are you lonely tonight? Then why not enter a chat room? If you've got a computer and Internet access, then millions of people all over the world are just waiting to hear from you. If you haven't visited a chat room before, it is very easy. Your server may have its own, in which case, just click on chat. Alternatively, use a search engine such as Yahoo and click on chat. From there you will have the choice of hundreds of different chat room topics.

Going into a chat room is a bit like going to a huge party where you don't know anyone. You walk into the room and panic. After you have given your personal details and chosen your password, just wait for a while to see what is going on before you start to take part. Remember this is live. It is happening in real time. When you type in a message, the other people can read it virtually immediately.

If you don't like what is going on or you can't understand it, it's probably because there are too many children just playing around. Choose another topic you are interested in and try that room. There are few rules. Just remember to watch your language and DON'T SHOUT. Typing in capitals means shouting and is considered rude. There are a few abbreviations which can help shorten your message and which you will need to understand. Here are some of the most common:

brb: be right back (if you have to go to the loo for a minute)
btw: by the way
cu: see you
lol: laughs out loud
myob: mind your own business
newbie: new user
pvt: private
rofl: rolls on the floor laughing

You never know – one evening you might find the person of your dreams. You won't be the first person to fall in love with someone they first met in a chat room.

13 Talking point

Have you ever taken part in a chat room?

Is there a chat room which you visit regularly?

What nationalities are the people you chat with?

Have you got to know anybody through a chat room? Have you ever tried to meet them?

Would you consider starting a friendship – even a romance – with someone you first met in a chat room?

14 Collocations

Look back at the text on chat rooms to complete these collocations:

1. This laptop comes with Internet . . . .
2. You can either . . . . or . . . . a chat room.
3. Which . . . . engine do you prefer?
4. You don't need to take . . . . if you don't want to.
5. What password have you . . . . ?
6. It's dead easy. Just . . . . on chat.
7. You may have to give some personal . . . .
8. The chatting happens in . . . . time.

15 If-expressions

Here are several 'if-expressions' in English which we use to talk about our future plans. For example:

Well, if everything goes according to plan,
I should be living in Morocco this time next year.

Complete the following conversations using the correct form of these verbs:

go fall fail work

1. So what do you see yourself doing when you get back home?
   > Well, if all . . . . . . well, I should be able to get my old job back. Touch wood!

2. So you're off to Australia for Christmas, are you?
   > Yes, if everything . . . . . . according to plan. We're just waiting for our visas.

3. So you've applied for the manager's job?
   > Yes, and if that . . . . . . through, I think I'll look elsewhere.

4. We're too late to get tickets for the final now!
   > Well, if all else . . . . . . , we'll just have to watch it on TV, then.

5. So you're thinking of building your own house. That sounds a bit ambitious.
   > Yes, it is a bit, but my father's a builder, and if nothing . . . . . . wrong, it should only take about a year or so.

6. What am I going to do about my boyfriend?
   > Tell him you're going to work in Greenland if he doesn't ask you to marry him – and if that doesn't . . . . . . , then nothing will!

Now go back and underline the full expressions with *if*.

Real English: Touch wood!

It is common when using *Touch wood* to touch a piece of wood at the same time. This is a common British superstition when talking about the future. For example:

I'm seeing the doctor tomorrow and if all goes well, I'll be back at work pretty soon, touch wood!

This is a very old superstition. The idea is that if you touch wood – the same material which the cross of Christ was made of – you will have good luck. Do you do anything like that?

16 Talking point

With a partner, decide what you think people in the situations below might be saying. Use some of the 'if-expressions' above.

1. a student sitting his final examination at university
2. a hitch-hiker on a motorway in France heading south with a sign saying "India or bust!"
3. a young couple who've just got engaged
4. when you see a flock of swallows in September in Britain
5. when you see a field with hundreds of large fat turkeys in November

17 The present perfect

Conjunctions

G38 **Use the following in the sentences below:**

a. I've finished my exams
b. I've saved up enough money
c. my brother's finished his military service

1. Once . . . . ,
   I'm going to buy a Bang and Olufsen stereo.
2. As soon as . . . . ,
   I'm going to organise a huge party for him.
3. The minute . . . . ,
   I'm going to have a year off and see the world.

Which of the highlighted expressions above is the most emphatic? Why?

Grammar in context 1

The present perfect has the idea of completion. Use the correct form of these verbs in the following situations:

open	finish	be
visit	discuss	get

1. Once . . . . filling in the form, let me have a look at it to make sure you haven't made any mistakes.
2. The minute you . . . . your exam results, ring me. I might have a job for you.
3. Once I . . . . on holiday somewhere, I never go back. I like to try a new place every year.
4. Let me know your decision as soon as you . . . . it with your wife.
5. As soon as I . . . . John in hospital, I'll ring you and let you know how he is.
6. You can't take it back to the shop, once you . . . . the packaging.

Now complete the following in ways that are true for you personally:

1. The minute . . . .
2. Once . . . .
3. As soon as . . . .

Now tell these to your partner and have short conversations about each one. For example:

As soon as I've saved up enough money, I'm going to buy a new mountain bike.
> Oh really? How much do they usually cost?
It depends on the type, but you can get them from about £150 upwards.

Grammar in context 2

Here are nine things which people plan to do. When are *you* going to do them? Try to start with:
As soon as, Once, or The minute ...

1. ring an old friend *(who?)*
2. fix something that is broken *(what?)*
3. travel the world *(where to?)*
4. get married and settle down
5. learn something new *(what?)*
6. buy a new car *(what kind?)*
7. buy some new clothes *(what exactly?)*
8. write to someone *(who?)*
9. retire

18 Talking point

Chat to some other students in your class about what you plan to do when this course is finished. Talk about how you intend to keep working on your English. Discuss the following and how important each is:

reading novels in English
going to an English-speaking country
making English-speaking friends
writing to people in English
listening to English language radio
going to films in their original version
continuing with an English course
buying English language newspapers
having English language radio on all day
keeping a vocabulary notebook

When you have finished your discussion, compare your ideas with those on page 149.

I'm Pierre. I come from Bordeaux. I try to watch CNN news every day. I have a friend in Norway and we keep in touch in English by e-mail.

Unit 10b : The world of work

perk of the job, isn't it? A proper contract? He's a real slave-driver. What do you do exactly? Pay tax. I'm usually home by four. What's the pay like? Sorry I
te. I'm a model in my spare time. How are things at work? If you pay peanuts, you get monkeys. What a nice uniform! Does it come with the job? I wish I h
t that Monday morning feeling. Anyone for coffee? What's your boss like? Could we possibly discuss my salary? It's enough to live on. Stress? We're very bu
ent. You don't know the meaning of the word. I'm rushed off my feet. Only two weeks paternity leave? We get a bonus at Christmas. It's a good firm to work f

1 Working conditions

Mark each of the following ideas from 1 (not important) to 5 (very important), depending on how important they are for you when you're looking for a job.

being able to work flexi-time
getting holiday pay and sick pay
earning a good salary
doing a really interesting job
knowing your job is secure
not being stuck behind a desk all day
doing something useful for society
being able to work from home
getting a company car
getting maternity or paternity leave

Compare your answers with a partner. What else would you add to this list?

I'm Nuria. I come from Spain. I'm living in Britain trying to improve my English. I've got a part-time job in a fish and chip shop.

2 Vocabulary

Complete the sentences with these expressions:

full-time	lots of benefits
paid holiday	unfairly treated
sick pay	income tax
maternity leave	contract

1. When my son was born, I took .... for three months and then went back to work part-time.
2. I've been there six years now, but I've never been given a proper ....
3. When I broke my leg, I managed to get two months' ....
4. .... starts at 20% and goes up to a maximum of 40%.
5. I appealed to a tribunal because I felt I'd been ....
6. I used to do only two days a week, but I work .... now.
7. I can't go away much, because I only get three weeks' .... a year.
8. The best thing about my job is that I get .... – a company pension, private health insurance and things like that.

Vocabulary discussion

What is the difference between a benefit (a perk) **and** a right? **Which of the following are benefits and which are your rights?**

a company pension	sick pay
a company car	maternity leave
private health insurance	holiday pay

Think of all the jobs you or your parents have done. How many of the sentences above were true for each job? Tell your partner about your answers.

3 While reading

A casual worker **normally works for a company, but without a contract of employment. He or she is not permanently employed and in many countries has few rights. Read the article opposite about two casual workers who had a problem with their employer. When you have read it, answer these questions:**

1. Why did Mrs. Carmichael and Mrs. Leese take their employers to court?
2. What was the judge's decision?
3. What are the implications of this decision for other casual workers?

4 Talking point

Have you ever done any casual work? How were you treated? What was the money like?

Who is the worst employer you've ever worked for?

Do casual workers get the same rights and benefits as full-time employees in your country?

5 Vocabulary work

Discuss these questions:

1. What is the difference between a full-time, part-time, and casual worker?
2. What are the usual reasons people get sacked?
3. What is the difference between getting sacked and being made redundant?
4. Do you know of anyone who has been unfairly dismissed from their job?
5. What benefits and perks would you like in a job?

Useful collocations

Complete these collocations from the text:

1. Workers should have a contract of . . . .
2. They won the . . . . . to the same benefits.
3. They were . . . . . . holiday pay.
4. They were refused a . . . . . . contract.
5. Workers can now . . . . . for the right to sick pay.
6. Workers can appeal . . . . . unfair dismissal.
7. You cannot be . . . . . . without reason.
8. This judgment is a . . . . . . breakthrough.

WE CAN WORK IT OUT

Two casual workers, who were never offered proper contracts of employment, yesterday won the right to the same benefits as full-time workers.

A judge said that because Mrs Carmichael, 35, and Mrs Leese, 36, had signed letters accepting jobs at Blyth Power Station, they should have been treated the same as any full-time employee of National Power. However, the two women were denied holiday and sick pay and other benefits normally given to full-time staff.

Despite taking income tax from their pay, making the women wear company uniforms, and giving them the use of company cars, National Power tried to insist that Mrs. Carmichael and Mrs. Leese never worked directly for the company. They were, therefore, refused a proper contract, and were not given any employment protection or benefits.

The judge's decision means that casual workers can now fight for the right to sick pay, holiday pay, maternity leave and other benefits. The judgment also means that casual workers can appeal against unfair dismissal by their employer if they are sacked without reason.

A solicitor acting on behalf of the two women said it was a major breakthrough in employment law, which was likely to have a very positive effect on the working lives of thousands of men and women employed on a casual basis.

6 How are things at work?

Match the common questions about work on the left with the typical answers on the right:

1. How are things at work?
2. So what exactly does your job involve then?
3. Have you been doing it long?
4. What are the hours like?
5. What's the money like?

a. It's OK. It's enough to live on.
It's not very good – more like slave-labour!
Well, actually, I don't think it's any of your business!

b. They're OK, the usual nine to five.
Awful. I don't usually get home until ten!
Great. I'm usually home by two or three.

c. Crazy! I've been rushed off my feet all week!
Oh, we've been pretty quiet, actually.
Oh, it's OK, the same as ever.

d. Well, I'm in charge of Accounts.
I do all the marketing.
I deal with all the complaints that we get.

e. Yes, it's about ten years now, I suppose.
No, I've only just started, actually.
Yes, too long!

In your country is it acceptable to ask someone how much they earn?
Are you happy to talk about how much you earn?

7 Reporting

G39 **In the text the judge said that the women** had signed **letters accepting jobs. The solicitor said that it** was **a major breakthrough in employment law which** was **likely to have a very positive effect on the working lives of thousands of men and women. What do you think their actual words were when they spoke?**

Here are some reports of speech. Write what you think the people actually said.

1. He said he was leaving for good.

. . . .

2. She said she didn't care.

. . . .

3. Then he told her he'd just won some money.

. . . .

4. She told him that it didn't make any difference.

. . . .

5. Then he told her he'd won £3 million!

. . . .

6. She told him that money had no effect on her.

. . . .

7. Then he told her he'd lied to her.

. . . .

8. She said he'd lied to her ever since they met.

. . . .

9. He said there was only one thing he hadn't lied about.

. . . .

10. She asked him what that was.

. . . .

11. He said he'd always loved her and that he'd always been true to her.

. . . .

12. She said she would forgive him if he agreed to stop spending all his money on lottery tickets.

. . . .

Grammar discussion

How did the verbs change?

Now discuss and agree the best way to report the following comments. Begin, And then he said . . .

1. "I'm emigrating to Australia."
2. "It's time to leave if we want to catch the train."
3. "I crashed my new Mercedes last week."
4. "You're silly not to have applied for the job."
5. "I'll see you later."
6. "I've made a terrible mistake."
7. "My house has been on the market for a week."
8. "There must be a mouse in the house."
9. "There's no time like the present!"

8 What do you do again?

With a partner, decide what these people do for a living.

Which of the jobs in the pictures would you most / least like to do? Why?

What do you think these jobs would involve? Could you or would you do any of them?

9 What's the job?

T61 Now listen to three of the people above talking about their jobs. As you listen, try to decide what the job is. Then compare answers.

1. . . . .
2. . . . .
3. . . . .

10 Role play

You are one of the people in the pictures in exercise 8. Spend two minutes thinking about how you would answer the questions in exercise 6, using the typical answers if necessary.

Your partner should then ask you the questions and try to guess which job you do.

11 The ideal boss

Match the pairs of endings to these answers to the question *What's your boss like?*

1. Well, he's not exactly the most	a. sit at his desk and give orders! talk to the other guys about football.
2. He's awful, a real	b. domineering. bossy and dictatorial.
3. Dreadful! All he ever does is	c. on the phone to her boyfriend! jetting off to Paris and Rome on business trips!
4. Oh, he's great, he's a really	d. easy-going and easy to talk to. nice and friendly.
5. Oh, she spends the whole time	e. me about things that aren't my fault. everyone about spending too much money.
6. Terrible, she's really	f. approachable person I've ever met, but he's OK, I guess. intelligent bloke I've ever worked for, but I guess he's OK.
7. Oh, she's brilliant, really	g. dictator! slave-driver!
8. He's always getting on to	h. nice guy. good person to work for.

12 Talking point

Do any of those comments remind you of your boss or one you have known?

Tell your partner what kind of a boss you think you'd make and why.

Which person in your class do you think would make the best boss? Why?

Is it important for a boss to be friendly and approachable or is it OK if they're a bit distant from their staff?

Are there other qualities which are more important?

How many other words can you think of with a similar meaning to boss? For example: *head, employer, manager, supervisor, superior,* etc. Which do you prefer?

13 Boss jokes

T62 **Below are three joke answers to the question, "So what's your boss like?" Discuss with your partner which one you find the funniest and why:**

1. He's really flexible. He lets me come in any time I want before nine, and then lets me leave whenever I want after five!
2. He's so mean that if you're three minutes late for work, he fines you, and if you turn up five minutes early he actually starts charging you rent!
3. He's really hard on late-comers. Actually, one day one of his assistants turned up over an hour late, covered in blood, and as he staggered over to his desk, my boss went up to him and asked him where he'd been. The assistant apologised and said he'd fallen down three flights of stairs. "What?" said my boss, "that took you a whole hour, did it!"

Listen to the jokes on tape. Mark the stresses and pauses. Then tell them to each other in pairs with one student asking, *"So what's your boss like, then?"*

14 The future continuous

G40 **Notice the highlighted verbs in the following situations:**

Look, we'll be passing your front door, so it's no trouble giving you a lift.
The twins will be starting school this autumn, so I'll have a lot more free time.

Both situations are about the future (will **and** 'll). **In both cases the verb is extended in time** (passing **and** starting). **It is common for this future continuous form to be followed by a clause that begins with** so. **Form complete sentences by matching the two halves of the sentences below:**

1. I'll be doing some work in your area soon,
2. I'll be going back to Japan in the autumn,
3. I'll be meeting my boss next week,
4. I'll be doing a computer course in April,
5. I'll be writing my MA thesis all summer,
6. I'll be going down to my dad's next Saturday,

a. so I'll talk to her about my chances of promotion then.
b. so then I'll be an expert on the Internet.
c. so don't try and call me until Sunday night.
d. so I'll be working in the library a lot.
e. so I'll pop in and say hello if I get a chance.
f. so I'll try and get you a cheap Walkman, shall I?

Grammar in context

Now complete the following conversations by adding the appropriate sentences from above:

1. Well, I really like this Sony, but it's just too expensive really.
   > Well, look, ...
   Oh, that'd be great if you could. I'd pay you for it, of course.
2. So, John, when are we going to see you next, then?
   > Well, ...
   Oh great, try and make it around 12 or so and then maybe we could have lunch.
3. So, are you looking forward to the holidays then?
   > Well, no actually. ....
   Oh well, I'll be thinking of you while I'm lying on the beach.
4. So, you're still having problems getting on-line?
   > Well, actually, things are looking up. ......
   ....
   Oh well, that's a start, I suppose.
5. I'll give you a call over the weekend about the following week.
   > Yeah, that's OK, but ....
   Sure. I probably won't know what I'm doing until then anyway.
6. What? You still haven't been promoted! You must be really fed up.
   > Well, hopefully things will change. ....
   ....

15 Career plans

Walk around the class and chat to some other students about the kind of work you see yourself doing in the future, where you see your career going in the short-term, any long-term career plans you've got and so on. Try to use as much of the new language from this unit as you possibly can. For example:

If we meet in 10 years' time, if everything goes according to plan, I'll have my own company. I'll be driving a top-of-the-range Mercedes. I'll be living in a huge house with my own private plane. I'll own an island somewhere hot.

Vocabulary

Work or job?

Use work **or** job **to complete the following:**

1. He's never done a day's . . . . . . in his life!
2. Are you still looking for a . . . . , then?
3. It's quite hard . . . . . . finding a flat in a big city like Milan.
4. It's a dirty . . . . . . , but someone's got to do it!
5. I know the money's not very good, but at least you're getting some good . . . . . . experience.
6. Oh, the kitchen looks lovely now. You've made a really good . . . . . . of it.
7. I'm sorry, but I can't let you use the phone to ring Australia. It's more than my . . . . . .'s worth!
8. I've been up to my eyes in . . . . . . all week!

Phrasal verbs with *up*

In this unit we met save up, getting really fed up **and** things are looking up. **Use these verbs in the gaps below and then go back and underline the phrasal verbs.**

do	cheer	put	turned
beat	hung	come	bottling

1. This really strange thing happened last night. An old friend from school just . . . . up on my doorstep, totally out of the blue!
2. That was weird. Whoever it was on the phone just . . . . up as soon as they heard my voice!
3. Once we've saved up enough money, we're going to . . . . up our flat a bit.
4. Why don't I cook tonight, if you're not feeling up to it?
   > Wow! That's the best idea you've . . . . up with all week!
5. I wish you'd . . . . up a bit! It's really starting to get me down, seeing you like that!
6. I got mugged last year, and when I wouldn't give them my watch, they . . . . me up really badly.
7. It's not healthy, you know, ... up all your negative emotions like this. It's much better to just get things off your chest.
8. If you're stuck for somewhere to stay, we could always . . . . you up on our sofa.

Hopes and dreams

Complete these sentences about the future:

1. My parents have . . . .
2. I wish . . . .
3. I hope . . . .
4. I've always dreamed . . . .
5. One of my greatest fears is . . . .
6. I'm really looking forward to . . . .
7. I'm really dreading . . . .

a. I didn't have to go back to Japan next year.
b. great expectations for my future.
c. ending up on my own when I'm old.
d. the summer! It gets so unbearably hot here!
e. seeing all my old friends again once I'm back home.
f. of maybe one day going to live in Hawaii.
g. I can find a good job once I graduate.

Working life

Complete the story below by adding these missing words:

interview	sack	promoted	called
job	salary	unemployed	got
career	applied	manager	

When I first graduated, I was . . . . for three months. With a wife and child to support, I desperately needed a . . . . , so I . . . . for all kinds of things until eventually I got an . . . . with this big firm. It went well, and a week later I got . . . . back for a second interview, after which they told me I'd . . . . the job. I couldn't believe it! The starting . . . . was £25,000 a year. Everything went well for the first month – until the . . . . called me into his office. I was convinced I was going to be . . . . , but I actually ended up getting the . . . . ! I don't suppose it was wise telling him he was incompetent! Oh well, I never really wanted a . . . . in baby care products anyway!

Review : Units 9 and 10

1 Tenses

Choose the correct verb form:

1. They still haven't been fixing/fixed our TV yet.
2. The restaurant was redecorated/being redecorated, so we had to find somewhere else.
3. Bills have to pay/be paid within a month, or else they cut your electricity off.
4. I wish they'll/they'd do something about all the stray dogs in the park.
5. I see/I'll be seeing Bill later, so I'll ask him if he got your e-mail.
6. I thought the film will be/was going to be great, but it wasn't as good as the book.
7. As soon as I'll have finished/I've finished this course, I'm going to look for a new job.
8. Once I get back from holiday, I'm going to try/I try and find a place of my own to live.
9. That bridge should've been widened/been being widened years ago.

2 Multiple choice

Choose the correct alternative:

1. What would be really great is if my parents
   (a) will buy me a car!
   (b) bought me a car!
2. Shopping in the US is (a) much cheaper.
   (b) much more cheaper.
3. If it doesn't stop raining, I'm going to end up
   (a) going mad!
   (b) to go mad!
4. (a) All Kate ever does (b) All Kate is ever doing is get other people to do her job for her!
5. I'd like to end up with my own business, but
   (a) basically,
   (b) hopefully,
   (c) realistically,
   I'll probably have to work in the family shop.
6. The minute (a) I've finished (b) I'll finish this report, I'm going home!
7. (a) He told me to wait outside till he was ready.
   (b) He said me
8. Don't ring before 9. (a) We'll be having dinner.
   (b) We'll have dinner.

3 Expressions

The following common expressions all occurred in units 9 – 10. Use them in the sentences below:

a. just doing what I'm doing
b. don't let it get you down
c. wait and see
d. if everything goes according to plan
e. I know what you mean.

1. I'm getting tired of Mr Owens complaining about our department all the time.
   > Look, ... There's nothing you can do about it. Forget him!
2. I just can't believe that all the banks here shut at four! How can I get to one if I'm working!
   > Yes, ... It'd be far better if they were open in the evening.
3. So, what exciting plans have you got?
   > Nothing, really. To be honest, I'm quite happy . . . . for the time being.
4. So, you're going to be in Nepal next year, then, James?
   > Yes, ... !
5. So, did you get that job you applied for?
   > I haven't heard yet. I'll just have to . . . .

4 Conversation

Put the jumbled conversation below into the correct order. The first line is correct.

a. So, how are things at work?
b. I think of nothing else, actually! I've got an appointment with Personnel tomorrow so that might make a difference.
c. Dreadful, to be honest! I feel as if I'm going to end up having a nervous breakdown!
d. How will that help?
e. Well, I'll have the chance to talk about the problems in my department. They might listen. On the other hand, they might not!
f. Is it as bad as that? Have you had any more thoughts about leaving them?

1 a	2	3	4	5	6

5 Collocations

Match the verbs with the expressions on the right to make complete collocations:

1. deny	a. a flat nearer where I work
2. see	b. house
3. move	c. with all the complaints
4. buy	d. a problem
5. take	e. about her problems all the time
6. deal	f. a bit more of my wife and kids
7. tackle	g. things as they come
8. go on	h. a casual worker his holiday pay

6 Idioms

Match up the following to make complete idioms:

1. That bar has gone	a. of the family.
2. He let the cat	b. off my feet all week!
3. I'm the black sheep	c. off your chest.
4. I think I smell	d. my mind.
5. I've been rushed	e. out of the bag!
6. It's good to get things	f. a rat.
7. ... and to top	g. to the dogs.
8. I changed	h. the whole thing off ...

7 Real English

Match these 6 questions with the six responses:

1. So, when will you be able to go back to work?
2. So, what happened in court? Did they fine you?
3. So, was Ian interested in coming out tonight?
4. Have you tried talking about working in Wales with your girlfriend?
5. Where's Darren from? He's American or something, isn't he?
6. Do you know where the guys who wrote this book are from?

a. I think so. Well, I mean, he said he would try and come.
b. Yeah, I think one of them's a Kiwi and the other one's a Pom!
c. Yes, £500, and I've been banned from driving for six months.
d. No, I think he's an Aussie, from Canberra or somewhere.
e. In a week or two, I think – touch wood!
f. Of course I have. I mean, that was the first thing I actually did. But she just won't talk about it. Whenever I mention it, she changes the subject!

8 Vocabulary quiz

Answer the following 20 questions with a partner. Then compare your answers with another pair. Who got most answers right?

1. If I send you on a wild goose chase, what do you come back with?
2. Apart from people, what else might need a facelift?
3. Are shanty towns nice places to live or not?
4. What is the difference between working flexi-time, full-time and part-time?
5. If you find your boss domineering, does it mean you get on with him or not?
6. Is an optimist afraid of the future?
7. Is it only bosses who can be bossy?
8. When would a woman get maternity leave?
9. If women get maternity leave, what do men get?
10. If you find your boss approachable, does it mean you get on with her or not?
11. Name one other thing apart from water that an office can be flooded with.
12. If someone is in charge of all the complaints, do they make complaints or deal with them?
13. What is the capital of the country you're studying in? And what's the capital of Australia? Bulgaria? Chile? South Africa?
14. Give an example of a vicious circle.
15. Give one reason why you might appeal to a tribunal.
16. If your little brother gets away with murder, has he killed someone?
17. If you do most of the hard work on a job, does this mean you have done the rat work, the dog work, or the donkey work?
18. If I tell you that they've banned all on-street parking, who are 'they'?
19. Name three benefits you would get if you worked for a big company
20. Can you name three rights you would expect in your job?

Tapescript

Unit 1a

T1 Who's who? (page 9)

Kirsty

Kirsty? She's really interesting. She's quite sporty and musical as well. She plays the piano a lot. She's actually quite good. She's in her twenties and has got lovely shoulder-length blonde hair.

Nick

You'd like Nick. He's really nice. He's very easy-going. He's got a great sense of humour. He's only 35. He's got really short hair – shaved, I think. He's very interested in photography and arty things.

Jenny

Jenny is in her forties. She's a really energetic sort of person – always doing things. She's got a very warm personality and enjoys helping other people. She has short, dark hair and dark eyes.

Matt

Matt is still at university. He's really friendly and is one of the most popular people I know. He's very hard-working and serious, but he's also a lot of fun. He's got fair hair and he wears glasses.

T2 The Brother from Hell! (page 10)

Melanie: I can't remember. Do you take milk?
Simon: Please, but no sugar. Thanks. It's weird, you know, but I've been to your house three times now, and I still haven't met your parents.
Melanie: Yes, they're out a lot. My dad works for the BBC and my mum's a, she does sort of temping work for a company. You know, like an advertising agency. They're both really busy.
Simon: Oh, they sound really interesting.
Melanie: Do you think so? I find my dad a bit dull, to be honest. He works late every day, even works some weekends, doesn't read, doesn't go out. I mean, don't get me wrong, he's quite nice, but I don't know, I just don't have anything to say to him. I think the thing is, we just don't spend enough time together.
Simon: How old is he then?
Melanie: About 55, I think. I can never really remember.
Simon: Oh yeah.
Melanie: But my mum's lovely. She's really nice, a bit too nice though, sometimes, always trying to look after me. She worries about me leaving home. She's a bit over-protective, if you know what I mean. I'm an only child, so ...
Simon: Oh, I didn't know that.
Melanie: What? You mean you can't tell!
Simon: I don't know. I've never thought about it, I suppose.
Melanie: So, what about you? Have you got any brothers or sisters yourself?
Simon: Yes, I've got one of each, actually.
Melanie: Oh right. Older or younger?
Simon: My sister's two or three years younger than me, but my brother's quite a lot older. He's about 40 now.
Melanie: Do you get on with them all right? You haven't really talked about them very much.
Simon: Well, my brother, not that well, actually. He's different from me, a bit old-fashioned, a bit traditional. Well, actually, he's a bit, how can I put it, right-wing. You know – things aren't what they used to be, more police, death penalty – that kind of thing. He's a bit of a fool, actually.
Melanie: Oh, well, it takes all sorts, I suppose.
Simon: But my sister, she's great. We get on really well. We've got the same kind of sense of humour.
Melanie: Just a pity about the brother from hell, eh?
Simon: Yes. Oh, but he's not that bad. We get on all right, as long as you steer clear of certain topics. Anyway, you were telling me about your parents.
Melanie: Oh, there's not much to tell, actually.

Unit 1b

T6 Giving bad news (page 18)

1. Can you give me a lift home?
   > I'm sorry, I'm afraid I can't. I lost my licence last week – had a bit too much to drink and got stopped by the police!
2. Do you think I could get that camera back off you sometime soon?
   > I don't know how to put this, but I think I lost it last night while I was out. I'm really sorry, but I've searched everywhere and I can't find it. I'll get you another one. I'm extremely sorry.
3. Have you heard from Jan recently?
   > Well, actually, I haven't – not for about six months – we had a bit of an argument last year.
4. Is your grandfather any better?

> I'm afraid not. We're very worried about him. But then, he IS 90.
5. So, has Peter had his results yet?
   > Well, yes, I'm afraid he has. He didn't pass – so he's got to re-sit part of his exams in July.
6. Are you feeling all right, Steve?
   > Well, actually, no. I've just had some very bad news.
7. Hello, how are you?
   > Oh, fine thanks. Well, actually, I think I'm getting the flu, so I'd stay away if I were you.
8. I thought you had a dog.
   > We did. But unfortunately it ran out into the street and was run over. I'm afraid we had to have it put down.

Unit 2a

T8 So what shall we do tonight? (page 24)

Dan: So what do you feel like doing tonight? Any ideas?
Helena: Well, I'd quite like to see a film, or, I don't know, see if there's any good bands around, if you're into bands.
Dan: Yes, that's an idea. What kind of music do you like, then?
Helena: Oh, all sorts, really, you know, a lot of pop and I quite like blues and jazz and things like that.
Dan: Oh, really? I'm more into dance music myself, so maybe ...
Helena: Well, if you'd rather, we could always go and see a film. I like really scary things.
Dan: What? You mean like *Halloween?*
Helena: Yes, that kind of thing, and I also quite like action movies, you know, car chases, guns, bombs, anything that's fast and exciting.
Dan: Oh, right. To be honest with you, I'm not really that keen on violent films.
Helena: You're kidding! And I thought this was going to be the perfect relationship!
Dan: So did I! But it doesn't sound like we've got all that much in common, really, does it?
Helena: Oh come on, there must be something we can do!
Dan: Let me think. Well, I suppose we could always go clubbing.
Helena: What? Somewhere like Paradox?
Dan: Is that the new place that's just opened?
Helena: Yes, just last week. Right, so how about going clubbing, then?
Dan: OK. Why not? Do you go much yourself?
Helena: No, not all that often, actually. A couple of times a year, I guess.
Dan: Oh, me too now, but I used to go a lot more when I was younger – almost every weekend. The thing was, though, it just got to me after a while, staying out dancing all night and then having to go to work first thing in the morning. I'm getting a bit too old for it now.
Helena: Oh, well, that's that off the menu then! So, what shall we do then?
Dan: I don't know. Couldn't we just get a video, and a curry, and have a nice quiet evening in in front of the telly?
Helena: Oh, you've got to be joking! We're not in our graves yet. I mean, that's the kind of thing my parents are probably doing right now! Look, it's not what I'd normally do on a Monday night, but let's give clubbing a go! It might be a laugh.

T11 Not really keen (page 26)

1. I love nearly all winter sports.
   > Really? I'm not really very keen on them, myself. I once broke my leg skiing and it put me off – for life!
2. Going out with a crowd of friends and having fun, that's what I really like doing.
   > Do you? It's not really my kind of thing, I'm afraid. I prefer to go out with just one or maybe two people. I hate crowds.
3. I'm really interested in politics.
   > Oh, it's not really my kind of thing, I'm afraid. I don't really understand what makes all the parties different. They all seem the same to me!
4. I'm really into older music, you know, before 1967.
   > Are you? I'm not really that keen on anything before 1980.
5. My favourite kind of things are comics and cartoons.
   > I don't really like things like that myself. I don't see the point of them. I prefer a good novel – the longer the better!
6. I'm really into roller-blading. It's a bit like roller-skating.
   > Are you? It's not really my kind of thing. I'm always worried I might get hurt.

T12 Not as often as I used to (page 29)

Interview with June, the bus driver.

1. How often do you work in the evenings?
   > Not all that often, actually, just when I have to. Some people like the extra money, but I prefer to be at home with my kids.
2. How often do you get up early on Saturdays?
   > Oh, all the time! My boys play football every Saturday morning, so I've got to be up by 8.

3. How often do you see your parents?
   > Well, they live in Wales, so, not as often as I'd like to. I suppose I see Mum and Dad two or three times a year.
4. How often do you have your hair done?
   > Oh, about every fortnight. It depends really. If I'm going out somewhere, I might have it done specially.
5. How often do you see your best friend?
   > Whenever I can. She lives quite near me, but she's a nurse, so she's got to work at weekends quite a lot.
6. How often do you go away for the weekend?
   > Oh, only a couple of times a year. It's difficult when you've got children.
7. How often do you go to the cinema?
   > Oh, hardly ever. I usually wait till films come out on video and then get them for an evening.
8. How often do you go clubbing?
   > Not as often as I used to. Before I got married, I used to go out every weekend.

Unit 3a

T14 Who did what? (page 40)

Speaker 1: It was total chaos. We had all our things lying around all over the place, making it impossible to get in or out of the house. It took forever to get everything all boxed up and into the van. We had to make five trips just to shift everything – and then there was the unpacking! What a nightmare!

Speaker 2: It was a real weight off my shoulders. Things had been bad for a while and I'd just got to the point where I just couldn't stand it any more. Every day there was hell, but then once I'd handed in my notice, I felt free again, and the future suddenly looked a lot brighter.

Speaker 3: I had my last one and stubbed it out, and then I felt really pleased with myself, but a couple of hours later the craving really started and I found myself absolutely dying for one. I was so tempted during the lunchbreak, but I managed to get through the whole day without one, and after that it was plain sailing.

T15 Forty a day!!! (page 41)

Phil: Just time for a quick smoke. Oh sorry, do you want one?

Jason: No, thanks. I gave up years ago.

Phil: Good for you! I've given up even trying to give up!

Jason: Yeah, it's a nightmare, isn't it?

Phil: Tell me about it! I don't know how you managed it.

Jason: Well, it's funny, but it was my job that did it. I mean, I'd been smoking for years, and you know it's destroying your lungs, don't you, and I knew I wouldn't be able to become a fireman if I didn't give up.

Phil: So what's becoming a fireman got to do with it? Is it the fire risk or something?

Jason: No, it's just that I knew I'd have to pass a physical to get in, and I wouldn't be able to do that if I was smoking 40 a day.

Phil: 40 a day! Just as well you gave up! So, how come you decided to become a fireman, anyway?

Jason: Mm, I'd have to think about that. I suppose it all goes back to when I got out of college. I wanted to do something exciting and different, you know, and a friend of my dad's was in the local fire brigade.

Phil: Oh, right. So, he helped you, did he?

Jason: Yes, he helped me get the job. I mean, I knew I didn't want to spend my life sitting in an office pushing bits of paper round a desk or stuck in front of a computer screen!

Phil: Yeah, I know exactly what you mean. I'm half-blind already! So, why did you decide to move to London, then? Was it for work or because of a relationship or what?

Jason: Well, it was mainly work, but also because I was just really fed up with where I was living at the time.

Phil: It was down in Crawley, wasn't it? It's pretty quiet down there, isn't it?

Jason: Quiet? Yeah, it's dead. There's absolutely nothing to do there.

Phil: So, was it the right decision, then?

Jason: What? Becoming a fireman?

Phil: No, no, moving to London, I mean.

Jason: Oh yeah, definitely. I love it. I don't think I could live anywhere else now.

Phil: No, it's the same for me. It gets you after a while, doesn't it? It's like a drug.

T17 Jokes (page 46)

1. How come you drive with your brakes on?
   > I want to be ready in case there's an accident!
2. How come you were born in New Zealand?
   > I wanted to be near my mum!
3. I wish I'd brought the piano with me.
   > How come?
   Because I left the plane tickets on it!
4. When I was a kid, I ran away from home. It took them six months to find me.
   > Six months! How come it took them so long?
   They didn't look!

T19 Saying you don't know (page 48)

1. You don't know anything about this party tomorrow night, do you?
   > I'm afraid not, but if you find out about it, let me know.
2. You don't know how this program works, do you?
   > No sorry, I'm afraid I don't. You could try asking Rob. He's our computer expert.
3. You know that guy I met last month in London? Can you remember where he was from?
   > No, how am I supposed to know things like that? I never even met him, did I?
4. Do you know Dennis's surname?
   > I've got no idea, but I'm sure I'd recognise it if I heard it.
5. Have you got any idea where Rose is?
   > Don't ask me. I haven't seen her all day.
6. Excuse me, do you know where I could get something to eat around here?
   > Sorry, I can't help you, I'm afraid. I don't live around here.
7. So, have you got any idea why you were made redundant?
   > No, I haven't got a clue. They just said it was because there was no work.
8. Do you know where my mobile is? I've no idea where I've left it.
   > How should I know? You had it last. You must've just left it somewhere.

Unit 3b

T20 Strong adjectives (page 53)

1. It must've been really hot in Greece.
   > Hot? It was boiling! That's why we made sure the hotel had air-conditioning.
2. Oh, you're from Sao Paulo originally, are you? It's a pretty big city, right?
   > Big? It's enormous! That's why I moved to a small town out in the country.
3. How's your flat? It must be a bit cold with all this snow we're having.
   > Cold? It's freezing! That's why I've decided to have central heating put in.
4. It's pretty quiet down in Devon, isn't it?
   > Quiet? It's dead! That's why I decided to move to the city!
5. You must've been pretty surprised when you read the report in the papers.
   > Surprised? I was shocked! That's why I contacted my solicitor straightaway.
6. It's a bit small in here, isn't it?
   > Small? It's tiny! You can hardly swing a cat in here!
7. So is he good-looking, then, your new boyfriend?
   > Good-looking? He's gorgeous! You'll die when you see him!
8. It must've been a bit scary, going so high up like that.
   > Scary? It was terrifying! There's no way you'll catch me doing that again!

Unit 4a

T22 Planning expressions (page 57)

Gavin: Well, tonight I guess I'll probably just stay in and have a quiet night in front of the telly. I'm a bit too tired to do anything really. Then on Saturday morning, I'm going to try to get up really early and go off and play football with some mates of mine in the park, which should be fun. Then Saturday afternoon, unfortunately, I've got to do some things around the house, because the place is a tip at the moment. Then, Saturday night, I've got a big night because a friend's having a party at her place and Karen's going to be there. And Sunday morning I imagine I'll need to have a lie-in just to recover, really, and then in the afternoon, I've got a friend coming over. And then, finally, Sunday night, I guess I'll probably just stay in and have an early night.

T23 Thank goodness it's Friday! (page 58)

Steve: Thank goodness it's Friday! This week's been dragging on forever.

Ken: Tell me about it! So what are you up to this weekend?

Steve: Oh, nothing special, really. This evening, I'm just going out for dinner with my parents.

Ken: Oh, that should be nice.

Steve: Yes, we're going to this little French place near where I live. The food's great there, and then tomorrow I've got to get up really early – at least for me! – and do some cooking, because I've got some people coming over in the afternoon. And I'll have to give the place a really good clean as well. And, I'm not sure, but I think we'll probably be going out after that – to see a film or something. We haven't really planned anything. What about yourself?

Ken: Well, tonight I'm supposed to be going out with some people from my old job, but I don't really feel like it any more. I'm feeling really tired.

Steve: So you're just going to stay in, then?

Ken: Yes, because tomorrow night I've got a big night. I'm going to my friends Pete and Rachel's party. It's on a boat.

Steve: Oh, that sounds great. Whereabouts?

Ken: Down by the river. You know, in the docks.

Steve: Oh yes, I know where you mean. I went to a

party there myself a while ago.
Ken: Right. Is it OK down there?
Steve: Yes, it's great, but it's not all that big. There's not that much room on the boat.
Ken: Mm, sounds cosy!
Steve: Oh, yes, you can get really close to people! Lots of sweaty bodies!
Ken: I don't think it's going to be that sort of party!
Steve: Well, you never know. If you're lucky, it might become one! – No, I'm only joking, it's actually a great place for a party.
Ken: Good. I'm really looking forward to it. But then on Sunday, unfortunately, I've got to do some things for work.
Steve: No rest for the wicked! Well, listen, I might give you a ring on Sunday, then, just to hear all about your quiet night out down on the river!

Unit 5a

T28 Lifestyle (page 72)

1. I hate going there but I'd run out of things to wear and, to be honest, some of my clothes were a bit – well, you know, so I thought I'd better have some clean shirts before work on Monday.

2. It's not something I normally do but I just felt like a bit of fresh air and it was a nice summer's evening and quite a few shops were open so, yes, it was really nice.

3. Not much really. I was quite tired when I got in from work so I just got myself something to eat and then wrote a couple of letters, read a bit, watched a bit of TV and before I knew it, it was nearly midnight.

4. Sorry I couldn't ring you last night, but Wednesdays are my evenings for Art History. It's something I've always been interested in so I thought I'd try this ten-week course that the university's running this autumn.

T29 The Worst Disco in Town! (page 73)

Lucy: Hey, Rose, there's a letter for you.
Rose: Thanks. You must've got in late last night. I didn't even hear you come in – and I went to bed after one.
Lucy: I did, actually, yes. I went and met some old friends from college that I hadn't seen for ages.
Rose: Oh, did you? That must've been nice.
Lucy: Yes, we had a drink and a chat and caught up with all the gossip. You know what it's like.
Rose: Uh-huh.
Lucy: Then we had something to eat and then another drink and then we ended up going on to this awful disco in town.
Rose: Oh, did you? Which one? Not 'Stardust'. No, surely not 'Stardust'?
Lucy: I'm afraid it was, actually – and it was really terrible, just full of kids and the music was so loud I could hardly hear myself think. It was like being back at school all over again. Kids of 14 acting as if they were 18!
Rose: I could've told you that!
Lucy: This boy came up to me – you know, bottle of beer in his hand, acting all macho, and asked me to dance! I bet he hadn't even started shaving!
Rose: And did you?
Lucy: What? Dance with him? Of course I did! Then I told him I was 35!
Rose: You're so cruel.
Lucy: Well, I just figured it was better he found out sooner rather than later that I was old enough to be his mum!
Rose: I thought you were supposed to be there talking to old friends.
Lucy: I was, but there was so much noise, you couldn't really have a proper conversation. And then to top it all, I missed the last train home and had to get a cab and didn't get in until three!
Rose: Didn't you? You must be feeling exhausted this morning, then.
Lucy: Yeah, I could do with another hour or two in bed, that's for sure. Anyway, what about you? How was your night?
Rose: Oh, it was OK. I just did a bit of shopping on my way home, cooked myself some ramen noodles.
Lucy: Cooked yourself some what?
Rose: Ramen noodles, you know, just Japanese noodles.
Lucy: Oh, OK.
Rose: They're really quick and easy, and then I just did a bit of tidying-up, you know, nothing amazing or anything, read for a bit, watched a bit of telly – some film – you know the kind of thing that's on late on Channel 4. Actually, I was so tired, I fell asleep in the middle of it!
Lucy: Oh, don't! You're making me feel even more exhausted!

T32 Linking ideas (page 77)

1. It was so cold, my hands felt like they were going to fall off.
2. I was so exhausted, I just went straight to bed as soon as I got in.
3. I was so hungry, I could've carried on eating all night!
4. It was so hot, I could hardly breathe.
5. His conversation was so dull, I could hardly stop myself from yawning.
6. I was so angry, I could've killed him!

7. I was so worried, I rang the police.
8. The film was so bad, I walked out halfway through.

Unit 6a

T 33 Hair today, gone tomorrow! (page 88)

Cathy: So, we've got to take this one and then change at Cannon Street, right?

Diane: Yes, that's it. Hey, did I tell you about what happened with me and my dad on the underground last year?

Cathy: No, go on, what?

Diane: Well, about a year and a half ago, I decided to get all my hair cut off, right? I always used to have really, really long hair – ever since I was about 14 or 15, you know – way down past my shoulders – parted in the middle like curtains. So, anyway, about a week after I had it all cut off, you know – really short – and I looked quite different.

Cathy: Yeah, I bet.

Diane: So, anyway, I was going home on the tube, and I was half asleep because it was 5 or 6 o'clock and I was just standing there, minding my own business – and little did I know that my dad was actually coming back from a business trip abroad, passing through London on the underground to get his train back to Durham. And guess what? He got into the same carriage as me! The doors closed behind him. So there I am, standing there face-to-face with my own father! I don't recognise him at first, but then I think, "Ah, that's my dad," and, of course, he's obviously only seen me with really long hair for the last ten years, and so I'm standing there, staring at him and he keeps on glancing at me nervously, thinking, "Who's this lunatic staring at me?" and I'm thinking – you know, it's the strangest feeling not being recognised by your own dad – so I just stood there thinking, "Well, shall I just get off at the next stop without telling him, or shall I risk giving him a nervous breakdown and a heart attack by saying, "Hello Dad"? But, anyway, eventually I went, "Hello Dad" and he went, "Diane!" and then said how he was getting really worried because he thought I was a pick-pocket or a drug addict or something who'd been getting ready to pinch his wallet or something – and, um, yeah, that was a pretty strange and funny thing.

Cathy: Yeah, really strange.

T34 Story-telling expressions (page 90)

A: Did I tell you about what happened to me in France last year?

B: No, I don't think you did. Go on.

A: Well, I was on holiday with my parents in this little village near the sea, and we ran out of French money.

B: Really? That's awful.

A: Yes, so we went into town to find a cash machine – which we did, no trouble. Anyway, when we put the card in the machine, it just started spitting out loads and loads of money.

B: You're joking! So did you keep it?

A: Of course we did! Wouldn't you?

Unit 7a

T37 Long time, no see! (page 105)

Sharon: Barry! Hi, how are you? I haven't seen you for ages.

Barry: Hello Sharon. Long time, no see.

Sharon: I know. So how're you doing?

Barry: I'm all right, thanks. And you?

Sharon: Yeah, not too bad. So, what've you been up to since I last saw you?

Barry: Not a lot – working mostly – I've been working really long hours this week, getting really fed up with it, you know.

Sharon: Really?

Barry: Yeah, but I went down to Kent last weekend, for my grandma's birthday party.

Sharon: Oh, how old was she?

Barry: 85. It was really great. We went for this lovely meal and then we went for a walk along the beach. It was good to get out of the city.

Sharon: I bet. I keep meaning to have a weekend away myself.

Barry: I know. You get to the point where you really need it, don't you? If you don't get out of London from time to time, it starts driving you crazy, you know. Anyway, what about you? What've you been up to?

Sharon: Well, on Sunday morning I went and saw that exhibition at the Royal Academy.

Barry: Oh yes, the one there's been all that fuss about – dead sheep and pictures of toilet rolls and things.

Sharon: Yeah, my friend Angela – she's at art school – she kept nagging me to go and see it, so I went.

Barry: And what did you think of it? Was it any good?

Sharon: Oh, I actually thought it was excellent, really good and challenging. There's only one thing that made you go 'yuk!' – the dead sheep. I think it's meant to shock you, though. Anyway, after that, I popped round and saw a friend of mine, Richard, for a bit and then we

Sharon: went up to Camden market to do a bit of shopping.
Barry: Oh yeah, it's nice up there on a Sunday, isn't it?
Sharon: Yeah, it's great. And then I spent the evening at my mum's, which was nice.
Barry: Oh, that sounds good.
Sharon: Yeah, and apart from that, I've been doing things for college, really.
Barry: Uh-huh, still being a good student, then. Oh look, there's my bus into town. I'd best be off. I'll see you soon, then. Bye.
Sharon: Yeah, OK, bye.

T39 Oh, that reminds me! (page 110)

1. I visited Alan in hospital last Friday to see how he was getting on.
   > Oh, did you? I keep meaning to go and see him myself. How was he?
2. I spent all day Sunday catching up on all my mail.
   > Oh, that reminds me. I must send in my passport application.
3. I went and saw that musical, *Chicago*, last week.
   > Oh, I've been meaning to go and see that for ages. Was it as good as everybody says?
4. I went round to Mike and Sue's the other day to see that new car they've been telling everyone about.
   > Oh, that reminds me. I must give them a call. I haven't spoken to them for ages.
5. I went down to Bristol for the weekend a couple of weeks ago.
   > Oh, really. I've been thinking about having a weekend away myself. Were you camping or what?
6. I just stayed in last night and watched TV. There's a great thing on on Fridays at the moment about Antarctica.
   > Oh, that reminds me. I must record that new thing on Channel Four tonight. It's meant to be really funny.

Unit 7b

T40 Recommending (page 114)

Conversation 1

A: I went and saw an exhibition at the Hayward Gallery earlier in the week.
B: Oh, did you? What was it?
A: It was a collection of photos from the first lunar landing.
B: Oh, really? It sounds quite interesting. What was it like?
A: Quite good actually, the photos were really great, quite amazing – some of them.
B: So you'd recommend it then?
A: Yes, you should go and see it.

Conversation 2

A: I went and saw that new exhibition at the National Gallery the other day.
B: Oh, did you? Which one's that again?
A: Oh, it was this collection of Flemish paintings from the seventeenth century.
B: Oh really? What was it like?
A: Well, I didn't think much of it myself. It was all a bit dull, you know.
B: So you wouldn't recommend it then?
A: No, I'd give it a miss, if I were you – unless you really like that sort of thing, of course.

T41 Recommending expressions (page 114)

1. It's OK if you're into that sort of thing.
2. It's a must.
3. I really recommend it.
4. I'd give it a miss if I were you.
5. It's well worth a visit.
6. It's not worth the entrance fee.
7. It's not really my cup of tea.

Unit 8a

T45 So what was it like? (page 119)

Conversation 1

A: Mm, this fish is really nice. What's yours like?
B: Well, I'm beginning to wish I'd had the same as you. I usually love chicken, but, to be honest, this is a bit bland. The waiter said it was in a delicious mushroom sauce, but it doesn't taste of anything.

Conversation 2

A: So, is the wine all right?
B: Mm, yeah, it's all right, but it's nothing special.
A: I see what you mean. £15 for this! It really is very ordinary.
B: Yes, it's a bit disappointing, to say the least. Shall we send it back?
A: No, I can't be bothered. It's not that bad.

Conversation 3

A: Didn't you go to see *Macbeth* last week?
B: Yeah, it was brilliant. I've been to it a few times before, but I think this was the best production I've ever seen.
A: Yeah, someone I work with went and said it was wonderful. I wish I'd been able to get a ticket.

T46 Not exactly Shakespeare! (page 120)

Paul: Guess what I went and saw last night – *Titanic* – it's on again this week at the Duke of York's.
Mick: Oh, yeah. I saw that when it first came out. What did you think of it? Did you like it?

Paul: Oh, it was great. I really enjoyed it. I thought the special effects were amazing, and the acting was brilliant. It's one of those films where, you know, when I first heard about how much money they'd spent on it, I just couldn't believe it, but it was really great. It was a bit like one of those old disaster movies, you know, like *Towering Inferno* or *Earthquake*, only better.

Mick: Really? I'm surprised. I thought the acting was a bit wooden myself, and the dialogue was just awful. I can't believe you actually thought it was worth the money they'd spent on it. I mean, didn't you find the whole thing just a little bit over the top?

Paul: Oh, no. Not at all. I thought it was brilliant.

Mick: But the acting was horrendous!

Paul: Well, I know it's not exactly Shakespeare, but it's not meant to be, is it? I'll tell you something weird though, there was this guy sitting next to us who snored all the way through the film!

Mick: Really? That must've been really annoying. How could anybody actually sleep through all that noise!

Paul: I don't know – just dead tired, I suppose.

Mick: Yeah, I guess so, but really though, didn't you think it was all just a bit too sentimental?

Paul: I know what you mean, but I honestly didn't. I really thought it was all done just right. It was so romantic.

Mick: Oh well, each to his own. Have you seen *Bomb Alert 2* yet?

Paul: No, I haven't even heard of it. Who's in it?

Mick: Um, Jean-Paul van Klam, he's great in it and, um, that woman from *Kamikaze*, you know who I mean. Remember? She was Turtle-woman too, although I must admit she wasn't very good in that.

Paul: Oh, her. So what's it like? Any good?

Mick: Yeah, it's great – if you like blood all over the place and that sort of thing.

Paul: Oh, it doesn't really sound like my sort of thing, actually. I think I'll give it a miss.

T49 Asking linked questions (page 125)

1. What's his house like? Is it big?
   > Yes, it's huge. It's got four bedrooms and an enormous garden.
2. What was that book like? Was it interesting?
   > No, it wasn't, actually. It was really boring. In fact, I didn't even finish reading it.
3. What's your new job like? Are you enjoying it?
   > Yes, very much. My boss is really nice and it's quite well paid, really.
4. What was Tunisia like? Was it warm?
   > Yes, it WAS quite warm, but not as hot as the last time we went.
5. What's this CD like? Is it any good?
   > Yes, I think it's great. The third track is brilliant.
6. How was the match? Did you win?
   > No, we lost three – one. It was just terrible. I can't believe it.

Unit 8b

T50 And when you can't answer (page 131)

1. Sorry, my mind's gone completely blank.
2. Wait, it'll come to me in a minute.
3. Wait, it's on the tip of my tongue.
4. Sorry, I can't remember off the top of my head.

T52 Contradicting (page 131)

1. You went to see that war film? It doesn't sound like your sort of thing.
   > Well, actually, I've always liked things like that.
2. So it's not a British film then? I thought it was.
   > Yes, it is. It's British, but it was financed by an American company.
3. So you can't make it tonight?
   > Yes, I can. I'm still coming. I'm just running a bit late, that's all.
4. You've never seen *Star Wars?* I can't believe it!
   > Yes, I have! I saw it ages ago. Everyone's seen it!
5. They didn't release the soundtrack, did they?
   > Well, actually, I think they did. I think I've seen it in a second-hand record shop.
6. That never came out on video, did it?
   > Yes, it did. And what's more, I've got it!

Unit 9a

T53 More sleeping policemen! (page 137)

Chris: Did you hear about that kid who was knocked down on Junction Road the other day?

Claire: Yes, it was awful, wasn't it? Still, it's hardly surprising, is it?

Chris: What do you mean?

Claire: Well, there are always accidents down there, aren't there, especially with the speed cars go at. And, well, basically, the crossing's in the wrong place, isn't it? I don't know why they've never moved it. I mean, it'd be better if it was exactly opposite the shops, wouldn't it?

Chris: Yes, I know what you mean. They could do something to slow the traffic down, couldn't they? Maybe they could put sleeping policemen there or something like that.

Claire: Yeah, maybe – maybe one every so often would help, but what would be really great is if they had one of those speed cameras.

Chris: Big Brother, you mean!

Claire: No, they really make a difference. You should see how they've slowed the traffic down where my parents live.

Chris: Yeah, I suppose you're right. I'm only against them because I got caught by one last month.

Claire: You're kidding!

Chris: No. A hundred and fifty pounds it cost me! A fine and six penalty points!

Claire: Oh, that's terrible!
Chris: Yeah, but it was my own silly fault. I mean, I should've known better, but going back to what you were saying about the crossing, you're right. It would be far safer if it was closer to the shops, because that's where everybody crosses, you know. That's where most kids cross, so it'd be more sensible if it was moved down.
Claire: Yes, I think that's the root of the problem. I mean, it does seem a funny place for a crossing. And I would've said the other problem with it is the fact that lots of cars park all round there.
Chris: Yes, that does make it difficult to see, I suppose. Apparently, the car that hit that kid had just driven off from there.
Claire: Oh, really? Had it? Well, you see what I mean, then.

T54 Disagreeing (page 139)

a. Well, I agree up to a point, but *(it's not as simple as you think.)*
b. Yes, I know what you mean, but *(it's time we did something about it.)*
c. Yes, but don't you think that *(we should wait till later?)*
d. Yes, but don't forget that *(everything costs money.)*

Unit 9b

T56 Complaining (page 145)

Complaining about a meal

Joan: How was the meal last night?
Mike: Oh, it was awful! The food wasn't very good. It would've been OK if that was the only problem, but the waiters were really rude as well. And then, to top the whole thing off, they tried to overcharge us. Then when we complained about it, they made it sound as if it was our fault!

Complaining about a situation

Terry: How's college going?
Julie: Not very well, actually. I've got a bit of a problem with my timetable this term. I mean, the last thing I need is three lectures on a Friday. I wish they wouldn't change the timetable every term. Last term was much better.

T57 Useful fixed expressions (page 146)

1. Doesn't it bug you the way shops always charge £9.99 when you know it's really £10?
   > I must admit, things like that don't really bother me.
2. Look, I'm really sorry. There's no way I can come to your party tomorrow night. I've got to work late.
   > Oh, well, don't worry. It's not the end of the world.
3. I really thought I'd got the job. I mean, my interview went really well, and then they tell me I'm not even short-listed!
   > Don't let it get you down.
4. I've got about five bills I'm supposed to pay by the end of the month. What do they think I am? Made of money?
   > Oh well, there's nothing you can do about it.

Unit 10a

T59 Now you're talking! (page 151)

Rachel: So, have you had any more thoughts about what you're going to do next year, then?
Nick: Mm. I don't know, really. I mean, I was thinking that it might be a good idea to do that art course I was telling you about, but it all depends on my results.
Rachel: So what about France? Weren't you talking about going to Paris a while back?
Nick: Oh, for that French course? Well, I would still like to do it, but I just don't know if I can afford it.
Rachel: Oh, I know what you mean. Money's always a problem, isn't it? I mean, what I'd really like to do next year is learn to drive and buy a car, but I'm not sure if I'll have the cash. The thing is, I'm just so sick of having to get buses everywhere.
Nick: Dreadful, aren't they? You wait half an hour and then three come along at the same time. So, you're basically just going to be staying around here, just trying to save up some money, then?
Rachel: Yes, I suppose so. It depends, really. I mean, if I can find a good job then I'll stick around, but otherwise what I was thinking of doing eventually is going back to Glasgow.
Nick: Oh right, because you grew up there, didn't you?
Rachel: Yes, that's right, yes, so I suppose I do see myself ending up there eventually.
Nick: Yeah.
Rachel: So, assuming you do this art course, what do you see yourself doing after that, in the long term?
Nick: Oh, I don't know. No idea really. I haven't thought that far ahead. I'll just take it as it comes and see what happens.
Rachel: Just listen to us, Nick! We just sound so boring! Why don't we go off somewhere together this summer, you know, maybe – I don't know – work abroad for six months?

Nick: What? You mean picking grapes in France? That kind of thing?

Rachel: Yeah, or, I don't know – working in a hotel in Spain, or ...

Nick: Or going to Australia. If the Aussies can work over here, why can't we go and get a job over there?

Rachel: Yeah, I'd love to do that. Where's the paper? What's the cheapest flight to Sydney?

Nick: Now you're talking!

Unit 10b

T61 What's the job? (page 160)

First job

A: So, what exactly does your job involve then?

B: Well, basically, I prepare all the prescriptions and keep a check on all the drugs we have in stock. I also give advice to people who come in with minor problems. You know the sort of thing – what cream to use for a rash, what to take for an upset tummy – that sort of thing. Sometimes, I'm just like a shop assistant, selling things over the counter; other times I feel like I'm a doctor.

Second job

A: So, how long have you been doing this, then?

B: All my life – since I left school. I worked with my father, and now I've got my son working with me. I really enjoy working with wood. I love taking a piece of wood and turning it into something useful. I learned everything I know from watching my father and the older men at work. Now, it's great passing on my skills to younger guys.

Third job

A: So, do you enjoy doing what you're doing?

B: Yeah, well, I mean, somebody's got to do it, haven't they? Just think, if nobody did it, what would the place be like? I mean, when I was a boy, if you dropped something, the police would be after you, but these days people don't care. They just drop everything – coke cans, cigarette packets, newspapers, everything, you name it, I've picked it up. Mind you, I've found the odd £20 note. I'd never work indoors. I just couldn't stand it.

Grammar Introduction

Vocabulary – words and collocations

You already know a lot of English grammar, and you probably keep a vocabulary notebook, so it is easy to think that the two best ways to improve your English are to improve your grammar and learn new words. But there is another thing you can do which is even more helpful, especially now you already know quite a lot of English. You need to notice **collocations** and record them in your notebooks. So, what are collocations?

We hardly ever use one word on its own. You will usually meet a new word in a text, where it is used with other words. So, it is always better to learn **groups of words which are often used together.** These groups of words are called collocations.

Fill in one word in each of these:

I must've . . . . . . a mistake.
Have you . . . . . . your homework?
He's a really . . . . . . smoker - at least 20 a day.
Shall we . . . . . . a . . . . . . break?

You already know 'chunks' of language. For example:

make a mistake	do your homework
heavy smoker	have a short break

These are all collocations.

If you learn words one by one, it is easy to make mistakes when you use the words later. You might, for example, say *I think I did a mistake*, or *I haven't made my homework*. If you learn words in groups, you will not make as many mistakes.

There are lots of different kinds of collocations. It is a good idea to have a different section in your notebook for collocations of different kinds. Here are some of the most important kinds:

curly hair	(adjective + noun)
pay the bill	(verb + noun)
theme park	(noun + noun)
highly offensive	(adverb + adjective)
on either side of	(prepositional phrase)
on the other hand	(adverb phrase)
talking to some old friends	(verb + adjective + noun)

The most important kind of collocation you need to learn is *verb + (adjective) + noun*. For example:

apply for a new job

Notice that you may know all the words in a phrase, but not recognise the phrase **as a single chunk. Learning it as a chunk is very important.** Notice the opposite of *a light colour* is *a dark colour*, but the opposite of *a light meal* is *a heavy meal*. You cannot translate *light* into your own language until you know what word is used with it. That is why collocation is so important. If you write collocations in your notebook, make sure you translate the collocation **as a single chunk.**

Grammar – the verb

You have met lots of English tenses – the present continuous, the present perfect, the present perfect continuous and so on. You might think the system is very complicated. In fact, it is fairly simple. There are only three really important patterns that you need to understand.

Continuous forms

Here are some examples:

The present continuous:
Oh no, it's raining again.

The past continuous:
I was working all last weekend.

The present perfect continuous:
There you are! – I've been trying to ring you all morning.

In every example the speaker sees the action as extended between two points in time, so a continuous form is used. This is also true for events organised before now which will happen after now:

We're having a few friends round on Friday. Would you like to come?

The game is being played next Tuesday.

The continuous always emphasises that the speaker thinks the event is extended over a period:

Next week I'll be lying on the beach in the sun.

Perfect forms

The present perfect:
Oh, you've changed your hair. I prefer it that way.

The past perfect:
Steve told me, but I'd already heard from Amanda.

The present perfect continuous:
There it is! I've been looking for that everywhere.

In every case the speaker is looking back on an earlier event. In spoken English we often notice something now which makes us comment on what happened earlier. The sentence often links the cause of the present situation, or the result of what happened earlier:

The journey only takes me 20 minutes now because they've opened the new road at last.

We've moved, you know, so I have to come on the train nowadays.

Simple forms

These are used if the speaker is giving a summary, or overview of the whole situation. Different kinds of overview all use the simple form:

I see what you mean.
I never eat meat.
I promise I won't say a word to anybody.
I play tennis at least once a week all year round.
It takes about two hours, depending on the traffic.

If you use another form it adds extra meaning, so the simple form is the basic form. It is the most common form of the verb in English.

Grammar – the noun

There is only one really important grammar pattern with English nouns – the difference between *countable* and *uncountable* nouns.

Countable nouns are things which exist in units:

books, days, children

or which we think of in units:

ideas, plans, opportunities

Because countable nouns are about units, you can have one – a book, an opportunity *(the singular)*. Or you can have more than one – six days, three children *(the plural)*.

Uncountable nouns are things which we do not usually think of in units:

luck, happiness, water, sand

Some words have two different meanings, one countable, and one uncountable:

1. Do you think there is life out there in space?
2. There's a free space next to that red Volvo.

In (1) space = the single, great cosmos.

In (2) space = the marked area where you can leave a car in the car park. You can count the spaces in the car park.

So, it is not words which are countable or uncountable – it is the particular **meaning** of the word. Some words have two very similar meanings, but the grammar is different:

1. I've only played two or three times before.
2. Hurry up – we haven't much time. The train leaves at twenty past.

In (1) times = occasions. You can count how many times you have done something.

In (2) time = the abstract idea of time. You can measure it, but you can't count it.

1. I'm very fond of cheese.
2. France is sometimes described as the land of 200 cheeses.
3. You need a very strong cheese for this recipe.

In (1) you are talking about cheese in general.

In (2) cheese = different kinds of cheese. You can count Camembert, Roquefort, Brie, etc.

In (3) you are contrasting one kind of cheese – strong – with another.

Learning rules / noticing examples

Two things are very important if you want to improve. Firstly, you need to hear and read a lot of English. It doesn't matter if you don't understand everything; if you understand part of what you hear or read, that is enough to help you improve. Secondly, you need to *notice* the language you meet. If your teacher says, "*You made a mistake,*" you need to notice that the expression is *made* a mistake, not *did* a mistake. If you do not notice something, you will not remember it.

With grammar, it is also very important to notice the examples you meet. Again, you need to notice whole expressions, and record them in your notebook **exactly as you find them.** Record examples you meet like this:

It's time you stood on your own two feet.
I searched high and low for it.
OK, I can take a hint.

Not like this:

To stand on your own two feet
high and low
take the hint

Do not change them so that they look like a dictionary. Changing them makes them more difficult to remember, and when you use them later, there is more chance that you will make a mistake. If you write a translation, translate the phrase as a single expression.

Slowly, you will begin to see groups of examples which are similar in some way. If you can see a pattern, and you can describe it, the description is a 'rule'. A 'rule' is nothing more than a description of some examples which are similar in some way.

But remember that examples which are similar in one way may be different in other ways, so your 'rule' may be only partly true. Even the rules in grammar books are often only partly true.

The real examples come first; rules come later, so the examples are more important.

With vocabulary, notice and record words in chunks – collocations and expressions.

With grammar, notice and record the examples in context, exactly as you find them.

Noticing and recording language in chunks will help you learn more quickly, and make fewer mistakes when you use English yourself.

Grammar Commentary

Unit by Unit Grammar Notes

G1 Modifiers (page 11)

Modifiers are words such as *very, really,* and *quite.* They are used to 'modify' – strengthen or weaken – adjectives.

Really and very

She's very nice. He's really bossy.

These two modifiers are used to make positive or negative adjectives stronger. However, with 'extreme' adjectives – *boiling, fantastic, delicious, huge, tiny, freezing,* etc – you can only use 'really'. *It's very huge* or *It was very fantastic* sound very strange.

It's really boiling today, isn't it?
It's really delicious, this soup.

Quite

The meaning of 'quite' depends both on the way it is pronounced and on the context you hear it in.

John's quite creative – he paints and draws.

In the sentence above, *creative* would be stressed and the sentence means you think that John really IS creative. However, in the sentence below, *quite* would be stressed and the sentence now means you think Pete is creative, but not particularly creative.

Pete's quite creative, but he's not Van Gogh!

a bit too

She's a bit too nice, if you know what I mean.

The structure *a bit too + positive adjective* is usually used either to slightly disagree with what has just been said, as in this example :

She's very good-looking, don't you think?
> Yes, a bit too good-looking, if you ask me. I mean, she's very big-headed about it.

Or to add an extra comment to a statement we have already made. For example:

She's really talkative . . . actually, she can sometimes be a bit too talkative, now I come to think of it! I mean, she just never shuts up once she gets going!

G2 Present simple/continuous (page 12)

The present simple is the most common tense in English. The present simple here is used to talk about things that the speaker sees as facts about life – things that are always, normally or usually true:

I find my dad a bit dull.
(always, not just at the moment)
Do you get on with them all right?
(generally)

The present continuous, however, is used when the speaker sees the action or event described as only being temporary, as something already in the process of being completed.

She's being really nice at the moment.
(which is strange, because normally she's horrible!)
He's working this weekend.
(but he doesn't usually, it's only a temporary arrangement)

Remember that the difference between the present simple and present continuous is about how we see an event. Both forms can be used about the same event, for example:

Jane's living in Greece.
Marie lives in Greece.

The difference is probably that Jane has a job in Greece for a year, but Marie is married and has a family there. The fact is the same, but the way the speaker sees the situation is different.

G3 Comparatives (page 20)

I get on a bit <u>better</u> with my mum than I do with my dad.
Everything's very much <u>cheaper</u> than in the UK.
I thought he was a bit <u>younger</u> than me – not <u>older</u>!

All the comparative words above are short – two syllables or less. To make comparatives like these, *-er* is generally added to the base form such as *cheap* or *young:*

dull	duller
long	longer

However, remember the irregular ones:

good	better
bad	worse

If the base form of the adjective is longer – three or more syllables – then the comparative is formed by adding *more* before the base form. For example:

I found this book a lot <u>more interesting</u> than the last thing I read by her.
Most of the other people there seemed quite a bit <u>more experienced</u> than I was.

Remember that as well as making adjectives into comparatives, we can add a second adverb or adverb phrase to adverbs describing how things are done. For example:

It was <u>a bit harder</u> to do than I'd expected.
I get on with him <u>much, much better</u> than I used to.
He finished it <u>much more quickly</u> than I thought he would.

G4 Using auxiliaries (page 25)

If an auxiliary verb is used in the initial statement, the response will use the same auxiliary:

So + auxiliary + I

I'm going to stay in tonight and do nothing.
> Oh, so am I.
I've just booked my summer holidays.
> Oh, that's funny, because so have I.

If we want to agree with a negative statement, however, the pattern is:

Neither + positive form of the auxiliary + I

I don't like things that are too sweet.
> No, neither do I.
I can't stand sea water.
> Oh no, neither can I.

If no auxiliary verb is present in the initial comment, we agree by adding a 'dummy auxiliary' *do:*

So + do + I

I prefer coffee without milk.
> Oh, so do I.

I never go abroad.
> No, neither do I.

Notice, that if the initial comment has more than one auxiliary verb, we agree by using the first of the two auxiliaries:

I've been thinking about moving house.
> Oh, that's strange, because so have I.

I haven't been feeling all that well just lately.
> There must be something going round, because neither have I.

Finally, note that it is very common in spoken English to simply use *Oh, me too* to agree to a positive statement and *No, me neither* to agree with a negative one.

I love fish and chips./I've been there loads of times now./I can speak a bit of Japanese.
> Oh, me too.

I don't like him much./I can't stand this kind of music./I haven't seen her for ages.
> No, me neither.

G5 The -ing form (page 27)

The *-ing* form is used for many different reasons. It is used in lots of useful *go*-expressions:

go fishing	go shopping	go skiing
go bowling	go cycling	go riding
go travelling	go swimming	go diving

It is best to keep a list of any of these expressions that you meet and try to learn them as whole phrases.

I'm really into surfing the net and skate-boarding and things like that.

I can't stand having to get up at 6 every day.

It can also be the subject of a sentence:

Learning English isn't as easy as you think!

Having to give him the sack was the hardest thing I've ever done in my life!

Being married has really changed him.

Notice that the *-ing* forms are often part of a clause, as underlined above. Traditional grammar books called this form the gerund.

G6 Much / many (page 33)

In spoken English *much* and *many* are rarely used in positive sentences. They can be, but generally only in fairly formal situations – at meetings or if you are making a speech; or in reports or serious articles. For example:

Much attention has recently been paid to the increasing numbers of women in sports such as kickboxing.

Many observers have recently commented on the large numbers of middle-managers now facing unemployment.

In positive sentences in normal, everyday spoken English, it is much more common to use *a lot of* or *lots of*. In very informal English *loads of* is used.

We've been getting lots of complaints recently.
Lots of people have commented on that just lately.
Don't panic, we've still got loads of time left.

Look at the way questions with *much/many* in them are answered in both a positive and a negative way in everyday, informal spoken English:

Do you see much of Mary these days?
> Yes, quite a bit, actually./No, not really.

Have you got many lectures this week?
> Yeah, loads!/No, not that many, thankfully!

G7 Used to (page 35)

I used to collect cans when I was younger . . . but I grew out of it after a while.

Used to + verb is used to talk about actions we did a lot in the past but don't do any more.

It is usually used with a time expression. For example:

When we were kids, our parents used to take us to France most summers.

I used to go to church, but I haven't been for years.

Didn't you use to do things like that when you were younger?
> Oh yes, all the time.

I didn't use to smoke when I was younger, but I stupidly started a few years ago.

G8 Would (page 35)

Would (or *'d*) is used when the speaker wants to make a statement sound more tentative or hypothetical:

Would you mind if I left a bit early today? I've got a doctor's appointment.
(I understand it might not be possible)

It'd be great if you did come and stay in the summer.
(though, of course, I realise you might not be able to)

I'd quite like the green one, if you can find it.
(but don't worry if you can't)

However, there are also lots of useful expressions using *would* which you should just try and learn to use as whole chunks:

That'd be great.
I wouldn't mind.
I would if I could.
I'd quite like to.
It'd be nice if you could.
I wouldn't do that if I were you.

It is a good idea to listen for and collect other expressions using *would*.

G9 Question tags 1 (page 42)

In positive sentences containing an auxiliary verb, the question tag is made by making the auxiliary negative and adding the relevant pronoun:

It's getting much colder, isn't it?
> Yes, it's freezing out today.

In negative sentences, a positive auxiliary is used:

You haven't seen my glasses anywhere, have you?
> Oh, I think I saw them in the kitchen.

When there is no auxiliary verb in the sentence, the dummy auxiliaries *do, does, did, don't, doesn't, didn't* are used:

Keith lives with his parents, doesn't he?
> Yes, but he's trying to find a place of his own.

That came as a bit of a surprise, didn't it?
> You can say that again. I couldn't believe it.

Notice that when question tags are answered, we don't normally give a purely grammatical reply such as *Yes, it is* or *No, I haven't*. Instead, we tend to answer the question with a *Yes* or a *No* and then give more details. This helps to keep the conversation going.

G10 Question tags 2 (page 42)

If we want to express annoyance or surprise, we can use a positive tag with a positive sentence.

My money worries are over. I got paid last week.
> Oh, you did, did you! Well, where's that £50 you owe me then?

Oh, you're Korean, are you? Sorry, but I assumed you were Japanese.

Here are some grammatically unusual but common question tags. The first kind are real questions, not just conversational prompts:

I love it up there in the mountains, don't you?
I'd love to go to Cairo sometime, wouldn't you?

The second uses *shall we* as the tag with suggestions using *Let's:*

Let's just go through it all once more, shall we?
Let's give it one more go, shall we?

Finally, the third is used with commands, requests, or instructions:

Don't do it again, will you?
Close the door, will you?
Give me a minute, will you?

G11 Gerund and infinitive (page 46)

Sadly, there is no easy way to learn which verbs are followed by gerunds and which by infinitives. The best thing to try to do is to learn useful chunks that you can use a lot:

I'll try to do it later.
I managed to do it in the end.
I must remember to call her.

I love living here.
I've finally stopped smoking.
I started doing it years ago.

It is also worth remembering that there are lots of adjective expressions which are followed by a preposition plus gerund:

I'm not very keen on cooking.
You must be tired of people always asking you where you're from.

There are two or three common verbs which can be followed by gerunds and infinitives.

Look at these examples:

I clearly remember swimming in the sea near our house.
(it happened in the past)
I must remember to call my mum tonight.
(in the future)
Have you tried asking the guy next door?
(Have you already tried this method of solving your problem?)
Just try to forget about it.
(in the future)
I just totally forgot to pay the phone bill.
(I should've done it, but didn't.)
I'll never forget climbing that mountain in Peru.
(I still remember it and I expect to remember it in the future.)

G12 The past perfect continuous (page 52)

The past perfect continuous is generally used to talk about the background to an event in the past or to explain why this event happened. It usually describes the events or actions leading up to something which is the main focus of our story or description.

We hadn't been getting on for a long time, so we decided to go our separate ways.

So how come you didn't have any money?
> Well, I hadn't been working much, and I'd been having a lot of problems with my car.

This contrasts with the past perfect simple, which is used to describe a single event which then had a result in the past. Look at these examples:

He looked really weird and then I suddenly realised he'd shaved his beard off! (just once!)

I wasn't feeling well . . . I'd had a cold for months. (not 'I'd been having a cold' - having a cold is not something you can DO over and over again)

Remember that the past perfect is always connected to other events in the more recent past.

G13 Second conditionals (page 54)

Second conditionals are used to talk about situations which the speaker sees as unlikely or hypothetical.

There are several very frequently used second conditionals. For example:

I wouldn't do that if I were you.
I wouldn't bother if I were you.
I would if I could, but I can't.
It'd be great if you could.
It'd be terrible if they did.
I'd die if that happened to me!

One thing to remember is that when we report first conditionals, they then have the same grammar as second conditionals:

He told me that I could if I wanted to.
(His actual words: *You can if you want to.*)

I always used to think that if I needed her, she'd be there for me.
(My actual thought: *If I need her, she'll be there for me.*)

We also use the same grammatical structure to talk about typical things that happened a lot in the past. For instance:

When I was a kid, if it snowed, we'd all go out and have huge snowball fights.

If my dad ever got really angry with me, I'd run upstairs and then I'd hide under my bed.

Note that in these examples, 'if' means *every time* or *whenever.*

Whether you use a second conditional or not is very much a matter of choice. For example, logically, you would expect people to use them when talking about winning the lottery, but actually you often hear people saying things like this – *'If I win this week, you won't see me back at work next Monday!'* or – even more optimistically! – *'When I win, I'm going to tell my boss what he can do with his job!'*

G14 The future (page 60)

When you are trying to decide which form to use to talk about the future, the most important thing to think about is WHY you think the actions you're talking about are going to happen. Here are some guidelines to help you:

'll - the normal, everyday, contracted form of *will*

That's the phone. I'll get it.
I think I'll have the chicken.

'll describes a decision or opinion made at the moment of speaking.

Going to + verb

Ugh! I think my tooth's going to fall out.
I'm going to hand in my notice at work next week.

Going to is used when there is evidence now for the future event – something you can see or feel – or to talk about a decision you have already made on your own.

The present continuous

They're leaving next week sometime.
I'm seeing her for lunch tomorrow.

The present continuous is used to describe events that have already been arranged with other people.

The present simple

My class finishes around 9.
She arrives on the 2nd.

These events are seen as facts, particularly facts connected to timetables – of movies, lessons, trains, boats, planes, etc.

G15 Spoken grammar (page 62)

I've got (somebody) (coming round).

This structure is mainly used with the verbs *arriving, visiting* and *coming*. Here are the most normal uses:

I've got my mum arriving tomorrow.
I've got some friends coming round later on.

I've got to + verb (or I have to + verb).

This structure is used to talk about things you don't want to do, but feel are necessary.

I've got to do some things for work.
I've got to take my kids to school tomorrow.

It is also used to explain why you can't do something. For example:

Hey, we were wondering if you wanted to come out with us tonight?
> Oh, I'd love to, but I'm afraid I've got to work late today. Maybe next time.

I'm supposed to be . . . -ing, but . . .

Supposed to be is used to describe arrangements you have already made with other people and which you haven't changed yet, but which you now feel could be changed. The structure is often used with a *but*-clause explaining that you no longer feel like keeping to this plan.

I'm supposed to be meeting some friends tonight, but I don't really feel like it any more.

It is also used with a *but*-clause saying that you haven't definitely decided yet.

I'm supposed to be going round to see him later, but I'm not entirely sure.

You can also say *I might go round to see him later,* or *I might be going round to see him later.*

G16 Just (page 66)

I just stayed at home and watched TV.
I just had a quick cup of coffee, that's all.

Just is often added to statements to make the subject sound small, unimportant or uninteresting. This is a feature of spoken English. Here are some more examples:

I'll just pop out and get a paper, then.
It's just a wasp. Don't panic!

Do not confuse this use with the way *just* is used with the present perfect simple to mean *very recently* as below:

I've just seen Dave. He said to say 'Hello'.
He's just this minute left, I'm afraid.
I'll phone you just after the plane's landed.

Just is also often used with the present or the past continuous tense to mean *at this/that very moment:*

We're just going to have lunch.
I was just leaving when the phone rang.
We're just getting ready.

G17 Responding (page 74)

Notice that when no auxiliary verb is present in the initial statement, we respond using the dummy auxiliary *'do'*. It is also very common to add a follow-up question or comment. For example:

I went off to Margate for the weekend.
> Oh, did you? That must've been nice.
Yes, it was lovely.
I speak pretty good Russian.
> Oh, do you? Where did you learn that then?
At university. I did French, Russian and Polish.

Be careful not to confuse *'had'* as a past tense verb with the auxiliary verb *'have'*. For example:

We had (main verb) a great meal over at Jim's.
> Oh, did you? What did he cook?
I've (auxiliary verb) got my new stereo at last!
> Oh, have you? I'd better come over tonight, then.

G18 I didn't . . . until . . . (page 76)

We use the structure *'not . . . until'* when we want to emphasise that we did something later than usual. For example:

I overslept this morning. I didn't wake up until 10!
I didn't start learning English until last year, so I'm quite pleased with how well I'm doing.

G19 Linking ideas (page 77)

Look at these two ideas:

It was very cold.
We needed two pullovers!

We can link these two ideas in one sentence using a *'so-clause'*. For example:

It was so cold, we needed two pullovers!

In spoken English, this is a very common way of expressing cause and result, with the *so*-clause explaining the cause. The *so*-clause may come first or second:

It was so hot, (that) I was sweating like a pig!
I was sweating like a pig (because) it was so hot!

It was so quiet in there, (that) you could've heard a pin drop.
You could've heard a pin drop (because) it was so quiet in there.

Notice that in normal spoken English, you do not need to use the linking words in brackets, as they are implicitly understood.

G20 Judging by appearances (page 78)

(S)he looks is always followed by an adjective:

She looks really nice and friendly.
He looks a bit stressed-out to me.

(S)he looks like is followed by a noun or a noun phrase:

He looks like a dentist or a doctor or something.
He looks like the kind of person who'll help.

(S)he looks as if (s)he is followed by a verb clause:

He looks as if he's about to cry.
She looks as if she's been running.

Note that in everyday spoken English, *'as if'* is often substituted by *'like'*:

She looks as if/like she's been working all day.

If someone *seems* a bit depressed, it is something you feel through knowing them, not just seeing them.

Dave seems a bit down at the moment. Is he OK?

G21 Expressions with modals (page 83)

There is a fine line between what is grammar and what is vocabulary. The expressions here are probably best treated as bits of vocabulary and just learned as whole, fixed expressions. These kinds of expressions are very useful in everyday English. Learning them will help you understand the meanings of the different modals. However, here are a few things to bear in mind:

1. *Must* is used to make guesses which the listener feels fairly sure are true, because of the evidence available.

   You must be joking! £100 for that?
   You must be American with an accent like that.

2. Similarly, *'must've'* is used to make guesses about the past, based on the evidence available.

   It must've been nice getting out of the city for a bit.
   You must've been really pleased to see her again.

3. *Could've* is used to talk about things you now feel were possible in the past, even if they didn't actually happen.

   I could've told you that!
   I could've helped you if you'd asked.

4. *Should've* is used to talk about what we think would have been a good idea in the past. It can be used to express regret or retrospective advice.

   You should've known better.
   You should've tried to get the price down.

G22 Telling a story (page 91)

Notice that when we give background details to our stories, we usually use the past continuous or *'used to + verb'*.

A few years ago, when this friend of mine <u>was coming</u> home from work, . . .
<u>I used to live</u> in this flat in down-town New York, and one day I <u>was taking</u> the subway uptown . . .
Last Thursday I <u>was riding</u> home on my bike . . .

When we introduce the problem in a story, it is very common to switch to present tenses. This makes this part of the story sound more dramatic and immediate.

When all of a sudden, this big, scary-looking guy <u>runs</u> up to me and <u>tries</u> to pinch my bag.
Then suddenly this girl <u>appears</u> from nowhere, and she<u>'s crying</u> and <u>screaming</u>, so I <u>ask</u> her what's up.

G23 Present participles (page 92)

It is very common to join two ideas together by using clauses using the present participle (*-ing* clauses). It is possible to add more than one clause, but we do not normally add more than three clauses at any one time:

I was just standing there, <u>waiting</u> for my bus, <u>minding</u> my own business.
She was driving along quite normally, <u>singing</u> along to this song on the radio, <u>feeling</u> pretty good, when all of a sudden . . .

G24 Past simple / continuous (page 97)

The past continuous is only used if the speaker wishes to emphasise that the action described was extended over a period of time. As a result, the past continuous is often used to describe an action which was already in progress when it was in some way 'interrupted':

I was driving through town when I got stopped by this police car.
I was just getting ready to leave when this brick came flying through my window!
I met my first wife while I was living in Paris.

Notice that the clauses here are linked using *when* or *while*. In certain contexts, verbs do not get extended in time – they just happen once. For example, it is correct to say:

I was finding the lecture really interesting until he started talking about bio-physics!

but not:

~~I was finding~~ the diamond when we were cleaning the flat.

You can only find a diamond once! The difference in grammar is because the meaning of *find* changes slightly in these different contexts.

The past simple is used to talk about things the speaker sees as complete, finished facts. These might be things that only happened once:

I found the diamond on the floor!
I crashed straight through the newsagent's window.
I broke my leg playing football.

Or they might be things that happened over a long period of time but which the speaker wants to talk about by giving an overview of the facts.

I lived in Nicaragua for six years in the 80s.
I worked on a farm for a few years after I left school.

G25 Or something / or anything (page 99)

Or something is added to positive sentences and questions to mean *or something else like that*. *Or anything* is added to negative sentences or negative questions.

I think he's a lawyer or a judge or something.
Have you got a screwdriver or something?
I didn't even kiss her or anything!
Didn't he even phone you or anything?

This feature of spoken English is not slang or 'bad English'. It is one of the ways we express 'vagueness' when we do not know precise details.

G26 Past simple/present perfect (page 107)

Both the past simple and the present perfect simple are used to talk about things that happened in the past. The difference is, however, that we use the present perfect simple if we see these events as somehow connected to NOW – perhaps we see a present result of these actions as in these examples:

Oh, you've had your hair cut. It looks great.
I can't play basketball today. I've twisted my ankle.
Is black tea OK? We've run out of milk.

The present perfect stresses that we have this experience and can talk about it NOW if the listener wants us to.

Well, I've worked in pubs before, and I've done plenty of washing-up in restaurants.

Oh, you play the piano! I've just started learning myself.

Note that when we use a finished time reference – *last Friday, in 1991, when I was at high school* – the past simple, not the present perfect, is used in British English.

She died in 1991.
They got married two weeks ago.
I knew Karen when we were at school.

G27 Present perfect continuous (page 108)

The present perfect continuous is used either when we want to show that an action which started in the past is still continuing now, for example:

I've been trying to find a job for months now!
My leg's been feeling funny for the last few days.

Or when we want to stress that we see the past action described as having been extended over a period of time – that we see it as having happened again and again and again. Notice that there is a present result in each of these examples:

I've been waiting here for you for hours – you could at least say you're sorry or something!

You seem out of breath. Have you been running?

With certain verbs, there is often only a very subtle difference between the present perfect simple and continuous. For example:

I've worked here for about twenty years now.
(It's just a fact. I see my job as permanent.)

I've been working here for about twenty years now.
(But I may be ready for a change now.)

Notice that lots of verbs do not work well with the present perfect continuous.

I've always liked this kind of food.
I've always ~~been liking~~ this kind of food.

The simple gives an overview or summary of the situation – you either like something or you don't.

G28 Adverbials (page 110)

An adverbial is an expression which functions as an adverb. Notice that time clauses usually come before clauses of reason.

I popped into Diane's <u>for a few minutes</u> just to see how she is.

I went into work <u>for the morning on Saturday</u> just to finish off a few things from last week.

G29 Adding a comment (page 111)

It is common to comment on the events described in a whole sentence by adding *which was + a descriptive noun/adjective:*

It was freezing in Chile, <u>which was a bit unexpected.</u>

I finally managed to ask for a pay rise, <u>which was a real weight off my shoulders.</u>

or we can add *which meant + subject + verb + object:*

It rained the whole time we were in Thailand, <u>which meant I didn't get much chance to go sunbathing.</u>

I failed three out of four of my tests that year, <u>which meant I had to re-take the whole year's courses.</u>

G30 Comparing (page 122)

Notice that in everyday spoken English, it is now very common to hear plural nouns and plural uncountable nouns preceded by *there's* instead of *there are*. Even well-educated, careful speakers will say things like:

It's a bit like Cairo or somewhere, only <u>there's a lot more cars</u> on the road there.

<u>There's hundreds</u> of sheep blocking the road down by the farm.
Business is OK, but <u>there's not as many tourists</u> coming this year as there were last year.

There are is also correct in these situations.

G31 *Must* for guessing (page 123)

We often make guesses about things we think are true based on the evidence available to us, and use *must* to show we are fairly sure, but not 100% certain that what we are saying is true.

It <u>must be</u> nice having a bit more space now that you've moved house.
It <u>must've been</u> really great in New York.

Remember that the opposite of *must* for guessing is NOT *mustn't* but *can't*:

You can't be serious!

You can't earn much working in a burger bar.

It can't have been very well made if it only lasted three weeks before falling to bits! (See also G21.)

G32 Conjunctions (page 125)

Although

In spoken English, *although* is followed by a main clause and usually introduces a clause that reduces the strength of the statement which comes before it.

I do like vegetables, although I must admit that I'm really more of a meat person myself.

It was lovely in Saudi, although the heat did get a bit much sometimes.

I really like my job, although a little bit more money wouldn't go amiss!

Considering

Considering is often followed by a *'how-clause'* and adds the meaning *which is strange when you think about it:*

The food there was really great, considering how cheap it was!

The party was pretty good, actually, considering there were only about twenty people there!

In spite of

In spite of is followed by a gerund or a noun clause and introduces an idea which has been thought about, but which doesn't affect the statement that comes before it.

She got great grades all through college, in spite of having to deal with all kinds of family problems.

Pete's Spanish accent is almost unintelligible, in spite of having lived in Madrid for three years!

G33 Past perfect (page 129)

The past perfect simple is generally used to talk about the background to an event in the past or to explain why this event happened.

It is usually used with other past tenses, and allows us to jump further back into the past from the main point in time that we're talking about.

My leg was killing me, because <u>I'd twisted</u> it at the gym the day before.

I had a dreadful headache, because <u>I'd had</u> a bit too much to drink the night before.

<u>I'd never done</u> anything like that before so I was really nervous about it.

G34 Suggestions with *if* (page 138)

Notice that the 'if-sentence starters' here are all second conditionals – a structure we use to talk about things we see as being hypothetical or imaginary at the time of speaking:

It'd be great <u>if the shops stayed open a bit longer.</u>

It'd be much better <u>if there was a gym.</u>

It'd be lovely <u>if I didn't have to get up so early!</u>

It is very common to find second conditionals beginning with the sentence starters given here, so try and remember the whole phrase in each case.

G35 Impersonal *they* (page 139)

They is the normal third person plural pronoun. However, it has another common use in spoken English. In certain situations where the sex of a person is unclear or where you do not wish to reveal it, it means *he* or *she*. For example:

Look at that person up there on the balcony. Oh, no! I think they're going to jump!
(You cannot see whether it is a man or a woman.)

My cousin's in town at the moment.
> Oh right. How long are they here for?
(I don't know whether your cousin is male or female.)

I'm meeting a friend of mine later on tonight.
> Oh right. Whereabouts are you meeting them?
(The person you are speaking to cannot tell whether *a friend* is male or female.)

If you have not met this use of *they* before, it is normal in both spoken and written English. There are even examples of this use in Shakespeare!

G36 The passive (page 141)

It is not helpful to think of the passive as being 'the opposite' of the active. We always use the passive for a very specific reason. Either we don't know who the doer of the action was:

My brother was killed during the civil war.
My car was stolen from right outside my house!

Or the action was done by a large group of people:

The stadium was built in the 30s.
(obviously by workmen)

At least three versions of this song have been recorded.
(obviously by musicians and singers)

Note that the active equivalents of these sentences use *they* as a 'dummy subject':

They built this stadium back in the 30s.
They've done at least three versions of this song.

We also use the passive when the doer of the action is known, but not relevant or important at the moment of speaking:

My car's being repaired at the moment.

Three of my teeth were knocked out last year when I was playing rugby.

This model was developed in our Seoul team.

Passives are more common in formal written English.

G37 Was / were going to (page 147)

This structure is often thought of as the 'future in the past' and is commonly used to report our past thoughts or words, particularly when they proved to be inaccurate in some way:

I thought it was going to rain, so I brought the washing in – just in case.

They'd told me I was going to be transferred to Mexico, but nothing ever came of it.

However, it doesn't always have to have a past time reference. It can be used to talk about things in the future that we've already decided to do, but now suddenly decide we might not do after all.

Do you want to come over later and eat something?
> Well, I was going to stay in and try and get some work done, but I guess I could always do that tomorrow instead.

Oh, it's funny you should call! I was going to call you later, but you beat me to it!

One of the most common uses of this structure is when you phone someone and they answer:

Oh, I was just going to ring you.

Have you noticed that certain people always say this?

G38 The present perfect (page 156)

After the conjunctions *as soon as, the minute* and *once*, it is common to use the present perfect to talk about a 'past in the future' point:

Once I've finished college, I'm going to go travelling for three months.

As soon as my bike's been repaired, I'm going to start cycling into work again.

The minute I've got over this cold, I'm going to take up jogging!

Notice that *once* and *the minute* are used here as conjunctions.

G39 Reporting (page 159)

When we report what someone said, we often use a past tense if they have used a present tense.

"I'm Canadian."
I phoned and told them I was Canadian.

However, real English often allows more possibilities than rules suggest. We often report things still using the tense they were spoken in. Thus, we might say:

He said he's Canadian.
He says he's Canadian.
He said he was Canadian.

This may be different from a rule you have read in a grammar book for learners, but these examples are correct! Look at the following correct ways of reporting *She's leaving on the 11.30 tomorrow morning:*

John says she's leaving on the 11.30 tomorrow morning.
John said she's leaving on the 11.30 tomorrow morning.
John said she was leaving on the 11.30 tomorrow morning.
John said she'll be leaving on the 11.30 tomorrow morning.
John said she was leaving on the 11.30 the following morning.

If you have learned rules for reported speech, remember that rules are designed to help you produce correct sentences. There may be many more possible correct sentences which simple classroom rules do not cover.

A further thing to bear in mind is the fact that we very rarely remember the exact words people say to us, and what we report is often a summary of what we remember.

He was talking about that job he's been applying for.

He was trying to get me to lend him some money.

Oh, he was going on about how much he hates life in London.

This is why it is useful to learn lots of 'reporting verbs'– *persuade, complain, urge, criticise,* etc. These help you summarise the content or mood of what people say. For example:

She complained that she'd been overcharged.
He warned us not to go any further.
They criticised us for not wearing the right clothes.

G40 The future continuous (page 162)

This structure is often used to talk about an event in the future that we see as already arranged but which now, because of what has come up in the conversation, we also see as the background to another newer event, described in the *so*-clause:

We've run out of milk.
> Oh well, look, I'll be going shopping later (I've already decided this), so I'll get some, if you want. (new decision/offer)

I really love proper pesto sauce.
> Oh, do you? Well, look, I'll be going back to Italy for a week in March (I've already decided this), so I'll bring you back some of my mum's special! (new decision/offer)

Expression Organiser

This section helps you to record and translate some of the most important expressions from each unit. It is always best to record words in phrases, rather than individual words. Sometimes you can translate very easily. Sometimes you must think of an equivalent expression in your own language.

1a

What do your parents do? . . . .
He runs his own business. . . . .
She works in advertising. . . . .
To be honest, ...
He sounds really interesting. . . . .
She looks really friendly. . . . .
Have you got any brothers or sisters? . . . .
How do you get on with him? . . . .
Not all that well, actually. . . . .
She's a bit too nice. . . . .
. . . . if you know what I mean. . . . .
He's a total pain in the neck! . . . .
He's got a really good sense of humour . . . .
. . . .
. . . .
. . . .
. . . .

1b

Haven't you heard? . . . .
I'm afraid not. . . . .
I'm sorry, I'm afraid I can't. . . . .
I don't know how to put this, but . . . .
I only know her by sight. . . . .
I don't know him, but I know of him. . . . .
We're old school-friends. . . . .
He's my ex. . . . .
Cheer up! . . . .
It's not the end of the world. . . . .
I laughed my head off. . . . .
We're on the same wavelength. . . . .
I'll pick you up at eight. . . . .
I'm up to my eyes in work. . . . .
. . . .
. . . .
. . . .

2a

What shall we do tonight? . . . .
So what kind of things are you interested in? . . . .
Well, I'm really into music. . . . .
Jazz and blues and that sort of thing. . . . .
I'm really interested in art. . . . .
I quite like reading too. . . . .
I'm not really keen on clubbing. . . . .
A couple of times a year. . . . .
Hardly ever. . . . .
Not as often as I used to. . . . .
We've got a lot in common. . . . .
We don't have much in common. . . . .
It's in perfect condition. . . . .
. . . .
. . . .
. . . .
. . . .

2b

I used to when I was younger. . . . .
I just grew out of it. . . . .
I would if I could, but I can't. . . . .
I'd quite like to go to the cinema tonight. . . . .
Well, we could always ... if you'd rather. . . . .
Do you go out much? . . . .
It's not really my kind of thing. . . . .
I don't know the first thing about opera. . . . .
I wouldn't go there even if you paid me! . . . .
How long did it take? . . . .
Do you want a lift? . . . .
That'd be great. . . . .
It's just not the done thing. . . . .
first thing in the morning . . . .
. . . .
. . . .
. . . .

3a

Why did you decide to do that, then? ....
How come you decided to go there, then? ....
That's a good question! ....
I'd have to think about that. ....
A friend of mine ....
I just felt like it. ....
I'd always wanted to. ....
It was a real weight off my shoulders. ....
Good for you! ....
Sorry, I've got no idea. ....
It's a nightmare, isn't it? ....
I wouldn't mind being a ... .
It's a really rewarding job. ....
It'd drive me mad! ....
The money's good. ....

3b

I'd been thinking about it for a while. ....
I just decided to give it a go. ....
I'd been meaning to do it for a while. ....
I'd just never had the time. ....
I'm trying to give up smoking. ....
It's easier said than done. ....
It was much better than I'd expected. ....
It was much nicer than I thought it would be. ....
Cold? It was absolutely freezing. ....
That's a wise decision. ....
We made the right decision. ....
I can't make an immediate decision. ....
He's a very heavy smoker. ....
It's a piece of cake. ....
on board a plane ....

4a

What're you up to this weekend? ....
I'm going away for the weekend. ....
I'm really looking forward to it. ....
I've got some people coming round. ....
I'm supposed to be going out tonight. ....
. . . but I don't really feel like it. ....
some friends of mine. ....
I've got to get up really early. ....
I might be going out later. ....
. . . but I haven't really decided for sure yet. ....
I haven't really planned anything. ....
I'd love to, but I'm afraid I can't. ....
I'll see what I can do. ....
I'll give you a ring tomorrow. ....
Tell me about it! ....

4b

I'm just going to stay at home. ....
Wait a second. ....
I've just got to make a quick phone call. ....
I just couldn't make up my mind. ....
I just couldn't believe my eyes. ....
Whereabouts is it? ....
When's a good time to turn up? ....
Should I bring anything? ....
We're having a family get-together. ....
I'll sort out the music. ....
. . . if you sort out the food. ....
There's no time like the present. ....
We all make mistakes. ....
You must be joking! ....
No rest for the wicked! ....

5a

So what did you do last night? ....
I just had a quiet night in. ....
I had an early night. ....
I went out for a drink. ....
I did a bit of cooking. ....
I went round to a friend's. ....
I got a taxi home. ....
I met some old friends. ....
I hadn't seen them for ages. ....
Oh did you? That must've been nice. ....
I didn't get in until 3 last night. ....
You did WHAT last night? ....
You went WHERE last night? ....
I got my haircut. ....
I walked out halfway through. ....

6a

Did I ever tell you about the time I ... .
Last summer sometime when I was on holiday in ... .
I was just minding my own business. ....
When all of a sudden... ....
So, anyway,... ....
Well, what happened in the end was... ....
I couldn't believe my luck. ....
It seems funny now, but it wasn't at the time! ....
He drives like a lunatic. ....
I'm dying for a coffee. ....
My feet are killing me. ....
Are you pulling my leg? ....
scary stories ....
He looked like death warmed up. ....
He had a heart attack. ....

5b

I could do with a holiday! ....
I could do with a bit more time. ....
He looks like a doctor or something. ....
We ended up going to a disco. ....
You must be mad! ....
You should've known better! ....
I can't believe it! ....
You can say that again! ....
Can I get you a drink? ....
They've just got engaged. ....
It's none of their business. ....
break the news ....
old enough to be his gran ....
to be honest with you ....
a man of 50 ....
I'm single. ....

6b

about 60 or 70 people ....
There were no toilets or anything. ....
It must've been in about 1994 or so. ....
He looked about forty-ish. ....
She's got reddish-brown hair. ....
Bye. Have a good journey. ....
I'll get round to it sooner or later. ....
What time does your flight get in? ....
Let's get down to business. ....
He went on a spending spree. ....
a boy of 12 ....
I try to travel light. ....
a guided tour ....
We get on really well. ....
He's a really nice bloke. ....

7a

Hello. Long time, no see. ....

I haven't seen you for ages. ....

You haven't changed a bit. ....

What've you been up to since I last saw you? ....

Not a lot. ....

It's very original. ....

I went round to Dave's for the evening. ....

I went to the opera, which was nice. ....

I've been meaning to do that for ages. ....

I've been waiting for ages. ....

I've been ill for the last fortnight. ....

What are you doing now? ....

Oh, that reminds me ... .

the other day ....

I was on the point of leaving. ....

....

....

....

....

....

8a

What was it like? Any good? ....

What did you think of it? Was it any good? ....

Oh, it was horrendous. ....

It was nothing special. ....

It was a bit disappointing. ....

It was a bit too slow for my taste. ....

It was quite good, considering how cheap it was. ....

Didn't you find it a bit over-the-top? ....

a bit too sentimental ....

I know what you mean, ...

. . . but I quite enjoyed it. ....

It was a bit like his other book, only better. ....

It's a bit like skiing, but not as difficult. ....

That must've been really annoying. ....

I work a six-day week. ....

translated into other languages ....

....

....

....

....

7b

So what was it like? ....

Would you recommend it? ....

I'd give it a miss if I were you. ....

It's not really my cup of tea. ....

It's OK if you're into that kind of thing. ....

It's well worth a visit. ....

I really recommend it. ....

It's a must. ....

It could have been worse. ....

It sounds quite interesting. ....

This is Clare, my next-door neighbour. ....

I get the impression you're a bit bored. ....

It's a work of art. ....

It's in original condition. ....

....

....

....

....

....

8b

It was banned in my country. ....

They dubbed it into French. ....

It's got subtitles. ....

The dialogue was brilliant. ....

It wasn't as good as I'd expected. ....

It's one of the best films I've ever seen. ....

I loved every minute of it. ....

I've heard it's awful / brilliant. ....

It's meant to be really good. ....

Who's in it? ....

What's it about? ....

What kind of film is it? ....

Wait. It's on the tip of my tongue. ....

It's brand new. ....

bad language ....

....

....

....

....

....

9a

It'd be really good if they ...
What would be really great is if they ...
I don't really have any strong views on that.
That's a difficult question to answer.
Well, I agree up to a point, but ...
Oh yes, I know what you mean.
It's hardly surprising, is it?
I wish they'd do something about it.
You're avoiding the issue.
It was my own fault.
I should've known better.
He's the black sheep of the family.
This town's dead at night.
global warming
on the other hand

10a

Have you had any more thoughts about ...
I'm perfectly happy doing what I'm doing.
I'll just have to wait and see what happens.
I can't really say yet. It all depends.
Ideally, I'd like to go abroad.
I can see myself going abroad one day.
If everything goes according to plan,
If all else fails,
If that falls through,
As soon as I've finished, I'll tell you.
environmental issues
a chat room
travel the world
It all happens in real time.

9b

It really drives me mad!
I don't know how you put up with it.
It's the last thing I need!
And then to top the whole thing off,
Things like that don't really bother me.
Don't let it get you down.
There's nothing you can do about it.
That's just the tip of the iceberg.
I can't be bothered.
It's a Catch 22 situation.
We took the wrong turning.
It's a vicious circle.
We had to do a U-turn.
It was a one-way street.
the inner city

10b

What do you do again?
How're things at work?
Oh, I've been rushed off my feet all week!
What're the hours like?
. . . They're OK. The usual nine to five.
What's the money like?
It's OK. It's enough to live on.
So, what does your job involve, then?
He's awful, a real slave-driver.
She's a really good person to work for.
She's on maternity leave.
I get three week's holiday a year.
It's a perk of the job.
private health insurance
in 10 years time

Answers to jokes:

Page 20: "The only trouble was when I took her home, my dad didn't like her!"

Page 54: "Are you feeling better?"

Page 116: " . . . but I'm afraid the bad news is that Pandino was a local street cleaner."

Answers to Shakespeare Quiz on page 124:

1. cruel 2. wicked 3. name 4. music 5. madness 6. gold 7. self 8. love

Acknowledgements

The authors and publishers thank everyone who agreed to be photographed and the following for permission to use pictures:

John Connor Press Associates (87, 97, 109); Press Team Scotland Ltd (34); Simon Ward (61); Michael Wagner and Mark Wilson (32, 44); Allstar Picture Library (15, 126, 127, 128, 132); Greenpeace UK (19, 87, 140, 162); Christie's, London (112); Superstock Inc (115); Russian State Museum, St Petersburg (115); Big Pictures (47); The News of the World (14); Photofusion (16, 23, 43, 50, 62, 63, 65, 66, 77, 87, 143, 150); 'Away from the Flock' by Damien Hirst, courtesy of Jay Jopling (London) (113); The Wellcome Trust (93); The 104 Theatre Company (78), The Ronald Grant Archive (124); Allsport UK (31, 32)

All other photographs and illustrations by Anna Macleod.

The authors and publishers would like to thank the following teachers for their valuable input on this material at various stages during production:

Jeff Stranks of the Cultura Inglesa in Rio de Janeiro; Tim Bromley of the Bell School, Bath; Alan Battersby; Rachel Appleby of International House, Budapest; George Woolard of Stevenson College, Edinburgh; Karl-Heinz Ribisch, Vienna; Kitty Lowenstein, Vienna; Madeleine du Vivier; Amanda Prothero, Brighton; Clare West for her careful proof-reading and valuable editorial input.